D0343139

Move On Up

Cohen, Aaron (Writer on
Move on up : Chicago
soul music and black cul
2019.
33305247943859
sa   06/30/20

Move On Up

Chicago Soul Music and
Black Cultural Power

AARON COHEN

The University of Chicago Press
Chicago and London

The University of Chicago Press, Chicago 60637
The University of Chicago Press, Ltd., London
© 2019 by The University of Chicago
All rights reserved. No part of this book may be used or reproduced in any manner whatsoever without written permission, except in the case of brief quotations in critical articles and reviews. For more information, contact the University of Chicago Press, 1427 E. 60th St., Chicago, IL 60637.
Published 2019
Printed in the United States of America

28 27 26 25 24 23 22 21 20 19   1 2 3 4 5

ISBN-13: 978-0-226-17607-9 (cloth)
ISBN-13: 978-0-226-65303-7 (paper)
ISBN-13: 978-0-226-65317-4 (e-book)
DOI: https://doi.org/10.7208/chicago/9780226653174.001.0001

Library of Congress Cataloging-in-Publication Data

Names: Cohen, Aaron (Writer on music), author.
Title: Move on up : Chicago soul music and black cultural power / Aaron
    Cohen.
Description: Chicago ; London : The University of Chicago Press, 2019. |
    Includes bibliographical references and index.
Identifiers: LCCN 2019004420 | ISBN 9780226176079 (cloth : alk. paper) |
    ISBN 9780226653037 (pbk. : alk. paper) | ISBN 9780226653174 (e-book)
Subjects: LCSH: Soul music—Illinois—Chicago—History and criticism. |
    Soul music—Social aspects—Illinois—Chicago. | Soul music—Political
    aspects—Illinois—Chicago. | Soul musicians—Illinois—Chicago. | African
    Americans—Illinois—Chicago—Music—History and criticism.
Classification: LCC ML3537 .C63 2019 | DDC 306.4/842440977311—dc23
LC record available at https://lccn.loc.gov/2019004420

♾ This paper meets the requirements of ANSI/NISO Z39.48-1992 (Permanence of Paper).

CONTENTS

The sounds of Chicago soul have always felt as expansive as a drive through this city's neighborhoods and down its wide boulevards. Vocal groups harmonizing about yearning for, or losing, eternal love defined the early 1960s, and singer-songwriters with acoustic guitars and a broader lyrical vision closed the decade. Some records' muscular brass sections propelled dancers; slower ballads highlighted intricate string arrangements. Even the blunt word "funk" signified, and combined, everything from small African percussion to interstellar explorations. R&B star Jerry Butler took in large pieces of it all. When he used his music to become an agent for wider changes, he did so in the city that always surrounded him.

Almost sixty years after Butler and his early group the Impressions signed their first recording contract on Michigan Avenue's "Record Row," his career outside singing was just as significant as his hits. He organized a songwriters' workshop that created a repertoire for artists who followed him. Then, after largely stepping away from concert stages and studios in the 1970s, he went on to become a successful entrepreneur and politician. Butler was elected to the Cook County Board of Commissioners in 1986 and served there for three decades, so he could have been justifiably proud when we talked on an Independence Day afternoon in 2016 as he neared retirement from public office. But hubris has never been his style. Instead, Butler's conversational voice merely hinted at his onstage baritone; quick-witted asides poked at a more serious tone. He also credited much of his accomplishment to his community.

"I'm always prejudiced when I talk about Chicago because I think it's such a great city," Butler said. "Most of what's done in this city is prompted by politics, and most of black politics is supported by music. And so the music and politics kind of walk hand in hand down Michigan Avenue."

Move On Up: Chicago Soul Music and Black Cultural Power details these meetings of music and hope for social progress. Mass movements and localized efforts for dynamic change helped create R&B in Chicago. Here too, musicians acted as change agents. Still, compared with other cities, surprisingly little literature describes how musical and social forces combined in this metropolitan area during the 1960s and 1970s. As a teenager I read *Sweet Soul Music*, Peter Guralnick's 1986 intermingling of southern R&B and the civil rights movement, and wondered how such reporting would describe the urban North's culture and its struggles. But since the late 1990s considerable work has focused on developments in soul music from such hubs as Memphis and Detroit. Suzanne E. Smith's *Dancing in the Street: Motown and the Cultural Politics of Detroit* and Charles L. Hughes's *Country Soul: Making Music and Making Race in the American South* are examples from two historians. Chicago has not been as fully investigated as these southern and midwestern counterparts, despite its large size, voluminous output, and intense political exchanges. That comparative lack of attention has been true even for local institutions. While I was growing up in Evanston, just north of Chicago, local artists' contributions were never part of my schools' curricula in the 1970s and 1980s (although a terrific soul singer, Patti Drew, lived just a few blocks from my classrooms).

These musicians had numerous traditions to draw from, such as gospel and blues, yet they had the confidence to declare their musical independence, recasting time-honored music to make it their own. A sense of autonomy also fortified the songs that came out of these neighborhoods through the heroic black educators, record companies, and performance spaces that African American Chicagoans owned and managed. The results helped shape canonical black American music through recordings that convey a full stylistic range. Musicians also intersected with Chicago activists, whether political or commercial. All of this occurred as African American media in the city evolved with advances in radio, television, film, and other industries. Black advertising firms in the city enlisted R&B studio players to promote a heritage along with marketing household products. The politics that Butler referred to include, yet are not limited to, elections and other forms of civic governance. His friend Curtis Mayfield wrote lyrics that came loaded with polemical discourse and lend this book its title. But actions are as important as words. Musicians learning to become entrepreneurs or banding with like-minded collaborators can be as consequential as inspirational verses. Big changes can be sparked just from trying to work, or even dance, across neighborhood boundaries.

Move On Up focuses on the period from the time Butler's group first recorded in the late 1950s until he entered another kind of public service in the early 1980s. These twenty-five years in Chicago proved vital. A generation born at the tail end of the African American Great Migration created its art while contending with segregation, integration, and deindustrialization. Music ran alongside civil rights activism, and some performers contributed to that crusade. Like their contemporaries in the civil rights movement, these musicians displayed ample courage to cope with daunting oppositional force even when just getting together to perform or compose. In that way their artistry resembled the work of activists as they also took it upon themselves to make things better even in the worst of times.[1] The contributions of the city's musicians to such national currents as the late 1960s counterculture and black arts movement also created enduring artworks that deserve more attention, as do the stories behind their conception. As these campaigns turned toward commerce and achieving elective office during the 1970s and 1980s, musicians remained linked with these tides.

Black music in Chicago continued to evolve during the later 1980s and throughout the 1990s and 2000s, but I chose not to cover those years here because those eras deserve separate books. Although I discuss the beginning of the house scene and its ties to a previous generation of music makers, a comprehensive study of that genre requires a deep dive into its changing aesthetics and narratives—such as internationally celebrated DJs, rapid technological advances, LGBTQ performance spaces, and municipal licensing laws. Presenting the recent development of hip-hop and drill music in Chicago would involve analyzing the controversial lyrics as well as detailing at length celebrated personages and recent changes within the public schools. I mention a few current musicians in the final chapter because of the way they speak about enduring soul culture and demonstrate it through their work. That a couple of them are just starting their careers provides hope for the future.

My methodology stemmed from my work as a journalist, which meant speaking with as many participants as I could. So I included interviews with a range of people who made it all happen; my concentration is on artists, but entrepreneurs, fans, media figures, activists, and one original *Soul Train* dancer also provided valuable observations. A few became famous early in their careers, and many others were connected with people who emerged much later. At the same time, I wanted to focus on the Chicago area rather than attempt overly broad comparisons or contrasts with other cities. Some of these interviews stemmed from my contributions to magazines and newspapers (*DownBeat*, the *Chicago Tribune*). Along with enabling access, these assignments spurred my determination to undertake this larger endeavor.

Each encounter reaffirmed my conviction that the music and the circumstances surrounding it told a bigger story than could be presented through a series of articles. I cannot say for sure if I had this project in mind when I visited Terry Callier in 1997, but I do know that he caused many people he met to think deeply. Some speakers contradict each other, while others voice confirmations. All quotations in *Move On Up* are from author-conducted conversations unless otherwise noted.

Popular and academic media brought up additional insights, which sometimes ran counter to, and at other times agreed with, the book's primary witnesses. These include newspaper archives (such as the *Chicago Defender* and *Chicago Tribune*) as well as national magazines with a focus on African American topics (*Ebony* and *Sepia*) and a host of music journals. Musicologists, historians, sociologists, and political scientists occasionally corroborated these testimonies and reports, and sometimes they argued against them. My idea was to balance journalistic approaches with academic techniques and discourses to tell a story that should have more than one dimension. I used a similarly inclusive method in my previous book, which looked at the creation of Aretha Franklin's *Amazing Grace* album and discussed its influence.

Recent cultural histories of Chicago also helped guide my framework. Chief among them has been George Lewis's 2008 study of the Association for the Advancement of Creative Musicians, *A Power Stronger Than Itself*. While I could never claim any kind of insider status—such as Lewis has achieved within the AACM—his presentation of the voices of participants, along with his assessment of the media and scholarship, is a paradigm. Discussing popular R&B artists requires different prose style and terminology than does writing about experimental jazz musicians, but in Chicago the two genres actually cohered, a point Lewis highlights.

I also model my approach on the work of historian Sheldon Cohen, whose writings about colonial-era Americans who are worthy, albeit lesser known, shine a brighter light on that time than the standard Great Man view of national progress (he is also my dad). This demonstrates another reason for focusing on the voices represented in this book: all the artists made often stellar albums and singles that deserve wider attention, in homes and on dance floors. Mostly the chapters are arranged chronologically, but like a classic 1960s R&B dance groove, the narrative calls for some stepping backward and sideways in time. I'll leave it to readers to decide if I share Jerry Butler's geographic prejudice about our city's status. My intention is for *Move On Up* to jump-start conversation.

ONE

Hallways and Airwaves:
Changing Neighborhoods and Emerging
Media Inspire New Music

Sometime in early 1958, five singers and their manager navigated a stretch of Chicago's South Michigan Avenue known as Record Row. Confident, persistent, and with nothing to lose, they hoped that one of the equally undaunted companies lining the street would change their fortunes.[1] Had they traveled the entire mile and a half of the street, they would have ambled from Roosevelt Road on the north to East Twenty-Fifth Street on the south.[2] Collectively known as the Impressions, these vocalists, in their late teens and early twenties, were from the Cabrini-Green public housing project on the North Side. Curtis Mayfield was not yet sixteen. Decades later, he recalled snow up to their necks that Saturday morning. But it proved little hindrance as he carried his guitar and amplifier down the street.[3] Eddie Thomas, the group's manager, came from the South Side. He was about ten years older, and his education in the music business combined street smarts with improvisation. They recalled that their first stop was a company called King, but its roster was full. Then they called on Chess Records—same response. Next they approached a record company named Vee-Jay on the other side of the street.

"We went over there, and I introduced myself to Calvin Carter, who was the A&R director at the time," Thomas recalled. "I told him I'd like to bring my group over. So we set up a date to bring them in. And we went back over to Vee-Jay Records; a cold winter night too. Snow on the ground. And we did a couple songs and he said, 'Man, your group is sounding good.' And I said to Curtis, 'Go and do "For Your Precious Love."' We did one take. Where's the contract? OK, they signed us up."

As Jerry Butler remembered it, their interests were to be heard and not to be cheated. Almost fifty years later he recalled, "We just wanted to see if someone would listen to our songs without a [hidden] tape recorder going in the drawer."[4]

This sequence of events and its aftermath—a hit song, international fame for the group, and solo careers for Butler and Mayfield—plays out like the kind of life-defining moment confirmed through collective memories. Legends do tend to conflict with other published narratives,[5] but several singers, instrumentalists, and producers who grew up in Chicago at that time experienced similar moments. Some of these artists and producers worked on or near Record Row, others worked throughout the city. Many of them lived through the circumstances that led to the recording of such songs as the Impressions' "For Your Precious Love." Major social shifts ran underneath that tune's four chords, Mayfield's lyrical guitar lead, and the group's incantatory harmonies.

Those harmonies convey understated power. No big vocal leaps or instrumental flourishes were needed to make "For Your Precious Love" a departure from the doo-wop that came before it. While only a few people were on hand for the recording, a community generated the circumstances for this song to be created—and for a larger audience to hear it. Not only had the Great Migration from the South dramatically boosted the black population of this midwestern city, but the Impressions' generation forged an identity through music. Diverse circumstances strengthened Chicago-area teen culture during the 1950s and 1960s.[6] Songs frequently arose within the hallways of public housing projects or schools, places full of teens with plenty of ideas, and varying religious denominations informed young singers' vocal training and inflections. The process of recording "For Your Precious Love" also reflected bigger changes. This single was cut for an African American–owned company, Vee-Jay, that was a landmark operation but not the only one of its kind. Emerging radio personalities provided airtime for records like these and spoke the same dialect as their listeners. These media voices would promote new economic resources and political advances as eagerly as they broadcast R&B hits. The real financial beneficiaries of these developments would always be questioned—these were commercial enterprises, not social missions. But whether or not everyone acted in harmony, and even if a burgeoning movement did not yet have a name, this record announced a push forward.[7]

On the eve of the civil rights movement in the 1950s, many Chicagoans had a great deal to push against. Schools in African American communities faced overcrowding and other entrenched difficulties. Barriers to equal employment were visible throughout the city; Butler remembers walking downtown and seeing signs that barred blacks from applying even for dish-washing jobs. His memoir describes the racism he encountered as a student at Washburne Technical High School, a vocational institution near Cabrini-Green.[8] He knew that the program could take him only so far, since white-dominated unions ran apprentice programs specifically to keep blacks out of skilled trades.[9] Butler, like other black musicians from his generation, remained steadfast.

Black musicians who came of age in Chicago from the 1950s through the 1970s usually were either part of or not far removed from the mass move-ment of hundreds of thousands of African Americans who left the South for the Midwest's largest city. As journalist Isabel Wilkerson noted in *The Warmth of Other Suns*, the Illinois Central Railroad "carried so many south-ern blacks north that Chicago would go from 1.8 percent black at the start of the twentieth century to one-third black by the time the flow of people finally began to slow in 1970."[10] By the 1950s, moreover, these new Chica-goans would "arrive with higher levels of education than earlier waves of migrants and thus greater employment potential than both the blacks they left behind and the blacks they joined."[11] They also tended to have more education than the city's white immigrant arrivals.[12] Parents sought to pass this advantage on to their offspring, although they faced institutional bar-riers within a school system that was 90 percent segregated by 1957 (and remained so sixty years later, when the city's public school students were 47 percent Latino, 37 percent African American, and 10 percent white).[13] As the National Association for the Advancement of Colored People (NAACP) reported, "In cost and quality of instruction, school time, districting and choice of sites, the Chicago Board of Education maintains in practice what amounts to a racially discriminatory policy."[14]

The fight against discrimination became as internal as it was organi-zational. Leon Forrest, who grew up on the South Side in the 1940s and 1950s, argued that his family and neighbors took on structural disadvan-tages through survival strategies and mutual support systems. In his essay collection *Relocations of the Spirit* he wrote, "More than anything else we believed that the individual had to find something within himself, some talent, moxie, intelligence, magical nerve, swiftly developed skill, educa-tion, knack, trade, or underground craft and energize it with the hustler's drive."[15] Indeed, these are qualities that most musicians have needed. But black artists in Chicago who developed these attributes could also rely on some reinforcement.

While Forrest illustrates how such performers had to build such qualities from within, some institutional support also existed for the kind of education he mentioned, and many times that came down to committed faculty. Families of young musicians in Chicago sought out the high schools in African American neighborhoods that had solid music programs and teachers who were more than adept. Saxophonist Willie Henderson and trombonist Willie Woods still credit the discipline they learned from band teacher Louis Whitworth at Wendell Phillips High School in Bronzeville. Captain Walter Dyett, who taught at Wendell Phillips and DuSable high schools from 1935 into the 1960s, became one of the most admired teachers. A graduate of VanderCook College of Music with a master's degree from Chicago Musical College, Dyett's students included Nat King Cole, saxophonists Johnny Griffin and Von Freeman (also an arranger at Vee-Jay), and many other jazz heroes. Dyett also taught future R&B musicians like violinist-turned-guitarist Bo Diddley and Morris Jennings, later a Chess Records session drummer.[16] Many of these artists have commented on their teacher's musical expertise, tough methods, and warm heart. His professional background and a supportive community embodied the qualities that later scholars of education would describe as essential.[17] Another drummer, Marshall Thompson, who would switch to singing, added that Dyett's pedagogy might seem unorthodox to some: "Capt. Walter Dyett started me off," Thompson said. "He was one of the greatest musicians in the world. He'd throw that stick at you if you played the wrong note. He'd throw that stick right at your face. It was amazing, we had a thirty-piece orchestra and he could tell who was playing wrong."

Budding musicians also honed their skills through higher education. Between 1941 and 1964, the proportion of blacks who completed college rose from less than 2 percent to greater than 5 percent.[18] As part of this trend, in 1950s Chicago more college and postgraduate educational opportunities became available to African Americans. Roosevelt University was founded in 1945 as faculty left the city's YMCA College to protest that institution's quotas on black and Jewish students.[19] By September 1954, Roosevelt could boast of a fall enrollment of 3,500 students in its schools of arts, sciences, commerce, and music.[20] This was part of a local wave of 90,000 college students, including 11,600 in the city's three junior colleges.[21] Alabama-born James Mack was one such student. His classical music education included bachelor's and master's degrees from Roosevelt in the 1950s. During the next decade he would mentor a host of future R&B stars at Crane Junior College before becoming in demand as an arranger.[22] Another arranger, Charles Stepney, attended Wilson Junior College and Roosevelt. In the late 1960s he would apply experimental compositional theories to R&B, blues, and rock.[23]

Religious Foundations Reflect Multiple Sources

Migrants and their children also heard or participated in older traditions, from blues to singing in the many churches on the West and South Sides. Curtis Mayfield and Jerry Butler had abundant experience with church music (Mayfield also expressed his admiration for blues musicians).[24] Mayfield was born in Chicago in 1942, and a few months later Butler, at age three, arrived from Mississippi with his mother and father.[25] As teens, both performed in Mayfield's grandmother's Traveling Soul Spiritualist Church. But while soul music is rooted in gospel, a common depiction of "the black church" as a single entity is misleading. The influence of Sanctified and Baptist shouts and rhythms on gospel and R&B has been described frequently, including in my previous book.[26] But denominations in black Chicago represented a cosmopolitan mixture, as did the music that resulted from this diversity. These churches and their differences reflecting class, theology, and missions had expanded since the beginning of the Great Migration.[27] Eugene Dixon, who would become known as Gene Chandler, sang in a Baptist choir. Marshall Thompson said that the Chi-Lites used Catholic liturgical singing as their model. The Flamingos, who formed on the South Side in 1952, belonged to the Church of God and Saints of Christ, which incorporated Jewish theological and musical influences in its services, and the group retained these minor-key refrains in its R&B ballads. Maybe these cries also reverberate in the eerily beautiful a cappella opening of the group's "Golden Teardrops."[28]

Dells singer Chuck Barksdale imitated the bass voices he heard in his church, but he also insisted that his group's vibrant harmonies derived from a denominational cross-pollination. "I was raised Methodist, I became a Muslim," Barksdale said. "Mickey McGill was a Seventh-Day Adventist, Marvin Junior was a Jehovah's Witness, and Johnny Carter was Hebrew. So we had five different situations going on, but we never had an argument about our religions. Everything that God puts together is going to be right. Mathematics is exact."[29]

Other musical influences from churches were not so straightforward. In north suburban Evanston, Patti Drew grew up singing in Mount Carmel Baptist and Bethel African Methodist Episcopal congregations. In the 1960s her jazz-inflected delivery shone on such hits as "Tell Him" and "Working on a Groovy Thing." Drew claimed that since her style did not come unadulterated from a purely Baptist or Sanctified Gospel tradition of ecstatic spirituality, her work was not easy to market as hard soul. She said her approach also derived from the "very plain, very straight" style of her main childhood church, but she also said she admired jazz stylist Nancy Wilson.

Religious roots involved more than just singing or transforming the rhythms and phrasings of a traditional repertoire. Churches back then, and today, provided either a rudimentary musical education or a gateway to alternative music schooling. This offered a rich reservoir from which African American youths could claim more music as their own. As a child, Barbara Acklin sang in the New Zion Baptist Church choir and studied classical music there too, although she later mentioned preferring "soulful pop."[30] Singer-songwriter Lowrell Simon's experience in church furthered his education: his hearing another performer in the church prompted him to ask his grandmother, a housekeeper, to pay for voice lessons.

Neighborhood Bonds and Collisions

Even as young people, some migrants brought southern traditions with them, which became enhanced with urban sounds. Mississippi-born McKinley Mitchell sang gospel before he relocated to Chicago in 1958 and wrote "The Town That I Live In," which a Record Row company, One-derful, released in 1962.[31] His elongated vocal lines and call-and-response delivery reflected his gospel background, yet the accompaniment from a horn section featuring saxophonist-arranger Willie Henderson and jazz trumpeter King Kolax represented different musical strains that also thrived in Chicago. The song's lyrics—which depict loneliness and dislocation—could have derived from migration and resonated among Latino immigrants in Southern California.[32]

For the generation that grew up in and around Chicago, the South and its attitudes often seemed not far away. Singer Eddie Perrell attended the city's McCosh Elementary School with Emmett Till, whose 1955 murder in Mississippi helped instigate the civil rights movement. Within Chicago, white resistance to African American migration and relocation took many forms. Lorraine Hansberry's classic 1959 play *A Raisin in the Sun* drew on her family's thwarted attempts to move into a white neighborhood in the 1930s. In Englewood on the South Side, crowds of angry whites vented their anger in 1949 when they only suspected a black family was moving into a home at Fifty-Sixth and Peoria.[33] White mobs continued to use arson and other acts of terrorism in trying to block integration of other South Side neighborhoods such as Park Manor.[34] Unscrupulous land speculators bought properties cheaply from white owners and sold them to black purchasers at inflated prices.[35] In 1948 the United States Supreme Court struck down the practice of white property owners' using restrictive covenants to prevent blacks from buying homes: *Tovey v. Levy* centered on the purchase of a residential building in Englewood.[36] But judicial fiat could not halt ongoing housing discrimination or white flight. As 50,000 whites left that neighborhood, its black population rose from 11 percent to 70 percent over the 1950s.[37]

Yet some African American artists who grew up in Englewood convey benign reflections. Speaking with them evoked not nostalgia, but a candid account of how they made connections within this time and place. Saxophonist Roscoe Mitchell said that at Englewood High School he was mentored on his instrument by the slightly older Don Myrick, years before they made their names in jazz and R&B.[38] Another singer, Jackie Ross, moved to Chicago with her mother, a gospel radio disc jockey in St. Louis, on the advice of family friend Sam Cooke. For her, Englewood was a step up from worse poverty, and white flight appeared not so burdensome. After a disastrous stay in the South Side's Washington Park area, the two of them rented an Englewood apartment from a Jewish family that vacated but left furniture behind. Still, Ross envisioned marriage as offering no relief from financial struggles when she wrote the witty "Hard Times," which she recorded in 1962 for Cooke's SAR label.

Gene Chandler recalled that prejudice in and around Englewood was visible then, but it seemed more a vestige than an inhibiting force. He had other concerns.

> When I went to Englewood, it was majority white. I was twelve years old. It was probably '52. My family decided to go to Englewood, and that's what we did. We had racial problems, yeah. I remember there was a club there about a block from me, and they put up signs, "For Members Only" to try to keep the black people out. Well, of course, I wasn't going into lounges anyway at that time. And it was soon changing; I think they ended up leaving the neighborhood or whatever the case might have been. So the usual racial conflicts were going on, and that was it. So I came through that. I came through the gangs because I was one of the gangs. We called ourselves the Latin Lovers. Because we didn't go out there to fight. We just enjoyed being around each other. But there were times we had to fight somebody just to let them know that we weren't punks.

Forming such bonds crossed neighborhoods and genders. As a teen in north suburban Evanston, Patti Drew said she was part of an all-girl gang called the Latin Ladies.[39] These were not outliers. British music historian Brian Ward compared the cohesion within black American vocal groups to that of street gangs as social institutions that often shared membership in the 1950s.[40] But neither Chandler's nor Drew's affiliations back then were much more than small, informal clubs.

Young performers also responded to a range of social situations just outside Chicago. In Evanston, Drew liked a combination of informal venues: along with the churches, she sang with the Evanston Township High School glee club and, at the behest of her gang, performed at Big Herm's fast food shack.[41] Arranger Johnny Pate grew up in Chicago Heights, thirty-one miles straight south of the city, during the 1930s and 1940s. He offhandedly described it as "sort of a segregated town, divided into sections. There wasn't a lot of discrimination; we all went to school together." The Dells (formed in 1952 as the El-Rays) started singing as teenagers in south suburban Harvey. For them, perceived class differences more than racial prejudice could have prevented their career from happening.[42] Their families did not encourage singing as a career move.

Artists pass through strata that their neighbors cannot penetrate, which was as true in the late 1950s as it is today. No whites-only signs were displayed in theaters, and artists were often able to work around the existing system of divided musicians' unions.[43] But their determination to succeed should not be taken as evidence that perseverance is the surest path to overcoming serious obstacles, as current pop psychology attests.[44] Many young people who experienced segregation did not see themselves as victims, despite the legal and unlawful forces that disenfranchised them. Musical excellence as a means of transcendence was just one response.[45]

Sounds of Public Housing

Chicago public housing increased in scale during the 1950s. The creation and legacy of the housing projects remain contentious, since crime, decay, and other social ills became their typically described characteristics. Also, historians have noted that political and other pressures prevented these public homes from being built in white areas, including a white-led race riot at Trumbull Homes in the South Deering neighborhood in 1953.[46] From 1954 through 1966, 99.4 percent of the Chicago Housing Authority's 10,256 family units—all but 63—were in largely black neighborhoods.[47] At the same time, CHA leaders constantly found themselves facing an indifferent, if not hostile, city council that resisted attempts to request more federal funding.[48] Nonetheless, at least during the first years of the CHA expansion, former CHA residents contend that the complexes "created a strong sense of community," as social welfare policy professor J. S. Fuerst noted.[49]

In terms of artistic output the most famous example of these projects was the Frances Cabrini Homes, which became Cabrini-Green. The original row houses were built in 1942 on seventy acres just southwest of the major three-way intersection of North and Clybourn Avenues and Halsted Street, somewhat close to downtown. Planned as a model for an integrated neighborhood of working-class families, the site was built in a largely Italian enclave.[50] About the time the Impressions walked down Record Row, larger high-rise buildings were constructed in their neighborhood, which had become predominantly African American.[51] Along with Butler and Mayfield, Cabrini-Green was home to an incredible concentration of future singers, including Otis Leavill, Major Lance, Terry Callier, and Larry Wade. Butler recounts in his memoirs that he did not really notice its "filth and dirt" before touring nationally with the Impressions.[52] In a 2016 conversation he mentioned that while he was living in Cabrini, he and the people around him had other concerns: "Everyone sees their conditions differently," Butler said. "I didn't realize that I was poor because everybody in the neighborhood was poor. So you didn't think about how poor you were, you just thought about, 'What am I going to do to succeed?' That was where we came from."

After Mayfield spent his childhood moving across the city with his mother and four siblings as they struggled against poverty, he said settling in Cabrini-Green "seemed like the greatest place in the world."[53] Fuerst describes how CHA-sponsored events at that time fostered a sense of community through activities geared toward young people.[54] He added that initially the CHA also had leaders who seemed concerned about the tenants' general welfare.[55] The idea of public housing as a means to encourage the kind of life that could make creating music possible came from the top down as well as from the aspiring singers. And as journalist Ben Austen described in *High-Risers*, his book about Cabrini-Green, the residents often took it upon themselves to organize events in the community and to look out for each other's well-being, as Butler's former neighbor, Delores Wilson, did.[56] But these reflections were not limited to this well-documented project: vocalist Bobby Hutton had warm memories of growing up in the Far South Side's Altgeld Gardens at that time, as did singer Maurice Jackson, whose family moved there when he was two years old. Jackson even recalled that in the 1950s it was "a paradise for black people."

In contrast to the South Side and Cabrini Green, the West Side had long been comparatively bereft of organized recreation or social activities. That part of town had no equivalent of such venues as Bronzeville's 3,000-seat Regal Theater at Forty-Seventh Street and South Parkway. Sociologist Allan Spear wrote in 1967 that as far back as 1908 "this neighborhood had lagged behind the South Side in institutional development."[57] Singer Mitty Collier, now a pastor, believes the differences between the South Side and West Side have continued. Her recollection also hints at class distinctions: "They were more glamorous on the South Side than on the West Side," Collier said. "Even now, I go over there to preach and even the people in church on the West Side is more southern atmosphere, country. Like when we'd play the chitlin' circuit and all the clubs were back off the road, off the highway, in the back with trees. The people who come to those clubs are like people on the West Side. When you got to the better upscale clubs, they were like people on the South Side."

But aspiring performers on the West Side also used what they had to their benefit. Schools were one example, even with the system's inherent and on-going inequalities. Bassist Bernard Reed learned how to read music during a Marshall High School summer program and looked up to the neighborhood's drum and bugle corps. In the mid-1950s future label executive Emmett Garner enjoyed singing competitions at Marshall, which guitarist Phil Upchurch attended too. Singer Marvin Smith, who also grew up on the West Side and attended Crane Tech High School, voiced similar sentiments: "I loved high school," Smith said. "When I went to school, there were a lot of singers around. We would sing in the corridors where you get the echo. Then when you sing in a vocal group, or just some guys getting together, you're going to attract a crowd. Once you attract a crowd, the pretty girls are coming around. Just like the basketball players and hockey players—we were stars around school."

Other entrepreneurs and institutions assisted young people on the West Side well into the next decades, sometimes unintentionally. Singer-songwriter Gavin Christopher said the blues bar Silvio's provided him with an alternative to the jazz vocal albums his uncle preferred during the mid-1950s. At about five years old, nowhere near old enough to go out drinking, he remembered listening to Sunnyland Slim and Koko Taylor outside the club during recess at his school.

Emerging Voices Recharge Radio

Radio connected the city and became an electronic forum throughout Chicagoland. Records cost money, and 1950s television, for those who owned sets, showed scant representation of African Americans.[58] Nearly every home had a radio, and the Federal Communications Commission allowed smaller stations to boom after World War II, with 200 to 1,000-watt stations going up fivefold from 1946 to 1951.[59] Nationwide, the number of stations in the country airing black programming went from twenty-four in 1946 to nearly six hundred by 1955.[60] In Chicago, black voices had been on the air decades earlier. In 1929 Jack L. Cooper became a DJ on station WSBC.

He went on to start the first African American daily news broadcast, which amassed national advertising.[61] And Cooper's ambitions extended outside the broadcast booth. He advocated for such causes as exhorting Dean's Milk to hire more black truck drivers.[62]

An upcoming generation of black radio personalities used their voices in the studio to signify change. Above all, they brought a speaking style that mirrored their local audience. Al Benson became the prime example. Previously known as Rev. Arthur Leaner, Benson played a mix of new jazz, blues, and R&B in the early 1950s, as his nephews George and Ernie Leaner helped him pick records from their Groove Record Shop in Bronzeville. On station WGES the Mississippi native spoke in what was recognized as a black American dialect, with its southern inflections.[63] Cooper, by contrast, spoke with more proper enunciation. The change carried cultural currency. Norman Spaulding's history of black radio in Chicago notes "the intermixture of Benson's southern style with the northern middle-class style that evolved into a Black urban language."[64]

While Benson's dialect attracted northern listeners, these audiences' musical preferences were changing, and local media started to go along with them. WBEE host Gregg Harris wrote in a *Chicago Defender* column on April 1, 1958, that he would ignore idiom boundaries and simply play "good music." He declared, "If you want to call it rock and roll, jazz, blues, 'pop' or whatever, that's your business. To me, it will be music and it will be good; it will also faithfully reflect what you indicate you want (by your letters and purchases) to hear."[65] The station also engaged in political and consumer activism, including airing a lengthy interview with a Chicago Urban League official, and it conducted surveys on the buying power of South Side consumers.[66]

Benson also hosted talent contests throughout the city, and clubs and high schools ran smaller versions. These events served as relatively egalitarian spaces for young performers, many of whom had more talent than connections. But Benson's competitions at the Regal Theater were the biggest. Mitty Collier entered a Benson-run event in 1959 as an eighteen-year-old college student from Alabama with a stunning contralto voice. As Collier related, Benson's ideals and business acumen were not mutually exclusive. After she won the talent show and received its prize of opening for Etta James and B. B King, in 1960 the DJ introduced her to a Chess Records talent scout. After numerous strong efforts, her hit singles followed three years later.[67]

Most likely a few underhanded favors were also exchanged between radio heavyweights and record companies. Later Benson would reveal to federal investigators that in 1960 he had been receiving roughly $1,000 a month from record companies.[68] Yet the money Benson accepted was just a part of his overall operation, according to one of his younger followers, WGES DJ Moses "Lucky" Cordell, who also arrived in Chicago from Mississippi. As Cordell told documentary maker Michael McAlpin, Benson had a true power to persuade on a higher commercial level: "Up to the point of his demise in broadcasting Al Benson called his own shots," Cordell said to McAlpin. "If you were going to reach the black community in Chicago, you had to come through Al Benson. . . . He talked to Coca-Cola and people of that size like they were children."[69]

For some struggling young singers, such clout was not so endearing. Vocalist Millard Edwards from the Sheppards and the Esquires considered Benson a bully for his enforced favoritism. Chuck Barksdale of the Dells just called him a crook. Still, it would have been difficult for a completely honest person to exist in that field—underhanded dealings in the music industry arose long before the first radio transmission.[70] Although both black and white radio programmers and employees received illicit payments for airplay, sometimes it was a matter of survival. As *Billboard* stated, "Black DJs often lived in squalor, earning as little as $30 a week in the '50s when payola wasn't illegal. It seemed as natural to pay DJs to play the records as it was to pay artists to record them."[71]

Benson's aggressive entrepreneurship crossed over into personal and unconventional political advocacy, which did not always profit him. In February 1956 (on George Washington's birthday), the DJ hired a plane to drop copies of the US Constitution on the Mississippi state capitol. Benson said he sought to penetrate "the Ironic Curtain of racial hatred and prejudice against Negroes in one of the forty-eight sovereign states of America."[72] He also integrated the Chez Paree nightclub, a 650-seat downtown venue that presented such postwar popular entertainers as Tony Bennett and Sammy Davis Jr. Benson and a group staged a sit-in and refused to leave until African American patrons were treated with respect.[73]

Not long afterward, another crucial event at the Chez Paree unfolded not in its show room, but in its outdoor parking lot. Eddie Thomas had a job parking cars there about the time Benson staged his demonstration. Born in 1931, Thomas had been accepted into West Point, but his stepfather, blues pianist "Big Maceo" Merriweather, suffered a stroke in 1946, and Thomas had to take on a series of jobs to support his mother.[74] "One evening in August I was parking cars and five kids from Cabrini-Green came over there," Thomas said. "They were looking for the manager, and since I was the only black person there parking cars at night, they came to me directly. And they said, 'Can you help us? We want to see the manager and be on the show with Sammy Davis Jr.' I said, 'I can't get to him right now because he's very busy, can you come back tomorrow?' I hoped they wouldn't come back [smiles], and bang, there they were the next night."

That group, the Medallionaires, rehearsed in Cabrini-Green's Seward Park recreation center. This field house offers fine acoustic qualities, specifically the way isolated vocals echoed through its gymnasiums and practice rooms, even sixty years later.[75] Thomas did become their manager, but when he saw them perform at a talent show, he noticed another Cabrini-Green–based group that beat them: the Roosters, who also practiced at Seward. Along with Jerry Butler and Curtis Mayfield, Tennessee-born singers Arthur and Richard Brooks made up the ensemble. Not lacking in aplomb, Thomas took them to the jazz club Mister Kelly's on North Rush Street in the posh Gold Coast neighborhood, where they could try out their music in front of a contrastive audience—even though the venue was just a short drive away from Cabrini. Thomas also suggested a name change to reflect their urbane aspirations: "I ended up managing the Roosters, and I said, 'You guys got a beautiful sound, you won the contest, but you should change your name. When I met you, I was very impressed with your sound, so why not change your name to the Impressions?' Everybody was doing doo-wops, but they had something like a musical choir in the background."

That choral intoning was intentional. The Impressions' harmonies on "For Your Precious Love" remained close to the gospel quartet tradition, but true spirit came from inside them. The song's basic elements do not deviate much from contemporary tunes that would have been part of the late 1950s radio playlists and jukeboxes: played in the key of C, it slowly descends and ascends among four chords (C, A-minor, F, and G). This chord progression (I–vi–IV–V) would commonly be called "ice cream changes" by more seasoned musicians as a slam on its seeming simplicity. But what made the song so distinctive was the way it was delivered. Butler's baritone avoided obvious highs and lows while conveying deep, quiet persuasion. Nor did the melody lose anything by not having an obvious hook (say, a middle eight in a thirty-two-bar form). As author Leon Forrest's bartender-playwright Joubert Jones narrates in his 1992 novel *Divine Days* (set in Chicago in 1966), "For Your Precious Love" can be pinpointed as the "first urban Soul song. . . . Slick, sleek too, ultra smooth, celebratory, sincere and foxy. Ice."[76]

Butler agreed that "For Your Precious Love" stood apart from the up-tempo tunes of the time, and that may have come from his method. He wrote the words at age sixteen as a kind of tone poem, with Arthur and Richard Brooks adding contributions to the melody. "I don't think I wrote a lot of poems, but I wrote a few," Butler said. "I was always interested in poetry. My mother always pushed poetry as a way of getting you to do something in public, and to recite poetry was that thing. And out of that, songwriting developed. That was our intent, to write something different [from other doo-wop songs]. When you listen to it, you hear that it was a poem—probably an ode would be the correct category."

Actually big enough to sound beyond any category, the song sat in the group's pocket as the Impressions hit Record Row.

New Record Labels Capture Youthful Sounds

Vee-Jay released "For Your Precious Love" in June 1958, and it ascended to number seven on the *Billboard* R&B chart and number eleven on the pop listing.[77] Competition proved equally intense locally and nationally as small Chicago record companies found growing audiences. These businesses also drew on a young talent pool for staff, such as Vee-Jay's recruiting ace teenage guitarist Phil Upchurch.[78] Although Vee-Jay and Chess were rivals, their emergence (Vee-Jay in 1953, Chess in 1950) arose from similar forces. Chicago's record industry dates back to the 1920s, with Paramount, Brunswick, Okeh, Decca, and Victor issuing jazz and blues artists.[79] Independent companies filled a pent-up demand for new music after World War II, and they were quicker than major labels.[80] Mercury, which went into business in 1945, ran its own pressing plants.[81] In this environment Leonard and Phil Chess (Poland-born Jews who immigrated to Chicago as children) and the African American married couple Vivian Carter and Jimmy Bracken who started Vee-Jay were not outsiders.

During the 1950s, the stretch of Michigan Avenue that had been home to car dealerships became the epicenter of the city's record industry. In the late 1950s, Chess moved to 2120 South Michigan Avenue, and Vee-Jay sat nearby at 2129. Vivian Carter had come to know the street well, since she won an Al Benson talent contest and in 1948 hosted a radio show as a prize.[82] After working in a millinery shop, during the early 1950s she went back to pursue a career in radio in northwest Indiana.[83] When she and Bracken established Vivian's Record Shop in Gary, they befriended Ewart Abner, who ran a record company. Abner told musicologist Portia Maultsby that he gave the couple the idea of starting their own company and offered to help them, bringing his earlier experience in establishing a label called Chance with Art Sheridan.[84] A few years later, Sheridan helped back Vee-Jay.[85] Another assist came from a pawnbroker who loaned Vivian and Jimmy $500.[86] Still, Butler recalled Abner as the real energy fueling these efforts. He described him as "one of the smartest guys who ever went into the record business. He came to the record business with the attitude 'I want to be big.' And he did that by recording all types of music."

While the Vee-Jay founders relied on that small network of supporters, they continued to fight inequities. The company struggled to establish its voice in an industry that saw whites in charge of not just the record companies, but also banks, credit agencies, and other firms that make business possible.[87] Vee-Jay's existence encouraged others, according to singer Shirley Wahls, who recorded for the company with the gospel group the Argo Singers. She remembered Vee-Jay as essentially the only significant black business of any kind that she encountered at that time, aside from small retail stores.

Nevertheless, these companies were not in the business merely to document and present great art or to build communities. They knowingly entered a system that depended on capital, and resources were not usually dispensed altruistically. Hints abound that Vee-Jay took part in this deviousness. For instance, company executive Calvin Carter's name appears before that of singer-songwriter James Hudson as the cowriter on the Spaniels' 1954 hit "Goodnight, Sweetheart, Goodnight." How much of the song, if any, Carter wrote remains anybody's guess. Since producers, managers, and radio personalities typically found ways to add their names to compositions as coauthors, Vee-Jay management was engaging in a standard practice. DJ Herb Kent uses harsher words to describe Vee-Jay's business moves in his 2009 memoir, yet he provides no details about the company's malfeasance.[88] Creative bookkeeping likely was in force at Vee-Jay when Butler, Mayfield, and the rest of the Impressions visited its office, even if there was indeed no tape recorder hidden in a drawer. There's just no way to put a definitive amount on how much any record company unfairly appropriated from artists. "They probably took advantage of us because we didn't know any better," Butler said. "And they didn't feel that they were hurting us because they were giving us an opportunity to be what we wanted to be. So it was fair exchange."

New technology also shaped those records during the late 1950s, especially at Chicago's Universal Recording Corporation on the Near North Side. Most of Vee-Jay's tracks were recorded at Universal, as were thousands of others from companies across the city. Engineer Bruce Swedien, who began at Universal in 1957, discusses these changes in his 2009 memoir, *Make Mine Music*. Swedien notes that when they began in the studios he and his contemporaries improved the clarity of musical instruments through such ideas as acoustic separation screens. Engineers experimented with placing microphones. The idea was to create a singular recorded sound rather than to duplicate a concert performance. A few engineers, including Swedien, looked into stereo recording that was more sophisticated than just reproducing what emanated from two speakers.[89] This was at a time when business media projected a boom in sales of high-fidelity recordings and major companies based in New York also investigated stereo for classical LPs.[90] In October 1958 the *Chicago Tribune* reported, "Industry optimists, anticipating a new billion dollar market, predict that sales of stereo recording equipment, only 100,000 units in 1956, will reach the 725,000 rate by 1960. This would mean a dollar volume of some 300 million dollars."[91] Even so, stereo recording for R&B records in Chicago remained a few years away.

As Butler remembered the recording of "For Your Precious Love," the configuration was simple: the Impressions' four voices, with accompaniment solely from Mayfield's guitar, bassist Quinn Wilson, pianist Horace Palm, and drummer Al Duncan. No sweeping orchestrations sweeten the sound. Those recent advances in studio innovation may have contributed to the sharpness of the instrumental section. An unadorned lineup was not uncommon for Vee-Jay sessions. Abner told Maultsby that gospel and blues groups came into the studio with their identifiable sound intact, so he and Calvin Carter would leave them to their work.[92] The results supported them.

That independence afforded to artists would continue in part because more African Americans in Chicago started their own music firms and obtained executive positions in larger operations. But the key is a sense of mutualism throughout these communities. Vee-Jay, and the Impressions' record for the company, embodied these essential connections, drawn from such institutions as schools, churches, and radio stations. Musical tastes were evolving, with a new generation growing up at the end of the Great Migration, but the passed-down traditions—jazz, blues, gospel—continued to inform younger artists in the years to come.

A big national change in R&B had emerged before all of this occurred. Artists' and small companies' hopes of receiving money for public airplay of their works became more attainable with the launch in 1940 of music publisher Broadcast Music, Incorporated (BMI). With BMI, songwriters in previously marginalized idioms such as R&B found a firm likely to be more amenable than the older American Society of Composers, Authors, and Publishers (ASCAP).[93] At that time BMI promised a more equitable fee structure for its members who were played on the radio, as opposed to ASCAP's paying more to better-known artists.[94] Curtis Mayfield and Jerry Butler would become affiliated with BMI.[95] This shift may have informed an article about a nationwide trend that received some attention in Chicago. As Hilda See wrote in the March 12, 1955, edition of the *Chicago Defender*, African Americans were achieving wider popularity as composers. She expressed concern about "ofays [whites] who are moving into the field."[96] See did not mention the rise of BMI, although she seemed to be alluding to it with her contention that black songwriters no longer had to be concerned about the dominance of songs from more exclusive Broadway and Hollywood hit factories. But with the wider popularity of traditionally black R&B, See concluded by warning about the potential encroachment of "white writers moving in on a field that began with the Sepians [blacks]."[97]

Maybe the future Impressions read See's article. It's anybody's guess if her concerns entered the consciousness of black youths like Mayfield and Butler. These young men were just beginning to respond.

TWO

I'm a-Telling You:
Artists and Entrepreneurs Step
Up in a New Decade

Eugene Dixon harmonized beginning in his teen years, singing in Baptist church choirs and then at Englewood High School, where he and Eddie Perrell rehearsed in the hallways with the Gay Tones. Then he joined a group calling themselves the Dukays. They began recording after he left to serve in the US Airborne Rangers. The singer rejoined them after his discharge in 1960, and they cut their mentor Bernice Williams's "The Girl's a Devil" on the small Nat label. One day in 1961 Dixon and the Dukays ran through a warmup vocal exercise. Soon enough, this repetition would become recognized around the planet.

"I wrote 'Duke of Earl' in one of our rehearsals," said Dixon, famously known as Gene Chandler. "I didn't write it, I just sort of thought of it. We were actually opening up our throats: do-do-do-do. And so we began to clown around and put harmony to it. I began to put lyrics to it. I know nothing about what was going on in England, but I know I had seen movies in there with dukes and there were earls. There's no such thing as a duke of earl. There's an earl of something, a duke of something. I realized all these things later. So they allowed me to continue to put the words to it. My mother came out of the room. She said, 'When did you all put that together?' I said, 'Just now.' She said, 'That sounds good.'"

By early April 1962, Dixon had taken on the name Gene Chandler, and "Duke of Earl" on Vee-Jay hit the million-sales mark while he was headlining a concert at the Regal.[1] Decades later, "Duke of Earl" has lost none of its charm: in the same key and basic chord progressions as "For Your Precious Love," its infectious melody and confident delivery set a strong direction for soul music. Chandler uses his voice like a saxophonist, his apparent ease never undercutting the song's inherent drama. With his tenor soaring above a baritone vocal ostinato background, Chandler's instrumental prowess matched the assured attitude he projected. Reformulating British heraldry and proclaiming himself the Duke "nothing can stop," he fashioned a romantic entreaty that becomes a boast no less than a promise that "no one can hurt you." "We'll walk through my dukedom and a paradise we will share," Chandler sings, pausing momentarily after "dukedom" to emphasize this new word and elongating "share" to suggest no doubt. The song had an impact not unlike that of Muhammad Ali's bold self-assertions (Chandler and Ali, in fact, were acquaintances). Chandler wore a tuxedo, top hat, and aristocratic monocle in promotional pictures and onstage. He personified this character of the Duke and had fun with it, too. This single by a black artist on a black-owned Chicago record label ruled the pop charts on its own terms.

That process of turning a vocal exercise into a hit song depended on collaboration, spontaneity, and confidence. These qualities have informed more than just this tune. Experienced musicians worked in studios with self-taught young performers as the city's jazz legacy pervaded some of these artists' records. This spirit also reflected the business side of Chicago's R&B scene throughout the early to mid-1960s. After "Duke of Earl," start-up companies looked to capture such success. Some achieved it immediately, others did not. But the energy that fueled this musical hotbed resonates through the wealth of recordings from that era. Emerging media, primarily AM radio station WVON, with its mix of music and social advocacy, expanded the reach of these sounds but also delivered contemporary activists' messages. The political stakes had also increased, and Chicago's black artists responded to these changes. Some became directly involved in the growing civil rights movement, others brought out a sense of consciousness through their lyrics. Musicians also fought for their own union's integration and the better-paying jobs they hoped would result. Even such cheerful musical gatherings as teen dances and record hops came loaded with significance. Movements and fashions became signifiers of identity in a city that frequently made these teens seem invisible. These young black Chicagoans' steps and styles would affect the world.

Chandler's artistic independence symbolized this movement. He became intertwined with two of the city's premier record producers, Carl Davis—a former assistant to Al Benson—and Bill "Bunky" Sheppard, who would rise to prominence during the 1960s.[2] "Duke of Earl" was recorded initially by Chandler's group, the Dukays. Member Earl Edwards (the Earl in the title) contributed to the composition along with Bernice Williams.[3] Davis approached Vee-Jay with the master of the song, and the label wanted to release it but could not do so as a Dukays record, since the group was signed with a rival distributor. That's when Eugene Dixon became Gene Chandler—naming himself after actor Jeff Chandler—and the company issued it under his name alone.[4] No one knew how the "Duke of Earl" single would fare. The Dukays held a place for Chandler to return.

The song's rapid ascent under Chandler's name meant he did not return to the group. By 1960, Abner had formed a partnership with distributors across the country and had firm ideas on how to reach white-oriented radio stations and record buyers. Vee-Jay had built up thirty-two distribution points that Abner said covered "maybe 200 to 300 cities."[5] That network of distributors, independent promotion representatives, and radio station DJs often came down to what Abner called personal relationships. More than twenty years after the release of "Duke of Earl," he reflected that, on a social level, young music fans clamored for at least one step toward integration.

"You know, white kids knowing the black kids' slang, whether they get it from playing in the playground, or whether they get it from being in school together, you follow me?," Abner said to Portia Maultsby. "Anyway, they would pick up on the black music. They would call a white station and say, 'You aren't playing so-and-so and so.' And the white station would say, 'What are you talking about? I don't have that record.' 'Well, you ought to get it.' Okay, and the white stations are always wanting to compete and be first in their marketplace, those who are daring and smart and innovative are going to get the record and they'll listen to it."

To be sure, white attempts to adapt, or imitate, black styles in America stretched back more than a hundred years before the rise of Vee-Jay and has continued for decades afterward.[6] But a few combined factors make Abner's observation distinctive. Here an African American–owned music business set itself up to profit from this trend. Also, he describes this company's using mass media to help shape the identity—as well as the buying power—of large numbers of teenagers (or preadolescents) as opposed to adults. Considering that this audience would have been at a more impressionable age than earlier generations' cultural consumers, these records would conceivably have made a bigger impact on mass consciousness. Detroit's Motown—which released its debut single in January 1959—would follow Vee-Jay's blueprint with phenomenal results.[7]

Chandler said he was too young to follow Abner's strategies and philosophy at the time "Duke of Earl" was released. But he admired how Abner pursued a crossover market and traveled to radio stations and record distributors across North America to do it. Using Chicago as an example, Chandler mentions the powerful AM pop station WLS. To approach such a station could be challenging for black artists. "Abner went out and hired some white promotion men to go to stations like WLS and around the country," Chandler said. "But you had to sell so many records. I think at that time 200,000 from black radio. Then you go to the pop stations and say, 'Okay. We've done 200,000 blah-blah-blah.' Because at that time, the black radio stations couldn't even really be heard north of downtown."

Jerry Butler's break from the Impressions occurred in circumstances similar to his friend Chandler's experiences. Vee-Jay maneuvered the singer away from the group, putting his name on top when "For Your Precious Love" was released. The company's stated reasons were commercial: casting individuals as stars made them easier to promote than groups. Butler objected to this placement, as of course did Mayfield, along with the other singers—Samuel Gooden and the brothers Richard and Arthur Brooks.[8] The Impressions continued recording and touring for about a year and a half until Butler decided to strike out on his own. By early 1960 the group, dropped from Vee-Jay, went on a hiatus. Butler hired Mayfield as his guitarist. Mayfield had begun writing songs, and four of their composing collaborations appeared on Butler's 1961 album *Aware of Love*. According to Butler, Caribbean-influenced pop like Harry Belafonte's became a key musical inspiration.[9]

That album also contains the Mayfield and Butler-written "I'm a-Telling You," which described the tribulations of low-wage employment. It would be Mayfield's first noteworthy message song. Their friends across Chicago would have connected with the lyrics. A series of recessions between 1957 and 1962 were substantially hard on black workers, since factories had been leaving cities at a faster rate. And while the unemployment rate in Chicago's Cook and nearby DuPage Counties rose from 2.7 to 6.7 percent from 1957 to 1958, for African Americans it rose from 8.1 to 20.1 percent.[10] All this would have added pressure on blacks who were able to obtain factory jobs, such as singer Tyrone Davis, who in the early 1960s was working in a West Side steel foundry and performing on weekends, While race is not overtly mentioned in "I'm a-Telling You," the *a-* in its title, signifying a specific dialect, strongly implies a black perspective, as did Butler's baritone. Nonetheless, the song received airplay among the pop offerings at WLS, according to the station's "Silver Dollar Survey" list, with at least five weeks of broadcast on the station as of September 16, 1961.[11] Mayfield's melody may have mattered more to that audience than his downcast lyrics.

Ironically, the cover of the *Aware of Love* LP is a photo of a smiling white couple, with a focus on the woman's blonde ponytail. Such happy white pairs appeared on the cover of a few Vee-Jay albums released that year, including singer Dee Clark's *Hold On . . . It's Dee Clark*. For a black-owned company whose president Ewart Abner served on the board of the Chicago Urban League, the situation seemed paradoxical, though also typical of the times.[12] Financial goals and pop radio airplay trumped realism, since that packaging was an attempt to hide black identities and market to a crossover audience. As Butler explained: "That was in the day when folks said, 'You're going to hurt your sales if you put black faces in the record shops.' Especially the big stores like Marshall Field's. So some smart executive at the record company decided, 'We won't put black faces on the cover of the album. We'll just make it young white kids singing and the music inside will do the rest.'"

But during the early and mid-1960s, Vee-Jay had also treated black music as an international term, a forward-thinking move that has not received the attention given its pop acts. The company was among the first American labels to issue a Jamaican ska album (Mango Jones and Orchestra, *The Ska*, 1964).[13] The year before, Vee-Jay released *Africa Calling*, an album by the Dungills from the South Side Morgan Park neighborhood, a family orchestra that had performed and taught cross-continental music since the 1940s.[14] Still, the emphasis stayed local, with such R&B artists as Betty Everett. A former child Baptist gospel singer from Mississippi, Everett moved to Chicago in 1954 at age fifteen and racked up a handful of hits with Vee-Jay. One standout, "The Shoop Shoop Song (It's in His Kiss)," recorded in November 1963, became a top seller and remains a paragon of that era's girl-group harmonies, even with her name alone as the artist. Her fans in England were equally enthusiastic when she visited in early 1965 to promote the assertive kiss-off "Getting Mighty Crowded."[15]

"Betty Everett had a natural tear in her voice," said Butler, who became her duet partner in the early 1960s. "I used to make a joke that she was the black Dolly Parton. She just had a natural thing in her voice that's hard to duplicate."

Vee-Jay was also one of the few black-owned companies to release records by prominent white artists such as the Four Seasons. In January 1963 the Beatles became part of the Vee-Jay portfolio after the band's British label, EMI, received rejections from other American firms for US distribution.[16] With Beatlemania sweeping the country the following year, EMI's American imprint Capitol sued the Chicago company to release the band's records. Although Vee-Jay lost control of the Beatles after court battles in 1964, more devastating wounds were self-inflicted. For example, management relocated to Los Angeles that year, then turned around and came back to Chicago in 1965.[17] During these expensive moves, the federal government placed liens on its products at pressing and plating plants because of unpaid bills.[18] Abner's gambling addiction was also a factor in the company's

1966 bankruptcy; he joked thirty years later that he integrated the Las Vegas craps tables.[19] This habit did not prevent him from ascending to Motown's presidency in 1973.[20] All of this reaffirms not just the ongoing connections between Chicago and Detroit, but also the accuracy of Butler's and Chandler's characterization of Abner's acumen.

Mayfield Rises through New Ventures and Collaborations

About 1960, Curtis Mayfield became his own executive. With Eddie Thomas, he formed Curtom Publishing, named after themselves (Curt and Tom). Precedents existed for young African American artists' controlling their music, notably former Chicagoan Sam Cooke, who began releasing singles on his SAR Records in Los Angeles in 1960.[21] But Cooke was a star when he established his own company; Mayfield was in his teens, and Thomas had yet to turn thirty. "The first time I visited Washington, I went to the Library of Congress and asked someone to give me whatever information pertained to music and copyrights," Mayfield later told journalist Agnes R. Smith. "All I had in my assets column were those little songs I was writing then."[22]

Thomas added that they were both improvising. "We were going to the school of hard knocks ourselves, and we were learning," he said. "We were also learning that the publishing was very important to participate in, in regards to getting some returns. We knew that if we had a piece of our own label, we'd have a little more slice of the pie than just being artists on somebody else's label."

The Impressions had also reconvened, and after tireless roadwork and Thomas's promotional efforts, Mayfield's evocative, flamenco-influenced "Gypsy Woman" became a hit single in September 1961 for the ABC-Paramount label, reaching number twenty pop and number two R&B.[23] The record also served as an early sample of his particular style of guitar playing. The Chicago pop radio station, WLS, was slow to pick up on it. Instead, Thomas managed to build up the approach among friendly DJs in Baltimore, Philadelphia, and New York. Shortly afterward, Richard and Arthur Brooks left, but the group thrived with Mayfield, Samuel Gooden continuing as bass voice, and Fred Cash as tenor.

Other Chicago artists and executives soon shared national attention. The same October 16, 1961, issue of Billboard that noted that the Impressions' "Gypsy Woman" was a hit in Philadelphia included an article about the rise of Granville White, the national field promotion manager for Columbia Records.[24] In Chicago, big band veteran Riley Hampton had established himself as the main arranger for R&B sessions. Among others, he produced

Jackie Ross, who had a hit in 1964 with "Selfish One" on Chess. The song frames Ross's quietly expressive voice with an assemblage of strings, brass, and handclaps for punctuation. Ross remembers that Hampton's charts inspired her to think about studying score writing.

But Hampton was not the only vital arranger at this time. Jazz bassist Johnny Pate became his main rival. Pate had played bass in clubs in Chicago and in New York since his discharge from the army at the end of World War II. He also arranged for singers such as Joe Williams, who performed at the Club DeLisa on the South Side. The GI Bill funded Pate's musical studies at the Midwestern Conservatory downtown. His trio recorded and worked regularly at venues like the upscale London House. With a family to support, Pate started to emphasize arranging, since that job paid better than performing. His compositions also appeared on such albums as saxophonist James Moody's *Last Train from Overbrook* in 1958. Carl Davis approached Pate about arranging for him, and while Hampton may have been chagrined about sharing jobs, he was not in a position to block this move.

Soon Mayfield asked Pate to work on his own recordings and on compositions he had written for other artists. One of the first was "Monkey Time," released by Okeh in 1963, a dance tune featuring twenty-two-year-old former boxer Major Lance. The Impressions served as backup vocalists, amplifying and engaging in call-and-response with the leader and other singers while the horns suffused the multilayered sound with emphatic fills. Possibly, Pate's expertise in the bass clef solidified its pronounced trombone part. Carl Davis, who started working for the Columbia imprint Okeh in the middle of 1962, was the producer.[25] Here Davis announced that he would build a "Chicago sound" based on Mayfield's writing and coproduction. They would sign new, locally based, acts rather than luring established singers from other companies.[26] Pate's brawny and percussive horn lines blended with the joy of Mayfield's composing to become the template.

Although Pate had enjoyed being his own boss as an artist and playing jazz, he came to believe he could add his technique and improvisational experience to pop. "Naturally, I'm a jazz bass player, and jazz is where my heart is," Pate said.

> ABC-Paramount decided to hire me. Once I did the first date for the Impressions, they said, "We never sold Impressions albums like [we] sold these." I was really producing. They said, "We want to hire you as an in house arranger, but we want you as an exclusive." So I agreed, would get a salary and benefits. I was doing the R&B dates, and I would have them bring me a rough tape of the basic tune—a rough structure, which Curtis would do. I would build the

arrangement around that. There wasn't a whole lot of head dictating. How do you go in there? You've got a three-hour session and dictate? It didn't quite work that way. I would take whatever they had and try to do an arrangement. A lot of that, I would change keys to keep it from getting monotonous.

For Pate, working with Mayfield posed another challenge. Mayfield tuned his guitar in F-sharp, an approach that came about while he was growing up self-taught and had his strings correspond to the black keys on his mother's piano.[27] Pate's experiences in jazz jam sessions and conservatory training proved to be the ideal musical complement to Mayfield's autodidact background.

> When I learned to write, I learned according to intervals. In other words, a major scale is a simple thing. If you do it on the piano, you do a whole step, a whole step, a half step, a whole step, a whole step, a whole step, and another half step. OK, that's a major scale. Now, if you know where the fifth is in the key of C and you're using the interval system, you'll know where the fifth is in the key of B-flat. Or you'll know where the seventh is going to be. That's the way I write. The voicings that I use when I'm writing, after all these years, I don't use too many voicings. So if I know that much about it, I can continue to write no matter how it sounds. Curtis Mayfield did not tune the guitar the conventional way. I don't know what system it was, but most of the tunes he wrote were written in the key of G-flat or F-sharp or B-natural. These are keys that the average musician doesn't want to have to deal with because there are too many sharps and flats. But this is the way Curtis tuned his guitar. That's how he wrote, and that's how he sang. When I started working with him, I had no problem because I was dealing with the interval system, so an F-sharp could be no different than a C. F-sharp is the root and then there is no problem at all, you know where C-sharp is naturally going to be the fifth. You do it interval-wise. I've never had any problems with any singers if they want to do it in some odd key. Real musicians have no problems with strange keys.

Mayfield concurred when he spoke to journalist Sue Cassidy Clark in 1968. "Well, usually through most of my own original things have basic ideas and thoughts in terms of little interludes that I hear some of the instruments doing," Mayfield said to Clark. "Therefore I dictate these things to Mr. Johnny Pate. And he with his own way of bringing things about, comes up with beautiful things, there's a great collaboration there."[28]

"People Get Ready" remains a highlight of the Mayfield-Pate synergy. Recorded in January 1965, the song reached number three on the national

R&B charts, number fourteen pop, and reflected the songwriter's spiritual emphasis in vivid colors.[29] Its image of a train leaving for a higher place would have had special resonance for migrants and their children who had come up to Chicago from the South. The lyrics' relevance to the church-inspired civil rights movement has frequently been discussed.[30] But along with these words, the melody, paradoxically both languid and momentous, and the sweeping orchestration's emphasis on strings would offer inspiration to contrasting groups of local activists. In August of that year, five hundred advocates for open housing in the high-end North Shore suburbs sang a version with their own verses advocating integration as they marched through Winnetka, historically exclusive Kenilworth, Wilmette, and Evanston.[31] About four years later, supporters of jailed West Side–based Illinois Black Panther Party chairman Fred Hampton sang their version of the tune at a rally. Their lyrics demanded Hampton's freedom and urged listeners to prepare for a revolution.[32]

Shared Goals, Different Methods in the Civil Rights Era

Even though Mayfield's songs helped energize the civil rights movement, Chicago R&B artists were rarely featured performers at the large rallies in the city during the early and mid-1960s.[33] Mitty Collier, for instance, remembered singing at the movement's programs in Birmingham, Alabama, but not in the North—even though she lived on the South Side and recorded for Chess. Nobody recalled why these artists with local ties and youth appeal had not been included at the campaign's major events within this city. Historian Brian Ward suggests that, on a national level, civil rights organizations had class biases and strategic complications that hindered them from coming up with a plan to feature soul stars as morale boosters.[34] While friction existed among Martin Luther King's Southern Christian Leadership Conference, Chicago ministers, and regional politicians, none of these disputes had a direct influence on young singers and musicians.

Some of these musicians did aid the freedom movement behind the scenes. Butler donated funds for the August 28, 1963, March on Washington. Others chose divergent paths. For Chuck Barksdale that included advocating for black pride and self-discipline as a member in the Nation of Islam and selling copies of the *Muhammad Speaks* newspaper on the South Side with Muhammad Ali. Gene Chandler, who knew King, believed his own temperament prevented him from taking a visible role in any of the marches. Considering that he was just a few years away from his teenage gang, this may not have been surprising.

"I was one of those guys who didn't feel like I could take any licks, any punishment," Chandler said. "I would fight back. I was not nonviolent. So I remember we were going to march somewhere. Not here, somewhere else. And I told Martin, I said, 'Martin, I'm not sure whether I'll be able to take somebody spitting on me or hitting me with something from the sidelines.' He said, 'Well, Gene, I want you to be up front with us. But it's best that you get back to the middle or somewhere else because it's got to be nonviolent. You cannot retaliate.' And so that was the extent of my involvement. I couldn't march up front."

The movement also informed a music industry labor struggle as Chicago artists pushed to integrate the two American Federation of Musicians (AFM) unions. Since the 1930s, members of the black Local 208 had advocated merging with the larger white Local 10.[35] Those calls increased beginning in the 1940s and into the early 1960s. Throughout those years, financial stakes had become greater. In 1962 the *Chicago Tribune* reported that this city had become a "center or a hotbed of freelance composers of singing commercials."[36] Six downtown agencies dominated that field. The AFM controlled who got those remunerative advertising jobs, and its racial bias was clear.[37]

AFM member Pate contested the status quo. "[Local 10 was] one of the richest local unions in America." Pate recalled. "When I got out of the service in 1946, it was very seldom that you saw a black player on a jingle date. I wasn't one who was afraid to make a fuss, so I did a little screaming. Sometimes I would be the only black in the studio."

But Pate stood apart from some older black musicians like Captain Walter Dyett, who feared that integration would be counterproductive to building enduring black institutions such as fraternal societies.[38] These veterans maintained that self-sufficiency among African American artists remained key. Younger activists like flutist and educator James Mack disagreed and emphasized the benefits that would come with integration. Mack alluded to the Emancipation Proclamation centennial in 1963 in pamphlets rallying union members to the cause.[39] His view carried the day: on January 11, 1966, the AFM at last decreed that "every member of Local 10 and Local 208 shall enjoy and be entitled to equal rights, privileges and benefits in the merged union."[40]

The launch of radio station WVON on April 1, 1963, inaugurated another confluence of music and community engagement with call letters standing for "Voice of the Negro." The idea for such an outlet with those same call letters went back at least to the late 1940s. Two ministers had initially proposed the black-owned operation about 1948, but they wound up squabbling viciously with each other.[41] Leonard and Phil Chess bought a station at 1450 on the AM dial from L&P Broadcasting, which had run foreign-language programming. The new endeavor opened its offices and studios at 3350 South Kedzie Avenue, and some of its initial on-air hosts included Al Benson, E. Rodney Jones, Pervis Spann, and Bernadine C. Washington, who served as a fashion consultant and commentator. Benson remained at the station for less than a month, saying he wanted to refocus on his ministry, but his presence at the company's inception furnished a link to his earlier broadcast work and activism. On WVON music, commerce, and politics intermingled. Its playlists of black artists constituted an end run around the dominant pop stations. The *Chicago Defender* greeted WVON's launch with an article stating, "A new 24-hour-a-day radio station—with an eye on the lucrative Negro market and its emphasis on music, news around the clock and an aggressive public service program—makes its debut in Chicago."[42]

WVON quickly succeeded, so much so that Jones felt confident enough to cut self-mocking promo spots, including one with Nat King Cole claiming he'd never heard of the station (to which *Billboard* responded, "Our guess is he will").[43] Within four months the *Defender* reported that WVON was beating its rival WYNR in the C. E. Hooper ratings for radio by a count of 17.1 to 14.9 in the morning and 27.2 to 20.9 in the afternoon. The newspaper commended young DJ Herb Kent's pop and nostalgic "favorites of yester-year" format along with Spann's "colorful" language, which echoed Benson's initial appeal.[44] By March 1964, *Billboard* marveled that WVON had moved from sixth to second place in the city's music ratings—all while the black-oriented station had only 1,000 watts of broadcast power versus first-place WLS's 50,000 watts.[45] Ingenuity boosted its signal: although its Federal Communications Commission Class Four frequency was the lowest wattage the agency would grant, some unlicensed engineers amplified its range by an unspecified amount. These included Bill "Butterball" Crane, a technician-DJ, and teenager Larry Langford, who somehow eluded authorities' detection.[46]

The dichotomy between black on-air voices and white ownership did rankle some people. In Nadine Cohodas's book about Chess, *Spinning Blues into Gold*, she writes that program director E. Rodney Jones believed the top executives knew little about the South and West Sides.[47] On the other hand, Cohodas also submits that Leonard Chess felt that white upper management made the station more appealing to bigger advertisers.[48] Still, within Chicago in the early and mid-1960s there was no mention of protest against WVON's upper management in such black media outlets as the *Chicago Defender*. Forty years later Spann expressed discontent not so much with the

Chess brothers as with racist southern congressmen who he said pressured the Federal Communications Commission into not allowing black owner- ship of radio stations.[49] Also, at the time of its inception, few could have imagined the station's long-term influence.

On the street, money continued to change hands in exchange for ra- dio airplay, just as it always had, no matter what the station format. Exact amounts varied, as one source mentioned during an interview.[50] Another Chicago-based singer asserted that he could use the system to his advantage across the country, although he added that not everyone was so fortunate.[51]

"They call it payola, but it was pretty hip," the singer said. "But then again, it was friendship. Who are you friends with? Well, the program direc- tor is a good friend of mine, and I could ask him for a favor. In Chicago it was E. Rodney Jones, in Detroit it was Al Perkins, in Philadelphia it was Georgie Woods. So what I could do is, beginning on Tuesday so they could program my records on Friday, I would hit in all these major cities. There were guys going broke because they couldn't afford to keep up."

While the WVON staff and ownership's profit motives were front and center, the station also engaged the community in ways that were not purely commercial. The Chicago Urban League's Sherwood Ross hosted a weekly spot called "Current" to discuss racial issues.[52] In May 1963 the station donated $2,000 to the Southern Christian Leadership Conference to help assist black demonstrators who were arrested in Birmingham, Alabama.[53] WVON's efforts to help the movement also became physically exhaustive: in December the station conducted a lengthy radiothon intended to add twenty thousand new members to the rolls of the National Association for the Advancement of Colored People. Martin Luther King publicly acknowl- edged that WVON raised money for the 1964 Mississippi Freedom Sum- mer.[54] That the station remained linked with the movement in the South reaffirmed the connections forged during the Great Migration.

Not everyone appreciated these efforts. For example, James Allen wrote to the *Chicago Defender* railing against the "vulgar" playlists on WVON and WYNR: "In a successful union of the theory and practice the owners of these obnoxious stations have managed to corner the market of radio listeners by giving them a steady, heavy diet of militant pro-integrationist propaganda— as if the civil rights issue was simple and existed in a vacuum and a similar dose of the cheap, crude music which sells best to Negroes."[55] Allen's race is unknown (although few readers of the *Defender* were not African American); but, either way, it serves as a reminder that activist fervor remained far from universal.

Modern Operators Guide Musical Changes

Notwithstanding its specious politics, Allen's complaint regarding chang-ing musical values points to shifts that actually had occurred. A growing generation of African Americans kept developing music that they could call their own, that was not just a continuation of their parents' preferences. Ra-dio airwaves also soared over physical and language barriers.[56] Syl Johnson epitomized the transition from blues to R&B.

Johnson, who was born in Mississippi in 1936, moved to Chicago with his family at age fourteen.[57] Within a couple of years he was playing guitar and harmonica for such South Side bluesmen as James "Shakey Jake" Harris. Yet he departed from the familiar twelve-bar and sixteen-bar blues progres-sions in April 1959 when he recorded "Teardrops" at Universal Recording. The song, which Johnson wrote with Howard Scott, is a pop ballad; King Records tacked on a light chorus, maybe to distract from the lead singer's southern inflections. Overall, it's the sound of a twenty-three-year-old Chi-cagoan transitioning in style and claiming his own legacy.

"That was blues all right—but say you're Mr. [Henry] Ford," Johnson said,

> Ford Motors' son comes along, makes the Navigator with power windows, power doors. So I'm extending what the older people did. And it came with rhythm; that's why they named it rhythm and blues. We dealt with the beat, different changes. Blues was I, IV, back to I [progressions]. When we could know how to read notes and make chords, we discovered that we could hear gospel; gospel had other chords in it. So we blended gospel and some jazz chords in there, and I know I kept the blues in my sound. I just didn't play the simple I, IV, V, the simple changes. And the people love it. 'Teardrops' is not blues, that's calypso, cha-cha with a funky beat. That's the way I wanted to do it when I started playing, and that was in 1959 when I made my first record. I was hearing it all in my soul, heart, and mind.

For a few years Johnson drifted among independent record companies, including Cincinnati-based King's Federal imprint, which also had an of-fice on Chicago's Record Row. He was far from alone. This was a heady time for small-scale music entrepreneurs in Chicago, whose owners, Robert Pruter observes, "usually got into the business as a sideline to their main enterprises—insurance, coal, construction, whatever."[58] Pruter counts at least twenty-two R&B labels from this period spread across the city and sub-urbs. That "whatever" turned out to be considerably broad. Early in the 1960s, a raconteur named Arrow Brown devised Bandit Records: by the end of the decade it had apparently become financed through the illicit earnings of women who lived with him in a Bronzeville graystone.[59] Whether or not these ventures were profitable, their results sometimes endured in unexpected ways, such as in the bidding wars of collectors.[60] Individual talents and the odd cheerfulness of, say, Bandit's youthful Majestic Arrows group did not require huge recording budgets.

Chicago also had a number of wholesale stores and independent truckers that became known as one-stops. These benefited small-scale R&B operations that needed an alternative to major distributors and retailers who were not eager to extend lines of credit to start-ups. When record seller and future songwriter Jack Daniels got out of the navy in 1959, he helped his brother-in-law Willie J. Barney set up his own kind of distributor, Barney's One-Stop. Soon they expanded to three locations, along with a wholesaler with record racks in his truck. This kind of underground economy burgeoned outside the notice of the *Billboard* chart compilers.

"The term 'one-stop' came from the fact that a lot of small record stores, you buy wholesale records from the distributors down on Record Row," Daniels said. "All State, United, Liberty, MS, Garmisa, all sold or distributed certain artists, records by certain artists, certain labels. And you would have to go by each one of them and pick up your list of records that you needed to sell. They could come by Barney's and get everything at the One-Stop. That's how, that's why they became one-stops. You could get it all right there."

This kind of cottage industry refuted an editorial in the June 1961 issue of *Ebony* claiming that African Americans had not become sufficiently entrepreneurial. Ironically, the magazine's office at Johnson Publications, 1820 South Michigan Avenue, was practically next door to the heart of Record Row. The article, headlined "The Need to Produce," argued that while there had been a slew of black doctors, scientists, and labor leaders, "the Negro is mad at himself for not making the commercial grade."[61] After acknowledging that African Americans were regularly denied access to capital from lending institutions and excluded from business organizations, the article argues for collective action and asks government organizations for government agencies. Its unnamed author concludes, "Surely, a people that can convert its consumer power into a weapon so potent that it desegregates lunch counters in Dixie can develop its producing power regardless of economic detours."[62] But plucky music entrepreneurs also knew that they presented a risky investment by the very nature of their business, so why approach traditional lines of capital in the first place? Conceivably, at that time class differences also separated the aspirations of *Ebony* editorial writers from many of the underground characters who tend to thrive in the music industry.

For some of these tiny operations, low overhead shaped the sound of their products throughout the 1960s. One of these was Down to Earth Records, which Walter Gardner owned with his trumpeter brother Burgess Gardner. One of its singles, General Crook's "Gimme Some (Parts I and II)" from 1970, is a stripped-down guitar-driven funk track that the singer came up with spontaneously late one night while returning home after visiting a girlfriend. The small-scale operation meant that a recording could be made almost instantly. "We had such a good relationship because there was nobody in between us," Crook said. "You know, I would write the tune, call Burgess up and go out to his house. And we'd put it together and go in the studio and record it."

Syl Johnson recorded a few tracks at One-derful, which became one of the most notable black-owned record companies to emerge in Chicago in the early 1960s. Ernie and George Leaner entered the business by starting at the Groove Record Store in the 1940s. They moved into distribution when they formed United in March 1950. In 1962 the Leaners positioned themselves vertically by setting up the One-derful company on Record Row, about one block south of Johnson Publications. Their connection to their uncle, media giant Al Benson, helped. Like Vee-Jay, the Leaners' operation encouraged flexibility. They could respond quickly to what was happening in popular music, as they did early on with the high-energy dance hit by the Five Du-Tones, "Shake a Tail Feather." The Leaners also owned imprints that specialized in R&B (Midas), blues (M-Pac!), dance music (Mar-V-Lus), early funk (Toddlin' Town), and gospel (Halo). Singer Otis Clay, who recorded "I Don't Know What to Do" for One-derful, said the company allowed its artists to just be themselves. That song, for instance, encapsulated his roots in driving rural gospel yet recast it all in pleading to a more earthly companion.

"One-derful had its own studio," Clay said. "You had that opportunity to write songs; we were putting them together. You had all the young writers and singers. We did this every day. We'd come into the studio, get into a creative thing. 'OK, I got this song.' We would put these songs down. It was my life for four years."

That close, informal atmosphere imbued the company's operations. Saxophonist Willie Henderson described how One-derful arranger Milton Bland accurately communicated his charts without writing them down. Pianist-arranger Larry Nestor joined One-derful in 1965 as a newcomer to R&B, and he remembers veterans like Monk Higgins and Clay as being exceptionally helpful. Guitarist Larry Blasingaine similarly recalls a feeling of camaraderie at the studio, calling it "one big family." He was a teenager at the time and learned valuable production techniques in this atmosphere.

Nestor adds that, as a boss, George Leaner remained unobtrusive. The pianist was routinely the sole white musician at One-derful, but he never felt ostracized. "They accepted me," Nestor said. "[Songwriter-producer] Jimmy Jones said to me, 'You're not white.'"

The Leaner brothers shared Al Benson's commitment to political and social advocacy—for instance, George Leaner raised funds for civil rights sit-in demonstrators[63]—but their activism went beyond just supporting organizations. Singer Beverly Shaffer was a teenager in 1965 when she responded to an article in the *Chicago Defender* seeking young people for its talent show at the Aragon Ballroom. DJ Herb Kent noted her performance and introduced her to George and Ernie Leaner. Shaffer then recorded a few singles at the studio in collaboration with Nestor and other musicians. Since One-derful did not have Motown's promotional muscle or its responsibilities, the company could be more open to giving a platform to young singers like Shaffer. The vulnerability she brings to the absorbing "Where Will You Be Boy?" reflects her feelings about a conflict thousands of miles away.

"They were the best, they were just like father figures," Shaffer said of the Leaners. "When I went down there, they said, 'Do you think you can write?' I said, 'I don't know, I never really tried.' So I just went home, and at that time the Vietnam War was going on, and I just sat and wrote 'Where Will You Be Boy?' I just wrote the title first, started humming, write a line, humming, write a line. Next thing you know, I had something. They were really impressed with me writing that and I was just fifteen. I didn't know, who would think that someone that young would be recording when there were the Supremes? There were artists out with that caliber, and I was just a fifteen-year-old lollipopping."

Dances Offer Alternative Spaces and Exchanges

Record hops and talent shows also served as a recreational alternative to the mess that often characterized the Chicago public school system, especially for African American families. In August 1963, civil rights organizations moved to oust Chicago Public School superintendent Benjamin Willis because of his refusal to support integration. Schools in predominantly black neighborhoods were overcrowded and lacked sufficient resources. Instead of letting black students attend schools in white districts, Willis shifted some black classes to the early morning, others to late afternoon. That proved unworkable, so he introduced cheap trailers that became known as Willis Wagons. Protests ensued, as did police brutality against protesters.[64] On October 22, 1963, more than 224,770 youths boycotted classes. Older students joined 20,000 marchers to protest downtown. In February 1964 about 180,000 students took part in a second boycott.[65] Meanwhile, WVON interspersed discussions of the school boycott with R&B records. Along with airing news spots every half hour during the early 1960s, WVON broadcast Wesley South's "Hot Line" open-ended forum immediately after Kent's program.[66] Such radio programming also provided a forum for voices that were largely ignored elsewhere in the media.

Even with systemic problems throughout the public schools, some students who later became musicians mention that the situation within their classrooms was not dire. Songwriter Raynard Miner, who attended Marshall High School during the early 1960s, disputes historians' descriptions of its condescending teachers.[67] Blind since childhood, Miner said he was just happy to attend a school where he was not treated differently because of his disability. Trombonist Willie Woods, who graduated from Wendell Phillips High School in 1964, recalled overcrowding when he was a student, but he also retained strong memories of some quality teachers, even under those conditions. Besides band instructor Louis Whitworth, he admired a physics teacher and an English teacher. He proudly recited a soliloquy from *Hamlet* that he had memorized fifty-two years earlier. "When I was in high school," Woods said, "there was a renaissance of learning."

Outside those spaces, segregation and racial animosity inhibited where young African Americans could travel within the city, even casually. Lowrell Simon sang with the Vondells in the late 1950s and early 1960s and lived in the South Side's Stateway Gardens housing projects. The group achieved a minor hit with the early soul song "Lenora," but despite this accomplishment walking a few blocks to watch the Chicago White Sox play at nearby Comiskey Park (in the Bridgeport area) was apt to be hazardous. The white neighborhood—home to Mayor Richard J. Daley—was noted for its overt hostility.

"You didn't go to Bridgeport," Simon said. "The police used to take us all the way over there when we used to sneak into the ballpark. They'd take us all the way over there and drop us off and let us out around the time for the game to end, knowing we had to come over to Stateway and get past all these white people. One time I was selling the *Sun-Times* and two white boys chased me, and I was scared to death—I thought I was in Mississippi."

A few black entrepreneurs realized how performance opportunities could enhance mutual support in these situations. The Teens with Talent program at a West Side YMCA provided opportunities for young prodigies like Larry Blasingaine to be mentored by older artists such as the Artistics. Albert Johnson and Johnny Nixon were responsible for the February 1963 Teens with

Talent concert at the 1,200-seat Studebaker Theater at the Fine Arts Building downtown, and it received glowing attention from *Ebony*.[68] Johnson and Nixon had gone to the West Side and invited gang members and school dropouts with musical potential to take part in the show, although most of the kids were, as *Ebony* noted, "from more stable circumstances."[69] The concert presented gospel, jazz, and blues and included such vocal groups as the Constellations. Bernard Reed, a member of that group, attests, "It gave us the chance to perform on a professional stage—it was a thrill for us to be there."

These musical and social events could not compensate for the failings of the public school system and the city leadership's inability to protect youths like Lowrell Simon. Nor did they always connect with political activism. But record hops hosted by Herb Kent, for example, among many other teen dances on the South Side and West Side, had significance in another way: as "community theaters." Pianist, musicologist, and former Chicagoan Guthrie Ramsey Jr. defines this term in *Race Music* as spaces where individuals become linked to a larger group through social exchanges, using music as a source of connected memory.[70] A new culture sprouted at African American teen dances, and it would unfold to subsequent generations, constituting a social cohesion that would be a step toward any kind of mass movement.

At the same time, Chicago's vibrant youth culture and its concentration of upstart black record companies made it the country's dance music capital.[71] Some of this influence came from sheer numbers: by 1963 the city's 923,000 African Americans represented a third of Chicago's population.[72] Such numbers would have yielded not just musical innovators, but also a robust audience for their creations. This audience constructed a culture around musical innovations, responding expressively in moves on the dance floor and in sharp fashions. All of these became assertions of identity in a city that largely considered these youths invisible.

One of the quintessential dance songs from 1964 was the massive hit "Twine Time," which Alvin Cash and the Crawlers recorded for Mar-V-Lus. The name derives from the twine, a dance that students at Dunbar High School devised and Kent picked up at one of his record hops. Andre Williams, who had been working in an artists and repertoire position at the label, wrote the song and had Cash record it.[73] Cash was hardly a singer, so his lines are calls to dance along with shouts and squeals. His limitations never mattered: tight—repeated short bursts from the horns punctuate a snaky, shimmying organ line. "Twine Time" became a huge hit, reaching number one on *Billboard*'s R&B charts and number fourteen on its pop charts. Even Chicago alderman Robert H. Miller impressed the *Chicago Defender* by doing the dance at a Christmas party he hosted.[74] Murray Kempton, among other writers, states that this dance was a distinctively black Chicago phenomenon, separate from the popular white dance of the time known as the jerk.[75] Jackie Ross, who recorded "Jerk and Twine" for Chess in 1965, disagreed and said her single was not an attempt to bridge communities. Although the twine was a South Side invention, she added that "everybody did the jerk." Either way, such dances advanced cultural affirmation in a city where such manifestations had to be built from the ground up.

Clothing fashions at Kent's parties on the West and South Sides also extended globally, even if that appropriation did not happen right away. These styles were split between the ostensibly rough "gousters" and the "Ivy Leaguers" who had more upscale aspirations. While nobody is exactly sure how the term gouster was transposed from Old English to 1960s Chicago, singer Gavin Christopher, a teenager then, identified with this set when he went to Kent's West Side dances, where he'd mingle with such singers as Major Lance and Billy Butler. Clothes became as much a personal and group identifier as musical choices. "We were gousters," Christopher said:

> The difference between gousters and Ivy Leaguers was we wore gangster-like clothes: fedoras, Italian knit shirts, double pleated pants with Stacy Adams shoes spit-shined to a tee—you dig what I'm saying? Ivy Leaguers wore bucks, khakis, and [high-end] Brooks Brothers shirts with button-down collars and mostly collegiate jackets and stuff like that. They liked to shop at Brooks Brothers, and we liked to go to [low-end] Maxwell Street to get our clothes. It was more to appeal to women. The tradition of a gouster was to have a little edge, to be hard-core, to be looked on as somebody with some clout and a gangster. We looked at Ivy Leaguers as namby-pamby. They wore pleat shirts. But back then the difference . . . was that masculinity in being a gouster; you related to gangsters.

Naturally Chicago's independent record labels tried to cash in on that outlaw appeal: One-derful released the Five Du-Tones' single "The Gouster" in 1964. Deep down, though, the mid-decade gouster/Ivy League divide was a fashion choice reflective of surface presentation, not deep class divisions. Kent mentioned occasional fights breaking out between the two Chicago teen dance factions but said they were mostly harmless.[76] The *Chicago Defender* first used the word gouster in a 1962 editorial by Marc Clemens, concerned less with social divisions than with sociable hygiene: "Be Ivy, be Gouster, be WWIG (Wear What I Got)—BUT BE CLEAN!!!"[77] Positive self-assertion ran throughout them all.

Years later, David Bowie drew from these black Chicago sounds and fashions to record an album he intended to call *The Gouster* but then remade as his 1974 rock-funk-disco hybrid *Young Americans*. The original LP was eventually included in his 2016 boxed set *Who Can I Be Now? [1974–1976]*. Most likely the concept came from his close attention to 1960s Chicago soul or more directly from Bowie's Chicago-born girlfriend and background singer Ava Cherry, who was a friend and musical collaborator of Gavin Christopher. Bowie's longtime producer Tony Visconti stated, "'Gouster' was a word unfamiliar to me but David saw it as a type of dress code worn by African American teens in the '60s, in Chicago. But in the context of the album its meaning was attitude, an attitude of pride and hipness. Of all the songs we cut, we were enamored of the ones we chose for the album that portrayed this attitude."[78]

Yet perhaps the widest cultural movement this social scene launched came at the end of the 1960s, when another WVON personality, Don Cornelius, took these sounds, dances, and styles and combined them with more overt social and political messages for his television program *Soul Train*. That show was also aimed at young adults, but its geographic and generational impact would reverberate further than anyone could have imagined.

THREE

We're a Winner:
Musicians, Activists, and Educators
Build an Expanding Industry

In fall 1969 *Chicago Defender* arts critic Earl Calloway visited Carl Davis's office at Record Row's 1449 South Michigan Avenue, previously the home of Vee-Jay. Davis had been an artists and repertoire director for Brunswick Records for about three years[1] in addition to running Jalynne, a music management and promotion firm, since 1965 and forming his own Bashie and Dakar recording labels. Calloway was impressed—not just with "the plush office, air conditioned with wall to wall carpeting."[2] And also not just with Davis's recording Barbara Acklin, the Chi-Lites, and Tyrone Davis, who had a gold-selling (500,000 units) hit in February of that year ("Can I Change My Mind").[3] Most of Calloway's subsequent article emphasized Davis's efforts with Operation Breadbasket, and he lauded the producer's organizational expertise. "'Whenever one thinks of a black business, he thinks of a dirty place with everyone running around not knowing what to do,'" Davis said to Calloway. "'It's my job to keep the attitude healthy and the people happy. I am not jealous when another black man grows because he has a mind just as I do. . . . The people here are together.'"[4]

Calloway's admiration was well placed. Within four months Davis would be promoted to vice president of Brunswick.[5] Sales had grown during the last four years of the 1960s, as they had for the record industry nationwide. Davis proved prescient about wanting to create a "Chicago sound." Nonetheless, the meaning of the term had become as complicated as the backgrounds and ambitions of the people who built it. Some looked at integrating different musical styles, others wanted to build up their own separate visions and identities. But Davis's quotation also reflects other currents outside that comfortable office.

While Davis's ascent as a black executive of a major record company was crucial for the city he called home, other African American musicians and entrepreneurs in the mid-1960s had their own productive ideas. This was a time when the rise of teen and young adult consumers fueled record sales not just for Davis but also for rival Chess. Even as these businesses followed corporate models, numerous smaller black-owned and artist-owned music labels arose throughout Chicago, even with the shady underworld that had always been a part of this industry. Although big and small firms controlled their work, R&B musicians had become more empowered in their financial dealings and in other collaborations throughout studios and clubs. Davis's beliefs and his confident demeanor reflected those of black educators who continued to help train the musicians who worked for him. These performers' considerable musical training or youthful adventurism created major hits and lyrical affirmations.

As Carl Davis's support for Operation Breadbasket revealed, all this occurred while the civil rights movement was becoming more visible in Chicago. Some in the music industry engaged with activists, others created the cause's soundtrack. The music also forged indispensable social bonds. Even in a racially divided city, a couple of observers from outside African American neighborhoods wrote about the way music created strong connections within these streets while it served as an invitation. The vibrant AM radio station WVON also continued conveying musical and political messages. Davis expressed a philosophy of wider outreach that had been growing in Chicago throughout the decade. Most notably, Martin Luther King brought the focus of the civil rights movement from the South to Chicago in 1966. Engaging with urban youth became key to King's efforts, as it was for R&B producers like Davis. Although the producer was a businessman whose job was to sell records, he and others, at least publicly, intertwined sales goals and expressions of social consciousness. From the mid-1960s into the next decade, the growth of soul culture would echo and feed into social and political progress—something Davis surely knew when he talked about the cooperative environment esteemed at Brunswick.

Musical and Educational Activists Set a Bold Agenda

Consider the career of James Mack. Crane Junior College on the city's West Side offered one means for the city's students to receive vocational training or transition into a four-year college program.[6] Its neighborhood faced serious challenges: in Crane's surrounding area of 300,000 people, about 22 percent of the population received support from the government's Aid to Families with Dependent Children, according to the college's dean James F. Groark in the *Chicago Defender*.[7] That same report lamented that students entering the college lacked required English skills. Faculty were quoted commenting on that problem.[8] One of them was Mack, chair of the music department, who bemoaned the lack of language proficiency but did not accept excuses.

Mack studied primarily European classical music. He attended St. Philip, a mostly white Catholic high school on the West Side, where he played the flute. Symphonic music on the radio inspired him to explore composers' techniques.[9] As an instrumental prodigy, Mack earned a scholarship to Roosevelt University after serving as principal flutist in the Chicago Civic Orchestra and singing opera as a bass baritone with Chicago's Grant Park Orchestra. After he received a master's degree from Roosevelt in 1954, he taught at the University of Chicago and joined the Crane faculty in 1959.[10] Mack wanted to teach his students the music that inspired him, but he shrewdly knew he could reach them best if he studied what they were hearing. He told writer Bill Dahl, "I'm entirely classically trained, my interest is entirely classical. In order to be able to get these guys interested in Bach, Beethoven, and Mozart, I had to develop some interest in jazz."[11]

Organization was part of Mack's pedagogy. His Crane student group, the Jazzmen—bassist Louis Satterfield, saxophonist Don Myrick, drummer Maurice White, and trumpeter Charles Handy—started winning competitions in the Midwest about 1962.[12] Willie Henderson, who played in the Crane funk group the Metrotones, said the lessons Mack taught him were "Be professional, learn what you do, be courteous, and watch out for people who are running a game on you." Mack also directed saxophonist George Patterson Jr.'s jazz group the Interpreters, and he brought his vocal quintet to harmonize behind them on their 1965 album *The Knack* (Cadet). This record's five stylistically diverse compositions included a mambo from pianist Thomas "Tom Tom" Washington.

In later years several of Mack's students at Crane would become invaluable in shaping R&B in Chicago and farther afield. Some remained musical traditionalists; others offered their own twists on African influences. Many delivered hit records through their work in the city's principal studios. These artists included jazz-soul singer Shelley Fisher and Brunswick's arrangers Henderson and Washington as well as trombonist-producer Willie Woods of the late-1960s Affro-Arts Theater and its house band, the Pharaohs. Four of Mack's students—Myrick, Satterfield, and the brothers Maurice and Verdine White—would go on to fame in the supergroup Earth, Wind, and Fire. But they all brought his lessons with them.

"James was a big guy in size, but one of the gentlest spirits you'd ever meet," Maurice White stated in his 2016 memoir, *My Life with Earth, Wind and Fire.* "That man is the godfather of much of the significant talent that came out of Chicago."[13] Woods remembers Mack's coming to his high school classroom at Wendell Phillips in the early 1960s to recruit students for Crane, and it was the teacher's confidence that won them over. "When he sat down, he gave us everything about music education," Woods said. "He said, 'Somebody sit at the piano and hit any series of notes.'" Then Woods demonstrated with hands spread as if they were on piano keys before continuing. "He said, 'Your baby finger is a C, next note up is an E-flat, next note up is a D.' We said, 'Maaan, this cat is bad!' He said, 'That's what you'll be able to do when you study with me.'"

A photograph that ran in a 1965 *Chicago Tribune* article about how Mack trained his Crane students for employment in the music business included Woods. "Our music department trains performers in both the classical repertory and the jazz idiom," Mack said at the time. "But when you look around, you find 95 percent of the musicians in the United States play commercial [popular] music. Despite this, there is no other school in the city that teaches a student to become a commercial musician."[14] Mack also describes how he emphasizes versatility—training musicians to play various instruments—as well as insisting that each student take a broad range of academic courses. Throughout, employability persisted as a dominant motif; at the end of 1963, the area surrounding Crane had sunk to seventy-first out of seventy-four Chicago communities in family income levels.[15]

Mack also nudged his students in other directions—away from sanctioned college activities. Willie Henderson and bassist Rollo Radford remember Mack's bringing students along to protest for the integration of AFM Locals 10 and 208. His daughter, Elaine Mack, who became a cellist, remembered her father's conducting informal classes in their home in the city's Hyde Park neighborhood. She says these sessions had a big impact on Washington.

"Dad was not just their teacher," Elaine Mack said, "he was also their friend, in regard of being encouraging, pulling out their innate musicality, and showing them different ways they could employ it. I'm sure that's how Tom Tom got inspired to arrange and write and do things. Because there weren't that many people who did this kind of work. It was new. We're talking black musicians back in the sixties. There wasn't that much opportunity to do what Dad did—bring the classical skills in with that music. There were plenty of guitarists and saxophonists, drummers and people who sang, and sang rhythm and blues. But how many knew how to write for strings?"

Racism also afflicted Chicago-area classical music ensembles. An editorial in the May 1963 issue of *Ebony* describes what happened when conductor Milton Preves invited black violinist Carol Anderson to play with the west suburban Oak Park–River Forest Symphony. The symphony board's president tried to prevent Anderson from performing, which caused an outcry among civic organizations and clergy.[16] Mack's imparting a classical tradition to young black musicians in 1960s Chicago made a liberating statement: no music should be out of bounds.

Partially because of Mack's advocacy, black musicians in Chicago could claim more professional opportunities during the latter half of the 1960s. Bassist Bernard Reed commented that he benefited from the musicians' union integration in 1966 and mentioned his jobs playing on commercials, where he received union scale for sessions. "Sometimes when you're black you find yourself left out," Reed said. "The basics of being with the union was the union was protecting you, making sure that you don't get run over, that nobody's misusing you—that nobody was taking your music and not paying you for it."

But despite Mack's arguments, some African American musicians in Chicago continued to disagree with their union's becoming integrated. Across the country, black musicians feared a loss of autonomy if their regional guilds merged.[17] This debate echoed the early twentieth-century divisions expressed between followers of Booker T. Washington and W. E. B. Du Bois.[18] Multi-instrumentalist Phil Cohran, who had been working in the city since the 1950s, remained an integration skeptic. Cohran felt that the black musicians who led Local 208 were stronger in Europe than their white union counterparts and that amalgamation would reduce their own influence. Also, Cohran believed that a separate black union had a sense of self-determination. Was it worth diminishing that in exchange for what he considered an inadequate deal? His frustration would become a catalyst to his cofounding the Association for the Advancement of Creative Musicians and establishing the Affro-Arts Theater on the South Side two years later.[19]

"[The union] promised [black musicians] radio gigs, [television's] *Bozo's Circus*, and a lot of things where we were banned," Cohran said. "A promise to me is for chumps—this is Chicago, you don't go nowhere on a promise. But they did, and I said, 'They spent $5 million to join the black and white unions together, and they didn't spend $10 to see what effect it would have.'"

Still, musicians' activism and their strategic arguments reflected the civil rights movement as it shifted its focus and embraced young people in Chicago. Martin Luther King relocated to the city in late January 1966 and lived in a West Side apartment in downtrodden Lawndale to bring more attention to urban poverty and the persistence of racism and housing segregation.[20] Earlier that month he had announced the formation of the Chicago Freedom Movement, which joined King's Southern Christian Leadership Conference with the locally based alliance of activists, the Coordinating Council of Community Organizations.[21] King's engagement with African American teenagers began right away. In February he visited Marshall High School, where students sang freedom songs and called him "Martin Luther Cool."[22] WVON had been enlisted to aid King's work. DJ Herb Kent served as emcee of his rally at Soldier Field on July 10, 1966, which thirty thousand people attended.[23] Behind the scenes, Kent, Bernadine C. Washington—the station's designated women's director—and owner Leonard Chess participated in a reception at the Pick-Congress Hotel before the rally.[24] When, during the week following the rally, there were riots on the West Side after police shut off a fire hydrant that young people had been using to cool themselves, WVON collaborated with civil rights ministers to call for calm.[25]

Despite WVON's influence and social consciousness among artists, civil rights leaders still did not feature nearby R&B musicians at major events during the mid-1960s. No Chicago soul singers performed at the Soldier Field rally—although politically outspoken vocalist Oscar Brown Jr., who did sing at the event, transcended genre. Traditional gospel and folk protest singers had been ingrained within the movement for years. Perhaps younger voices had not yet gained their elders' attention. Or maybe R&B was still seen as of the same lesser artistic value as pop and rock 'n' roll, even though all these idioms encompassed wide lyrical and musical ideas by the time King moved to Chicago's West Side. Possibly, lingering perceptions of class differences between soul music audiences and some potential middle- or upper-income contributors to the movement also had an impact.[26]

But WVON still led in covering King in Chicago as the twenty-nine-year-old Don Cornelius traversed the civil rights beat for the station. News director Roy Wood assigned him to King, since this rookie had no claim to more coveted slots playing music.[27] As a result, King's time in Chicago had unforeseen consequence. As part of his coverage, Cornelius met with one of the civil rights leader's Chicago corporate supporters, Sears Roebuck executive George O'Hare.[28] When Cornelius launched the *Soul Train* television program in Chicago four years later, he persuaded O'Hare to bring Sears on board as an initial sponsor.[29] Jesse Jackson recalled Cornelius's describing his mission to portray positive images of black youths on television after meeting with King at this time.[30]

WVON's promotion of the movement's values also was recognized in other media. Young adult author Susan Gregory documents this appeal in her memoir *Hey, White Girl!*[31] Gregory describes her family's move from north suburban Wilmette to the West Side because of her progressive father's work in the liberal-leaning faith-based Ecumenical Institute. When she attends Marshall High during the 1966-67 school year, she takes note of crime in the area, the school's crumbling infrastructure, its lack of resources, and the mixed quality of teachers. As the book's title indicates, she encounters hostility from some students, but she also describes feeling welcome from others who are part of a growing black consciousness movement. And she admires the school's music program. For Gregory, listening to WVON DJs and picking up their cues become keys to her acceptance. Although Detroit's Motown and Aretha Franklin dominate her narrative, she also mentions getting the chance, at a year-end school dance, to spin Chicagoan Ruby Andrews's hit "Casanova (Your Playing Days Are Over)" as well as the Ivories, a vocal group consisting of Marshall alumnae.[32] Her account presents a vision of the city that contrasts with typical portrayals. Although the book has its somber moments, she suggests that even in divided Chicago, soul music could connect young people from contrasting backgrounds.

Young Artists and Producers Assert Themselves as the Market Expands

In November 1967 the Impressions' irrepressibly uplifting "We're a Winner" broke on the airwaves—but not everywhere. The single may have frightened some white station programmers. "We're a Winner" alters the message of Mayfield's earlier "People Get Ready" and "Keep on Pushing." Those songs seemed universal, even as they echoed black gospel songwriters.[33] But "We're a Winner" denotes unmistakably African American dimensions, from the way Mayfield phrases "Lord have mercy" to a background shout of "sock it to me." Eddie Thomas's wife Audrey sang that backing line as friends and associates gathered at the session, which was meant to feel like a club gig. Meanwhile, Mayfield asserts that "we're true from the good black earth" and urges "keep on pushin' / like your leaders tell you to," full of verve and connoting a new attitude. Foregrounded call-to-action triplets by Billy Griffin's kick drum, along with Mayfield's distinctively tuned electric guitar lines (played by Mayfield or by Phil Upchurch), brashly juxtapose Pate's horn fanfares and tensile violins.[34] The title implies unified action: plural becomes singular: it's not "We Are Winners." So too do the crowd sounds throughout the song—rising at the very end. While "We're a Winner" continued to convey Mayfield's optimistic viewpoint, some pop stations, notably Chicago's WLS, did not play the song.[35] This was six years after WLS did put into rotation the Mayfield and Butler song about low-wage employment, "I'm a-Telling You."

Still, as Eddie Thomas said, WLS had never warmed to the Impressions in the first place. Whether the song's rallying cry led to its being stricken from pop stations' playlists across the United States became an issue at the time and for years afterward. In 1972 Mayfield commented, "When we get into music like 'We're a Winner,' or anything that's going to inspire oppressed and exploited people, there are going to be problems."[36]

Running somewhat counter to this claim, *Jet* magazine looked into whether there was a nationwide attempt to ban "We're a Winner" from the airwaves beyond Chicago.[37] The radio station personnel they quote— and their cities—remain anonymous, but across the country most of them claimed to be playing the record. It has a positive message, they said, and they had not received any white backlash.[38] There were exceptions. One is a station representative in "a smaller southern city" and another in a "major midwestern city" who states, "There has been a lot of race friction here, and we were worried that if we played this record we might get criticized for stirring things up. But now I'm beginning to think we ought to play it."[39] So whatever programming decision WLS made, the station's refusal on this song had shown that this formidable AM outlet could not claim complete control over young consumers. The same could be said for other stations that may have declined to play the record: playlist bans could not stop its ascent. "We're a Winner" rose to number fourteen on the *Billboard* pop charts and first place in its R&B ranking.[40]

Ironically, musicologist Arnold Shaw felt that the Impressions were not radical enough. Although his thoughts reflect a long-buried polemic, they serve as reminders that some on the left also slighted Mayfield's message at the time. In Shaw's 1970 book *The World of Soul,* his derogatory comments include calling the group "Oreo singers." He assumes that their performances would be picketed by black student unions during the era of large student demonstrations.[41] He cites the May 1969 hit "Choice of Colors" as an example of Mayfield's suggestion of education as the means of advancement (rather than, say, rioting) as an example of his moderate approach. Shaw's claim overlooked the African American students at Howard University who sang "We're a Winner" to celebrate their victorious demand for a black research institute.[42] Along with his insulting terminology, he ignored the assertiveness in Mayfield's lyrics. The evocative lure of the music also mattered: the Impressions' smooth delivery conjoined with Pate's sophisticated string arrangements could be far more effective in putting a message across than if the words had been shouted or framed in most other ways. But a few outliers in the Impressions' audience concurred with Shaw, including a "white kid dressed in revolution hip" in San Francisco who, according to *Rolling Stone,* derided the group as "black capitalists."[43] Neither of these viewpoints acknowledges a long history of African Americans' taking on such business endeavors as publishing their own literary works despite entrenched opposition.[44] Indeed, such ventures can prove more challenging than overt militancy.

For instance, along with the Impressions' music, Mayfield and Thomas's entrepreneurship addressed the "actualities of local, state and national power" that essayist Albert Murray called for in *The Omni-Americans*.[45] They exerted local control through starting their own business, not through the posturing Murray derided. "We're a Winner" was released just before they launched Curtom Records in spring 1968, using that song's title as the company's motto.[46] Mayfield also said they donated a percentage of the profits to the Southern Christian Leadership Conference.[47] The office was in the same South Side building as Curtom Publishing and was the successor to their previous attempts in the mid-1960s, including Mayfield, Thomas, and Windy-C. All of these released midwestern R&B artists, yet few achieved national traction. But they did have good relations with the larger distributor, New York-based Buddah.[48] Thomas had experience from promotions work for ABC-Paramount; Mayfield was a rising soul star. Through trial and error, they made it all cohere. "We didn't have the Brink's truck out front," Thomas said. "That was the basic challenge. But I've always been a fighter, infighter, low profile. And some of the jocks appreciated that, that warmth, that cordiality. That helped me a lot. Some felt sorry for me, too. I lived on the road, seven days a week. And whatever little money I had, I'd send some records in, and I knew their families, I knew their kids. My life was on the road."

The Burke family, who lived near the Curtom office, had a fruitful connection with the company during the 1960s, singing as the Five Stairsteps. They epitomized one narrative of working class–based ambitions and talent forming bonds and turning them all into lasting pop. Clarence Burke Sr., a detective with the Chicago Police Department, followed a time-honored path by showcasing his four sons (Clarence Jr., Keni, James, Denis) and daughter (Alohe) to a wider audience as they won a Regal Theater talent contest in 1965.[49] The elder Burke became acquainted with his neighbor, Fred Cash of the Impressions, who heard the group and—as Keni later told radio journalist Bob Abrahamian—brought them over to Mayfield's house that night for an audition.[50] The upbeat "Don't Waste Your Time" was released on Windy-C that fall. Windy-C folded because of distribution problems, but when Curtom formed, the Stairsteps returned. A new Burke, Cubie, appears on the album *Love's Happening*; at age two-and-a-half, Cubie was more gimmick than performer, but the band was renamed the Five Stairsteps and

Cubie. Perhaps, as Keni Burke mentioned, his early listening to Latin music informed the harmonies and dance tempos on the record.[51] He also said that Mayfield did more as a producer than fund the sessions—including giving him a bass when he was an adolescent.[52]

Other Curtom artists in the 1960s benefited from classical training. Holly Maxwell, who nailed and extended remarkably high notes on Mayfield's "Suffer," had sung at the Civic Opera House in Chicago at twelve and attended Roosevelt University. When the Impressions visited Howard University in 1967, Mayfield met music major Donny Hathaway. Hathaway moved to Chicago later that year to become a writer-arranger-producer at Curtom and sang "I Thank You" with June Conquest for the company.[53] He also helped arrange the Impressions' album *The Young Mod's Forgotten Story* and worked on multiple projects at Curtom. Mayfield described Hathaway as "a genius" and relied on his services, since Pate had an exclusive contract with ABC-Paramount, where he had moved into an artists and repertoire executive position.[54] "[Hathaway] had a lot of learning in him but he was instilled with a lot of depth of the religious feeling of black music," Mayfield later told Craig Werner in *Goldmine*. "This fella, you could just talk to him over the phone and play him a piece of music and he could call out every chord and every movement and where the fifth was and the augmented and tell you what key it was in."[55]

But Thomas knew that, with both Hathaway and Mayfield having such determined ideas, the protégé would not stay long with his mentor. Since independent R&B companies thrived in Chicago during the middle and late 1960s, a versatile musician like Hathaway could bring his prowess as a composer, arranger, and producer to numerous outlets. Along with Curtom, he worked as a copyist at Chess, and he arranged the strings on such records as singer Maurice Jackson's infectious "Step by Step" for the small Plum label. These were just a few of Hathaway's jobs across town.

Such enterprises burgeoned for a few key reasons. Worldwide, by early 1968 the annual sale of records was believed to be nearly one billion, and singles accounted for 530 million, the first time such a global study had been completed.[56] Widespread changes in the United States contributed to this market. Jon Savage mentions in *1966: The Year the Decade Exploded* that the civil rights movement's attacks on segregationist laws supported the ascendancy of black pop stars, although he specifies Motown artists and their southern counterparts.[57] Still, Motown sent a lucrative signal to independent entrepreneurs nationwide.[58] In 1964 Chess had already brought over Motown's Billy Davis to produce such hits as Jackie Ross's "Selfish One," which rose to number four on the *Cash Box* R&B charts.[59] In the baby boom's aftermath the nation's median age declined to 27.9, and 17.9 million Americans were between thirteen and seventeen. Such demographics also drove record sales. But ongoing fascination with soul music overseas also played a part. Reportedly, in 1966 R&B made up 40 percent of all singles sold in the United Kingdom.[60] Back in Chicago, where distributors, retailers, and one-stop operations were concentrated, such logistics played their part in making this surge continue.

For African Americans, the possibility of US Small Business Administration (SBA) loans in Chicago might have also helped start-up record companies. On September 1, 1966, the SBA raised its ceiling on direct loans to $100,000 and on participation loans to $150,000 (the former ceilings were $50,000 and $100,000).[61] By the end of that year the Economic Opportunity Act would provide loans of up to $25,000 to individuals throughout Illinois.[62] How many of these loans actually made their way to applicants, or if they were distributed fairly, remains questionable. In September 1968 *Ebony* reported that, during the first six months of that year, only 2.4 percent of $411.1 million in loans approved nationwide by the SBA went to black applicants. Eugene and Katherine Alexander, who owned the Parliament Recording Studio and Electronic Service Shop in Chicago, believed the SBA was inherently racist when refusing their loan to expand.[63]

Even if new black-owned record companies perhaps did not benefit from expanded SBA loans and other loan programs—such as those resulting from the Economic Opportunity Act of 1964—these programs did bring some money into the urban economy. This could have fostered the growth of local music, such as more people purchasing records from retailers or buying drinks at neighborhood spots. In Chicago, at least a few African American entrepreneurs who received SBA funds went on to hire musicians in the 1960s and the 1970s. In 1965 Vince Cullers, founder of the Vince Cullers Advertising Agency, was one of the first to receive such a payment ($15,000) under the city's urban opportunity program, which administered SBA loans.[64] In 1971 Barbara Proctor—once an executive at Vee-Jay—received an $80,000 loan to set up her own advertising agency, but only after she put herself on the job market and used the offers she received as personal collateral.[65]

By the late 1960s, for young artists hoping to get signed to any labels in Chicago, the process remained much as it had been when the Impressions walked down Record Row a decade earlier. Singer Cliff Curry, who grew up in Englewood, had been a member of a few vocal groups when he helped form the Notations. They recorded briefly for the obscure Tad Records on the North Side, but he knew the group would have to do better. So, he said, they made the rounds of Record Row about 1969. "Finding the label wasn't really hard." It was more or less disappointing because at that time you could go up and down from Roosevelt Road, Twelfth Street, all the way to Twenty-Second and Michigan—and a couple were on Wabash—you could go and just knock on doors and ask if you could audition. We got turned down a lot for whatever the reasons were, and that's part of it. But we never stopped, we kept going forward and we knew that eventually something would happen."

What happened was that more Chicago R&B artists took on entrepreneurial roles during the late 1960s. One such musician-entrepreneur, Syl Johnson, heard the Notations and invited them to audition for Twinight Records, just north of downtown. Johnson recorded for Twinight and worked there as a producer and a co-owner with Howard Bedno and Peter Wright, who established the company in 1967 as Twilight.[66] Since a California record company had already registered that name, the Chicago operation became Twinight by the end of the year.[67] Curry had an almost finished ballad, "I'm Still Here," which guitarist Brad Bobo and Johnson fine-tuned. The recording became a substantial hit: WVON gave it airplay in summer 1970, and it reputedly sold eighty thousand copies, reaching number thirty-six on *Billboard*'s soul chart in December of that year.[68] Curry's vocal plays with the steadfast 4/4 time kept on the high-hat; his abrupt high notes on the first beat contrast sharply with the drummer's emphasis on the third beat. The minimal arrangement—no brass or strings—highlights the song's emotional directness. But Curry's achievement came about inadvertently. Although he thought James Stroud would be the lead singer, Johnson heard something crucial that the Notations themselves did not. Curry's voice maintained a direct middle register that his Detroit contemporary Smokey Robinson, for instance, avoided. The results became one more legitimate claim for defining a local R&B aesthetic.

"When I wrote it, I didn't write it to sing the lead," Curry said. "So when we went to the studio to record, we laid the background down first so the lead would have something to go on. Jimmy did the lead, but Syl said, 'Jimmy, you did a good job, but I want this group to sound like nobody else out here. I want an original Chicago sound. And right now the background I'm feeling, but Jimmy, you sound like Smokey [Robinson]. So, Cliff, can you do the song?' Syl said, 'That little thing you did with your voice makes a huge difference.' I felt uncomfortable for about a year when we would do shows. We ended up with a hit because of it. That's what keeps us working across the country."

Another artist-driven enterprise, Giant Productions, formed in 1967 in Hyde Park.[69] The creative energy came from singer-songwriter "Joshie" Jo

Armstead, whose husband, Mel Collins, controlled the business side. Along with Vivian Carter, Armstead was one of the few black women in Chicago responsible for producing significant R&B records. When not on duty for the police force, Collins had been chancing different ventures, including producing blues vocalist-guitarist Fenton Robinson. But Armstead, who was ten years younger, thought, "I loved Fenton and I loved the blues, but that wasn't what I was hearing in my head." For Armstead, the newer R&B would prove engrossing. This included her performing her own songs, "Stone Good Lover" and "I Feel an Urge Coming On."

Armstead said that Collins recognized her voice from demo recordings of songs she had sent to Betty Everett (whom he had managed) in hopes that the popular singer would record them. But she was never one to just wait for opportunities. Born in Mississippi in 1944, at age nineteen Armstead sang in the Ike and Tina Turner Revue. Although she describes Ike Turner as generous in teaching her songwriting, he was not inclined to give Armstead credit for her contribution to the 1961 hit "I'm Blue (The Gong-Gong Song)."[70] She left to join her family in New York, where she met the songwriting team of Nick Ashford and Valerie Simpson. The three of them composed Ray Charles's "Let's Go Get Stoned" as staff writers for Scepter Records. She said that, while living in New York, her folks were "working people and wanted me to quit shucking and jiving and go get a job." So she moved to Chicago, where she slept on friends' couches until Simpson sent her a royalty check for $500.

Not having a bank account, she went to her friend Cubie Coleman to see if he would cash her check at his club, the Tiger Lounge. Coleman didn't, but he did introduce her to Collins, and their producing partnership took off with her handling the writing and him in charge of the finances. Armstead composed Ruby Andrews's "Casanova," which was a hit for Ric Williams's Zodiac company during summer 1967 and, as noted, became part of memoir author Susan Gregory's West Side playlist.[71] Detroit arranger Mike Terry inserted subtle twists such as hand drums mixed with violins to begin the song. Andrews's alluring but hard-line vocals ran alongside the bass line, and she glided across one treacherous verse that rhymes "contrary" with "extraordinary." Although writing it down took about ten minutes, Armstead said the ideas within the song had been rolling around in her head for years.

Andrews also had a wealth of experience that belied her actual age (barely twenty when recording "Casanova"). Also a Mississippi native, she recalled growing up on a plantation but said her aunt forbade her to enter the cotton field. Her family moved to Chicago when she was about nine and lived in a South Side cold-water flat. A Hyde Park High School music teacher taught

Andrews and her classmate Minnie Riperton vocal scales. Andrews says, "She took us as far in our range as we could go, and then we had to figure out how to get beyond that, how to make a smooth transition." Early on she formed connections in the urban Midwest that she had never envisioned in the rural South. She sang with the Vondells and had a background part on the C.O.D.'s popular dance track "Michael (The Lover)," but she felt just as enthusiastic about jazz musicians she met.

"There was a club called the Grass Hut, and I ran into Cannonball Adderley there," Andrews said. "They used to work at the Happy Medium on the North Side and would come south because their audiences were white up there, and being black they would come and hang out at the Grass Hut because they were classy black jazz enthusiasts. So I'm sitting there, like, 'Wow!' Talk about scared, I was seventeen going on eighteen."

Another Armstead associate, singer Garland Green, was also born in Mississippi (as Garfield Green) and moved to Chicago's Englewood neighborhood in 1958 at age sixteen. Green enjoyed hanging out in South Side poolrooms—because he liked the game and because staying indoors gave him sanctuary from the warring Blackstone Rangers and Disciples gangs. Green's singing in those halls got him more attention than his cueing: Argia B. Collins, a restaurateur and creator of Mumbo barbecue sauce who aspired to be a music producer, paid for his classical education at the Chicago Conservatory of Music. Green briefly studied piano and Italian opera there, although he ruefully said, "I didn't give it the concentration and time; I was a very young man." Yet conservatory training may have bolstered Green's vocal dynamics.

Green sang in small venues throughout Chicago. In 1967 he met Armstead and Collins at the Sutherland Lounge. Their biggest hit together came in late summer 1969 with "Jealous Kind of Fella," a domestic drama that Green, Armstead, and Rudolph Browner composed. At Green's insistence, Bernard Reed and Fred White made up the rhythm section on the session. MCA soon moved the song to its pop imprint, Uni. The song spent sixteen weeks on the *Billboard* R&B charts, and on November 1, 1969, it cracked the *Billboard* top twenty in its Hot 100 chart.[72]

Underhanded, if quotidian, business shenanigans ended these partnerships. When Green signed with Atlantic's Cotillion subsidiary in 1970, Syl Johnson claimed producer's credit. The singer said that Johnson did not perform such a role (Green's friend Donny Hathaway arranged his "Plain and Simple Girl" without charging a fee). Armstead and Collins's marriage and their Giant company were also breaking up about that time. After their divorce, Armstead became sole owner of their master recordings.[73] Ultimately, Giant's output and its impressive role in providing opportunities to Armstead, Andrews, and Green despite limited resources added up to its lasting impact.

Chess Records continued its global success alongside these burgeoning smaller companies. It opened new headquarters at 320 East Twenty-First Street in spring 1967. After it purchased the eight-story 3M company building for $425,000, its goal was to have all its pressing and printing facilities in one location.[74] The company invested about $750,000 to refurbish the studio so it could manufacture 375,000 singles and 19,000 full-length albums a day. Marshall Chess expected that 60 percent of its pressing would be done for other record labels.[75] At the same time, its sessions remained straightforward. Maurice White remembered that the studio taping stuck to four tracks: rhythm section on one, guitar or piano on another, orchestra on the third, and vocalists on the last.[76] He was watching closely and learning.

The Chess business plan developed as it expanded from its classic blues roster into the R&B of such singers as Jackie Ross. Billy Davis also served as a model for ascending black executives within the record industry, much like Carl Davis (no relation). After Billy Davis joined the company about the middle of 1961, he had moved up to running the artists and repertoire department and had formed a publishing company called Chevis Music (Chess and Davis).[77] Marshall Chess said hiring him "was the beginning of the shift into Mitty Collier and all that great soul music he produced. He was just a great soft-spoken guy from Detroit. He came to Chess because we put out Barrett Strong's 'Money,' which Billy and Berry [Gordy] produced, and it was on [Motown subsidiary] Anna Records, which we distributed. Billy took over the A&R department to get Chess to change into the new era, so we knew it was coming."

Although Davis was soft-spoken, he could also persuade the streetwise Chess brothers. He insisted that the company have a house band, which would include Maurice White and Louis Satterfield along with guitarist Gerald Sims and pianist-organist Leonard Caston Jr. Chess wanted all these musicians to punch a time clock. White and Satterfield protested,[78] and Chess relented.[79]

Another addition to the Chess staff, saxophonist-arranger Gene Barge, has said that he and Davis were "friends in one sense, but also competitors." Barge had no problem asserting himself. Originally from Norfolk, Virginia, he played in gospel and R&B groups, and his saxophone propelled Gary "U.S." Bonds's 1961 early rock hit "Quarter to Three."[80] After serving in the US Air Force and teaching high school, he moved to Chicago in June 1964 to work for Chess. Barge remembers flying into the city just as Martin Luther

King was holding a rally in Soldier Field.[81] He felt that his own experiences, and those of other musicians who moved to Chicago from the South at that time, contributed to their being socially active. For Barge, that would come to mean his involvement with the Southern Christian Leadership Conference's Operation Breadbasket a few years later.

"We were in the eye of the storm," Barge said. "A lot of people from troubled areas in America migrated to Chicago from the deepest part of Mississippi. We had more people from Mississippi in Chicago than they had in some of the bigger cities in Mississippi. A lot of those musicians, like [trumpeter] Burgess Gardner and [singer-guitarist] Little Milton [Milton Campbell Jr.], all these guys were Mississippi guys, and the trials and tribulations they were going through in the Deep South—or Arkansas and Alabama—they brought those on their backs to Chicago. Trying to fight through that maze of racism. So Chicago was always a hotbed, still is."

Little Milton's 1965 R&B hit "We're Gonna Make It" was one of Barge's first big producing jobs for Chess and might reference those tribulations. The coda's gospel call-and-response may have reflected civil rights-era optimism with its belief that a couple—or maybe a community—will leave poverty for a brighter future. In September 1965 Barge worked on former St. Louis gospel singer Fontella Bass's monumental soul recording, "Rescue Me." A cocomposer on "We're Gonna Make It," Raynard Miner (then twenty years old) wrote and played piano on "Rescue Me," which also featured Barge's saxophone, organist Sonny Thompson, guitarist Pete Cosey, and a rhythm section of Satterfield and White. The song is in A-major, and Bass's voice is a marvel: beginning with a demand, her tough lead turns into a gospel moan and ends with a hum that coaxes instrumentalists to drop out until all that's left are White's propulsive hand drumming and soft, descending notes from Satterfield's gurgling bass.

"It was around 6:00, 7:00 at night, I was at my piano, playing the piano hard, trying to get this right, that right," Miner said.

> And I hit it. When I heard it, I said, this is it, and I called Billy Davis up. It was "Take Me with You" at first, and we changed it to "Rescue Me." It was August, and Chess had built this studio across the street; it had no air conditioning. It was just a rehearsal studio, and I got together with Billy and played it, and BAM, that was the birth of "Rescue Me." Billy said, "I want you to show Fontella Bass this tune." I laughed at the name Fontella Bass—Fontella who? The magic of that tune, I'll never, ever forget how I felt and how the studio felt after we did two takes of "Rescue Me" and the rhythm. I made a mistake and said, "Let's kick it off again." I got through it all the way through, and the studio

was quiet for about thirty seconds; nobody could say anything. You knew this was it. I had other feelings about my songs being hits, but there was no way in the world . . . you just knew it.

Although Davis is cited as producer and Phil Wright as arranger, Barge says that all the musicians had input. Hearing that cohesion come through in this terrific single does not require any imagination.

"Working with the rhythm section, we rehearsed them for four days in the back room of the studio," Barge said. "And the sessions—we had discussions about what beats Maurice was going to play, what Satterfield was going to play. He was very dogmatic about his bass playing, always pushing to get certain bass lines in. Raynard and them came up with the bass line, and Satterfield picked it up, and that bass line was the whole song. We just worked them out, had fun doing them. When we got in to lay the tracks there were no problems because we had worked out all the kinks, all the arguments and fights about what we were going to do. Everybody was on the same page."

Cosey agreed: "We had a very tight, crack rhythm section. It didn't take us but a minute to scan the music and figure out what we wanted to do with it. That would save a tremendous amount of time and money for the producers. They were at an advantage using a rhythm section who already knew one another and who could read music and play the proper feeling and play the hit feeling."[82]

Barge added that the musicians went their own way after they were off the clock at Chess. Often they steered toward the changing Chicago jazz scene. This was when traditional musicians gigged in clubs throughout the city, while burgeoning experimental groups like the Art Ensemble of Chicago created new performance options. R&B session musicians sought out all these prospects. Barge says that Maurice White would "form a new band every week" before settling in as drummer for pianist Ramsey Lewis. Satterfield and Cosey also collaborated with Phil Cohran. Fontella Bass, who was married to Art Ensemble trumpeter Lester Bowie, told Michael McAlpin that informal studio jam sessions were more important than the tunes they recorded.

"In between songs everybody would kind of challenge one another in the studio, and we would do a jam session," Bass said to McAlpin. "And I'll play the piano and we'd be doing tunes like 'Round Midnight' or 'I Can't Get Started' or whatever tunes. And we would be playing it while they were getting things together in the control booth. And when they'd come through and say 'OK, we're ready,' then everybody would have to go back to the

Mickey Mouse music. But, you know, then maybe somebody else would mess up on the tape—we'd get back, you know, everybody'd want to play jazz and that type of thing. But it was great. But then that way we got to know one another. We talked about the music, what was going on around town."[83]

Pedagogical links also connect these sessions at Chess with teachers like James Mack. Raynard Miner credits Mack's student Satterfield with encouraging him when he crafted such songs as "Higher and Higher," which he wrote for the Dells. Jackie Wilson covered this song for a massive hit on Brunswick.[84] "Satterfield was cool," Miner said:

> Maurice was too, but Satterfield dug out what was hidden in me. The little simple things I would play, they would say, "How in the hell did he play this with that?" Because I had these different voicings that I was using on the piano. The meter was not quite normal. Satterfield said, "No, don't let that go, because it's you." When I did "Higher and Higher," we were all in the studio, and I was playing it and the musicians were saying, "What is he playing?" Pete Cosey said, "Listen to what he's playing." I was playing it crazy, but it was right. Third intervals and other things like that. Satterfield said, "Naw, that's happening." And I just blew up after that. He used to come over to my house and there was a little studio room that we had, and he would come over around 6:00 or 7:00 and we'd stay up until 2:00 or 3:00 in the morning, just going C to D, C to E, C to G, just playing in rhythm with that, just getting the gut of what we were trying to feel within. And we found out that the most simple things could be the most effective things in the rhythm.

Despite this creative freedom at Chess, Bass, Jackie Ross, and Mitty Collier have argued that they were not receiving sufficient royalty payments.[85] Ross contended that her claims about this caused her to be blackballed from the industry. She adds that Sam Cooke influenced her to be resolved. "I have my own selfology, just like everybody," Ross said. "I will say that after however many weeks 'Selfish One' was on *Billboard* and *Cash Box* charts, it beats me how all of a sudden that doesn't mean anything. If you deserve making a certain amount of money, if you wind up lousing it up, that's on you. But for somebody to take from you what is rightfully yours, that's not right."

Collier states, "With us being young, we accepted what they gave us. If they gave us an advance we thought that we were something. If they gave me $10,000 and a car, or a leased car, [with me] not knowing that these things would put me in debt for the rest of my life with that quarter of a penny they were giving us for royalties, and having their attorney as our attorney when you're supposed to have an attorney protect your rights, but actually protecting the rights of Chess, we didn't care—we had good clothes, a car, and had some money."

Nadine Cohodas examined these claims in her Chess history, *Spinning Blues into Gold*. She concluded that it would be impossible to prove them. Even assuming that any publicly available ledgers do not differ from possible secret ledgers, one would need to unravel accurate figures for basic details like sales revenues or royalty arrangements. How frequently Chess records gave artists cars and other gifts in lieu of royalties is unknowable.[86] Billy Davis told Cohodas that, at the time, Ross never complained directly to him about unpaid royalties.[87] Still, considering social norms, it is likely that Davis was not paying attention to her—it would not be the only time powerful men did not listen to young women's claims. Artists at the time, whatever power they had in the studio on the creative end, lacked the resources to pursue equitable treatment or simple payments due. But they deserve appreciation for trying.

Murkier still was the involvement of organized crime throughout the music industry. Music historian John Broven quotes Billy Davis as saying, "Why does everybody keep asking me about the Mafia? If I knew, I wouldn't tell anyway!"[88] Carl Davis's memoir mentions that the mobsters who were involved with Brunswick played a role in his being hired as its A&R director in October 1966. Carl Davis was managing Gene Chandler at the time, and he had the singer sign a recording deal with the company to cancel a mob hit on Davis's business associate Irv Nahan.[89] Further complicating matters, Chandler was simultaneously signed to Chess Records and to Abner's Constellation company (formed not long after he left Vee-Jay). Davis contends that his persuasive negotiating skills had a way of untangling commitments. Chandler is understandably more circumspect when talking about incidents involving organized crime and the record business. None of this diminishes the quality of the output Davis oversaw at Brunswick, nor does it detract considerably from what he meant to journalists such as the *Defender*'s Earl Calloway.[90]

Even though Davis held a high position at Brunswick, in 1967 he launched his Dakar Records, which Atlantic distributed. No one seemed to mind the potential conflict of interest.[91] This degree of autonomy amazed Marvin Smith, who sang with the Artistics. "Nat Tarnopol just gave Carl the right to do what he wanted to do," Smith said. "In other words, Carl was the man. He had the hand to do whatever he wanted because he was turning out the hits."

Like the Chess studio team, Davis's crew included musicians from other companies as well as upcoming younger performers. In 1964 he brought over Motown veteran Sonny Sanders to serve as arranger and producer.[92] Willie Henderson moved from being a house saxophonist to directing sessions for artists such as Tyrone Davis. Although Barbara Acklin was hired as a receptionist and background singer, she became accomplished as a singer-songwriter, including composing "Whispers (Getting Louder)" for Jackie Wilson in 1968. Her equally talented boyfriend, Eugene Record, composed her hit "Love Makes a Woman."[93] Poise oozes from every measure on that track. Acklin had been working at Brunswick since 1966, but it took her persistence (and duets with Chandler) to convince Carl Davis she could also sing.[94] Not only did she deliver, but the *New York Amsterdam News* observed, "To the young blacks of today, especially the girls, Barbara Acklin is an idol and believe me—she's quite an idol."[95] Whether she was admired for her singing, writing, fashion sense, or a combination of the three, such adulation was well deserved. After her own "Love Makes a Woman" in 1968, she continued writing with Record, who had come aboard with the Chi-Lites. Acklin later recalled to Robert Pruter that Davis said the pair "tended to write seven years ahead of ourselves. He said we were too deep."[96]

Bernard Reed had met Carl Davis five years earlier, just after the bassist graduated from Marshall High School and was singing in the Constellations. That group performed around town—from a record hop at the state's National Guard Northwest Armory on the West Side to the Regal Theater. Along the way, Reed studied the Impressions' harmonies and absorbed Johnny Pate's jazz-influenced techniques. After Reed switched to becoming primarily an instrumentalist with the Artistics, his sound combined raw funk and sophistication, unlike any other bassist in Chicago. His own sensibility as a composer resonates on such tracks as Jackie Wilson's "My Heart Is Calling," which Reed wrote with his brother, Danny Reed. As they were granted a semblance of creative freedom to work without overt supervision, their unassuming method built up a hefty songbook.

"We were the guys in the back room woodshedding on everybody's material," Reed said. "For two hours a songwriter would come in and work with the band on their song. They'd bring it to us in any form they had. Some would come in with their own chords that they could play on piano and guitar. Some only had the melody in their head, and they were good singers at expressing the words they had written, and we put the music behind them. We started stockpiling songs, and [Carl Davis's] Jalynne's [publishing] catalog became a catalog once a song was chosen to make a demo. And we made the demos, and the demos would go into the Jalynne catalog that they sent out to other artists looking for material."

While Davis mentions in his memoir that Chandler walked out on him after fighting with singer Otis Leavill in 1968 and took Reed with him, the bassist returned a few weeks later. Reed said that tensions kept brewing among the core group of musicians and Davis. Everybody involved was strong-willed. Also, Reed and his group felt confined and not fully credited for their contributions. A boiling point came in late 1968 when Davis released a single, "Soulful Strut." Essentially, it was the instrumental part of Acklin's "Am I the Same Girl" with new chords added by pianist Floyd Morris. Davis claimed that none of his acts wanted to put their names on it—Morris, for one, termed it bubblegum stuff, and he considered himself a serious musician. So Davis released it under the name Young-Holt Unlimited, a band that drummer Isaac "Red" Holt and bassist Eldee Young nominally led. Most likely, neither Young nor Holt played on the record—which hit number three on the US *Billboard* pop chart and would go on to be certified gold by January 20, 1969.[97] Reed argued that he cowrote the tune, saying it stemmed from his bass line groove, and he felt disturbed about his anonymity in accounts of its genesis. That anger would lead to his again leaving Brunswick to play on sessions for other companies.

Even with this discord, a sense of building still dominated Chicago soul. Carl Davis's management of the Brunswick office and the accomplished musicians on his staff represented just one pillar of combined artistic and entrepreneurial musical success in Chicago at this time, as did Curtis Mayfield and Eddie Thomas at Curtom and Billy Davis at Chess. Meanwhile, performers and audiences in venues across the city shaped the records from small labels. Aspirations were global. Their optimism was well founded, not just because of the march toward integration, but also because of the inherent quality evident in the music. The abundance of youthful energy and these spaces for spontaneity also supported it all. Some events that took place had no immediate impact, yet their reverberations would be felt well into the 1970s and beyond.

That was the case with a recording session at One-derful in July 1967. This date, unremarkable at the time, helped set off a crucial sequence of events, even though the resulting tape would be discovered only forty-two years later, after Larry Blasingaine mentioned it to journalist Jake Austen.[98] An upstart entrepreneur from Gary, Indiana, brought his sons with him to Chicago to record the Eddie Silver-composed "Big Boy." In some regards this family story echoed that of the Five Stairsteps: the father had expectations for show business glory and some small-scale political engagement. It was their first time in a professional recording studio, and some were eager to learn how it worked. Otis Clay remembered the family's inquisitive young vocalist named Michael bombarding him with questions. Nobody is sure why this charming single was never released. Probably the reasons are connected with George Leaner, who retired the following year. Jonas Bernholm has noted this group's playing in the Bonanza Lounge the following summer and recalled that they seemed more experienced than their ages would suggest. Shortly thereafter, the singers moved on from Chicago and at the dawn of the new decade would become known as the Jackson Five.

FOUR

Psychedelic Soul:
Chicago's 1960s Counterculture
Redirects Social and Musical Cues

Teenage singer Gavin Christopher dressed sharp at Herb Kent's West Side dances, but his outlook took a different turn when he joined Oscar Brown Jr.'s revue in 1966. The experience with the jazz vocalist–songwriter expanded his horizons, and so did his neighborhood excursions when they performed at a North Side club called the Happy Medium. His trip to a nearby area known as Old Town turned into a reinvention.

"The hippie thing started to happen, and I lost all the gouster identity because I started to hang out on the North Side with Oscar," Christopher said. "The Old Town area—everything became Wells Street, everything became the old army jackets, holes in the knees, walking down the street playing the flute. Everything became Lincoln Park, the be-ins, love-ins, that's what it became. Everything became crash pads."

Christopher's journey within this counterculture involved more than stylishly tattered clothes and easy social connections. With seemingly liberal politics and the expression of open lifestyles, some barriers cracked a bit. In that regard, Old Town in the 1960s resembled similar neighborhoods in San Francisco, New York, and Toronto. To be sure, its utopian ethos did not reflect daily life on Chicago streets, another similarity of this scene and its counterparts everywhere: idealism was fleeting. But if lasting interracial harmony proved elusive, the sounds that emerged shattered limited conceptions of black popular music. That change came about because of the musicians themselves. By the mid-1960s, some racially mixed bands in Chicago attracted broad audiences. The American Breed had a national pop hit with "Bend Me, Shape Me"; it included black bassist Charles Colbert Jr. (this group hailed from the notoriously segregated suburb of Cicero). Along with playing what had been accepted as white pop music genres (acoustic folk, garage rock), these artists and their producers also brought sophisticated string arrangements or European-derived folklore to their records. A few used lyrics and other means to address social issues that affected white and black America. For some of these artists, the experience became a launch toward stardom; others took a more difficult trajectory. Their training and their experiences in front of this city's audiences undoubtedly helped them over the long haul. As the decade progressed, so did musicians' efforts to seek integrative collaboration. Emerging folk and rock clubs on the city's North Side inspired a course for Chicago soul music that diverged from the strings, horns, and vocal harmonies of its recognized stars. Singer Terry Callier and the soul-rock band Rotary Connection were two such artists, as was their producer, Charles Stepney. Other musicians blended in rock, funk, and folk music—Baby Huey and the Babysitters, Gavin Christopher, Rufus (which Colbert cofounded), and Rasputin's Stash. They ignored or openly defied racial schisms while claiming their own stages.

The Offbeat Rise of Old Town

This scene emerged gradually. In the 1950s there was no "sustained integra-tionist subculture" in Chicago along the lines of the "somewhat integrated Bohemia of 1950s and 1960s New York" to nurture artists such as jazz mu-sicians. Thus writes trombonist-author George Lewis in *A Power Stronger Than Itself*.[1] During the mid-1960s, however, Old Town reaped media atten-tion as it offered a more integrated environment. In the 1950s, according to the *Chicago Tribune*, that area, particularly a stretch of North Wells Street near North Avenue, had been "a ragged, desolated stretch of old houses and little else." An early addition, Slim Brundage's beatnik-era College of Com-plexes, was a coffeehouse that hosted idiosyncratic lecturers.[2] Meanwhile, an older generation of socially conscious labor activists, the Industrial Workers of the World (the IWW, also called the Wobblies), hung on to its head-quarters in the area.[3] By the early part of the next decade, the *Tribune's* Paul Gapp writes, "Craftsmen and artists—many with little previous business experience—began operating interesting shops in low-rent buildings along the street. Offbeat saloons, restaurants, and other businesses followed."[4] In spring 1963, twenty-year-old guitarist Michael Bloomfield began managing the Fickle Pickle coffeehouse in Old Town and brought in such South Side blues musicians as Big Joe Williams.[5]

Gapp also noted the racial dynamic in this bastion of freethinking. Al-though the participants were largely white, this area was just a few blocks from Cabrini-Green. Gapp wrote, "The strip [of Wells Street] would be-come what it is today, in a purely physical sense: An unplanned buffer zone between the Gold Coast-Sandburg [Carl Sandburg Village apartment complex] swath of affluence to the east and the almost unbroken expanse of black poverty housing to the west."[6] That proximity was not without its tensions, such as a 1966 riot that started when black teenagers heard that a white high school student in Lincoln Park had thrown one of their classmates onto the train tracks.[7] But because of its position, Old Town appeared less exclusive than other North Side neighborhoods. Black media found the changes there encouraging for youthful entertainment. A 1965 article in the *Chicago Defender* made it seem like a lively and wholesome spot for teenagers. "What's happening hippies," the unnamed author wrote. "The Like Young is a swinging coffee house in Old Town for hippies under twenty-one (hey! finally got one!). The atmosphere is utter chaos, but it's lots of good clean fun."[8]

Even though *Ebony* touted upwardly mobile black strivers, a photo editorial in the July 1967 issue took an encouraging approach to the be-ins that Christopher described. The spread ran with a photo focusing on a young African American woman in a poncho holding flowers on Chicago's lakefront and urged "even the most conservative WASP, if he would let his tensions relax for just a moment" to focus on the positive philosophy of the movement and not be concerned with the drug intake. The editorial did lament that be-ins could not expel the country's racism.[9] Indeed, the next issue of the magazine questioned if there was anything that would connect white hippies and black youths.[10] Of course, this being 1960s Chicago, the trend got turned into an upbeat dance forty-five: Saxie Russell's two-part "Psychedelic Soul," which Eddie Thomas produced and released in 1968 on his Thomas Records.

Old Town's geography also motivated musical exchanges. Folk saloon the Earl of Old Town was only a few blocks north of the Plugged Nickel, which hosted jazz stars. While the doo-wop singers who practiced in relatively nearby Cabrini-Green's Seward Park field house customarily continued toward soul, some preferred a different tradition. Willie Wright, formerly of the Medallionaires, turned to folk at the suggestion of Chloe Hoffman at the Olivet Community Center, which offered a practice room and other resources. On his 1963 album *I'm on My Way*, he mostly sang Anglo-American ballads like "Wayfaring Stranger" and "House of the Rising Sun."[11] That album's liner notes attempted to describe him as a natural, or naive, talent, claiming that "though he never had a lesson, even musicians think he had a trained voice."[12]

Singer-songwriter Terry Callier, who grew up in Cabrini Homes' lowrise apartments, combined different strains of folk, jazz, and soul on his album *The New Folk Sound of Terry Callier*. He recalled that gospel groups were as popular as their counterparts in R&B. The lingering Italian American Catholic influence in the Cabrini–River North area also affected Callier. In 1997 he reflected on those beginnings: "I was socially challenged," Callier said with a laugh.

> I guess that's the way you'd say it now. It was easier for me to make music, write songs, than to make conversation, and once I discovered that, I kind of stuck with it. I started playing piano by ear at seven, eight years old. Then I studied piano with Sister Maria Theresa from St. Dominic's for a couple of years. Sister Theresa of the hard ruler across the knuckles, because she didn't fool around. I started my first vocal group when I was in the seventh grade, and I played the same triplet chords that everybody else was playing. Even at that time we were doing a lot of original material. We were doing songs that were popular because that's how to attract an audience, but we were doing original things even then.

As a teen, Callier auditioned for Chess, but his mother felt he was too young to pursue a performer's lifestyle.[13] Then he attended the University of Illinois at Urbana-Champaign during the early 1960s, where, in his words, he "started fooling around with a guitar on campus." Returning home for summer break, at the urging of a friend he began performing at the Fickle Pickle on State Street.

"When it was time for me to go back to school, I didn't want to," Callier said. "I told my mother, and my mother was very firm in her dealings. She said, 'You may not go back to school, but you have to do something.' I started playing four, five nights a week. At that time, there were so many places in Chicago that you could play every week for a couple months and not play the same room. The money wasn't great, but at that time it seemed like a lot."

Callier also heard Charlie Parker and Bud Powell records during his childhood visits with jazz-fan residents of his great-grandmother's boardinghouse in Bronzeville. But the singer had a more visceral response to jazz at the South Side McKie's Disc Jockey Lounge in 1963.

> John Coltrane and the quartet came in. I walked up to the door and there was the sound of hammering, and I was saying to myself, "What can they be building here? The show is supposed to start in an hour." The hammering was Elvin Jones nailing his drum kit to the floor. "Gee, what kind of music are they playing if he has to nail his drums to the floor?" I sat through that whole

evening and went back many times. And when they left I started looking for a day job because I had never seen musicians hurl themselves into what they were doing. It seemed to me like a perilous thing, because I couldn't see how that wouldn't take some kind of toll on them.

So Callier stepped away from performing and took a job as a laboratory technician. He kept practicing, constantly trying, in his words, "to emulate that intensity." When Callier played Old Town clubs again, a main spot was Mother Blues, a Wells Street venue that hosted folk, blues, rock, and comedy acts as it boasted of welcoming all ages. Owner Lorraine Blue introduced him to producer Samuel Charters, who recorded *The New Folk Sound of Terry Callier* in 1964, although the album was not released for a couple of years.[14] The arrangements on the record are sparse, and Callier performs mostly traditional repertoire like "Cotton-Eyed Joe," but his voice imparts a deep resonance. Unusual for the folk scene, two bassists accompany Callier and his guitar, a lineup that was his way of emulating Coltrane. Some songs, such as Kent Foreman's "Spin, Spin, Spin," are played in contrasting time signatures (4/4, 2/4, 6/8). But Callier's delivery, equally haunting and inviting, ties them together. Singer–civil rights activist Jimmy Collier arrived in Chicago from Arkansas and recalls being "in awe" of Callier when they both played in those coffeehouses.[15] A few years later Collier worked with the Southern Christian Leadership Conference to help recruit younger people into the Chicago Freedom Movement.

Callier's former neighbor in Cabrini, singer-songwriter Larry Wade, was living in the nearby Old Town Gardens apartment complex and would see his friend perform some of those tunes. Wade almost could not believe Callier's command of Old Town's performance spaces. "There was a place called Poor Richard's, had peanut husks on the floor and had an audience that came near and far to see him," Wade said. "The songs that he would play, stories that he would tell, only thing you could hear sometimes were the waiters and waitresses walking and cracking those shells. And they'd stop because they wanted to hear too. He had the most mesmerizing lyrics and stories in his guitar playing that brought you to tears."

Rotary Connection's Kaleidoscopic Vision

In 1967 a group of musicians, some of them Callier fans, came together at Chess as Rotary Connection. This band brought Callier's investigations into an amalgam of soul and folk while adding elements of psychedelia and classical music. At this time Chess producer Billy Davis had refocused his career on advertising and would soon depart for New York's McCann-Erickson, becoming the Madison Avenue firm's music director.[16] With Davis's departure, Leonard Chess's son Marshall moved up to the building's eighth floor, where his office adjoined the studio and the musicians' rehearsal rooms. He oversaw production on a new Chess imprint, Cadet Concepts, and sent lead sheets of compositions to Washington, DC, to establish copyright. Veteran Chicago arranger Charles Stepney was tasked with writing those lead sheets, for $15 each. Stepney may not have appeared to have much in common with the younger crew at the company. He was thirty-six when the division was launched; back then, this would have seemed like a generation behind the times. Stepney's discipline would also have seemed at odds with Marshall's free-spirited ethos. But they became friends.

"One day we were sitting in the commissary and he had this big, thick manuscript," Marshall Chess said. "And I said, 'What the fuck is that?' And he said, 'It's my thesis from college, it's a symphony I wrote.' I said, 'You wrote a symphony?!?! Have you ever heard any of that shit played?' He said, 'No, only in my head.' So I said, 'How would you like to work with me, I got this idea. . . .' And I told him about Rotary Connection, and that's how it began."

While that casual conversation sparked Stepney and Chess's creative partnership, it also stood against historic perceptions of black music composition in the city. About twelve years earlier, black writers of modern chamber music had no local outlet. Composer Edward Bland contended that African American composers of art songs at the end of the 1940s and beginning of the 1950s "were working in the post office or they had left Chicago."[17] According to dominant social prejudice, black musicians could only be jazz and blues artists. No welcoming performance venue for black composers of other music existed in those years, but teaching did offer an alternative to nonmusical employment or leaving the city. With new attitudes emerging in the later 1960s, Stepney had a place to bring modern classical concepts to pop music.

Stepney discussed his background and music theories in depth with a journalist only once—with Edwin Black, in *DownBeat*. The article mentioned his producing Ramsey Lewis and Phil Upchurch, as well as his experience in the "west side Chicago street school," playing vibes with saxophonist Eddie Harris in 1950s jazz clubs (the article did not mention Stepney's academic training at City Colleges of Chicago and Roosevelt University).[18] Stepney talks about using cluster overtones and resonant muting, which he gleaned from reading Henry Cowell's *New Musical Resources*. He did his own studies of extracting electronic sounds that were not limited to the new Moog synthesizers, an autodidactic approach that came from necessity. Stepney lacked the equipment budget of Beatles producer George Martin, whom he admired more than the Beatles themselves. So he had to improvise. "I can get excellent effects by altering and distorting legitimate sounds with tapes and stuff," Stepney said. "If you keep up on the latest developments in acoustics and electronics—you know, subscribe to various international engineering magazines—you can pick up all sorts of techniques."[19]

At some point Stepney encountered Joseph Schillinger's system of classical composition. Schillinger, an early proponent of electronic music, used mathematical formulas to show how writing music could go beyond accepted processes and stylistic norms. He also emphasized the spiritual aspects of music. Albert Murray derided Schillinger's theories in *The Omni-Americans*, writing, "As for swinging the blues, the affirmative beat of which is always geared to the rugged facts of life, if you run Schillinger exercises instead of riffing down home, you only *think* you're swinging."[20]

For Stepney, music was about including it all. His experience swinging in the city's jazz clubs provided a retort to Murray's statement. Stepney also introduced the system to jazz pianist Muhal Richard Abrams, who, according to George Lewis, would use it as part of his method in leading Chicago's Experimental Band and the Association for the Advancement of Creative Musicians.[21] The musicians at Chess saw that their producer devised avant-garde ideas without losing his musical identity. Phil Upchurch said that Stepney "loved odd meters, but they weren't odd just for the sake of it. The melodies moved the bar lines."[22] Sometimes he would arrange strings to form a countermelody that answers the tune, such as on the Radiants' euphoric single "Hold On."

Stepney's classical theory was just one element in the Rotary Connection idea. The name came from Roland Binzer, a Chicago advertiser and friend of Marshall Chess, who shared his affinity for the Rolling Stones.[23] This was a time when conservative scribes wrote frightened columns like one in the *Chicago Tribune* with the headline, "Are Hippie Motives Love or Fear?"[24] The media tone had shifted from the "good clean fun" line in the *Chicago Defender* just a couple of years earlier. Such alarmism from an older generation spurred Marshall Chess's rebellious streak. He brought a white garage band from the West Side together with Stepney's arrangements and two other Chess employees, vocalists Sidney Barnes and Minnie Riperton. Through the Old Town School of Folk Music education-performance space, he recruited Judy Hauff, a singer from South Dakota. Company session players, like Upchurch, also worked with the group in the studio.

Different impulses guided Barnes. He had grown up in Virginia and toured the East Coast as an R&B singer. In Detroit, he formed a production company with fledgling songwriter George Clinton and Mike Terry, a saxophonist who had also worked as an arranger with Jo Armstead. Barnes (and Clinton) wanted to embrace what was happening in and around rock, as Jimi Hendrix had been doing. Barnes drew inspiration from his mid-1960s visits to New York's Greenwich Village folk and rock clubs (also following Hendrix's steps). He took these ideas to Chess when Billy Davis hired him to be a writer, producer, and singer in early 1967. "I was always doing the R&B stuff because that's how I got into it," Barnes said.

> That whole circuit from the dingy clubs, the highest you could get was the Apollo, and you didn't make a lot of money, had to get to gigs as best you could, change in the back of the station wagon, hope the promoter pays you. You go to town and hope people don't harass you because you're black. Up until 1967—then the shit changed. And for me, I was brought up around white people and I get along with white people. I was cool with whatever came, and I dug country music. So I embraced harmonies of Crosby, Stills, and Nash, I loved Led Zeppelin, that whole thing. At that particular time that I got there, the whole business was different and made my whole way of writing songs and thinking about life a lot different. I was seeing it not from an R&B perspective.

Already an experienced vocalist, Riperton brought her own perspective to the group. The daughter of a Pullman car porter, she had been singing with the Gems on Chess since her mid-teens, auditioning for the group on the same day that President John F. Kennedy was assassinated, according to the group's leader Raynard Miner. She recorded as Andrea Davis and as a backup singer for such groups as the Radiants.[25] Her high-pitched laugh introduced Syl Johnson's single, "Different Strokes," a modest R&B hit in 1967 that would earn significant sampling fees for its creator some twenty-five years later. Although she had a wide range, her initial efforts as a solo lead in the mid-1960s met little reaction. When Marshall Chess approached her about joining Rotary Connection, she was working as the label's receptionist. Racial perceptions may have stalled her early solo career, as she later told British journalist Penny Valentine. She also questioned whether much would ever change. "I was doing what I'm doing now," Riperton told Valentine in 1975. "It wasn't what you'd call black music so therefore nobody knew what to do with it. I mean, in the record industry if you were black you were black and you couldn't be anything else. At that time you were Negroes, you weren't even human beings. That's the way it was then, that's the way it is now."[26]

Besides Riperton's singular vocal range, prowess, and stylistic choices, her background countered a general assumption about R&B singers. In another 1975 interview with British writer Chris Charlesworth, she responded disdainfully when asked if she had a background singing gospel. Riperton grew up singing in the choir of Chicago's Sixth Grace United Presbyterian Church, a denomination culturally removed from the Baptist and Sanctified congregations identified with creating and sustaining that idiom.[27]

"That's the old black story," Riperton said to Charlesworth. "Da gospel musik, no, no, no. In fact, I didn't go to that kind of church. I did visit them and I did sing in the choir but it wasn't one of those Baptist gospel things. As a kid I did just about everything I could, being a tomboy and doing acting and singing and ballet and dancing and whatever."[28]

The white rock musicians in Rotary Connection included guitarist Bobby Simms, bassist Mitch Aliotta, and drummer Kenny Venegas. Dells bass vocalist Chuck Barksdale had no idea what to expect when Stepney brought him to the studio to add his voice, but he found the end results, in his words, "fantastic." Judy Hauff was more attuned to the likes of (preelectric) Bob Dylan and Joan Baez.

Hauff also valued the idea of singing in an integrated soul-rock band, having earlier considered marching with civil rights activists in Selma, Alabama. She encountered some of the local white backlash to the movement when the group's rehearsals were held at the MB Club, a bar on Ninety-Third Street where Simms had played previously. This part of the South Side was transitioning to predominantly African American, yet the bar served as one small holdout for a few pockets of whites in the area. Nearby violent resistance to ending housing segregation also continued. Not long before Rotary Connection's formation, in summer 1966 white mobs attacked housing integration marchers in the Gage Park and Chicago Lawn neighborhoods.[29] Marshall Chess and his team set out to strike at least a small blow on behalf of progress.

"It was a key club because, 'We only let people who belonged to the club in'—riiiight," Hauff said sarcastically. "Bullshit. It was just flat-out racist. Of course Marshall knew that. I didn't know that. Sometimes we needed a rehearsal room that was not at Ter Mar [Chess Studio]. So Marshall just loved it when we all had to go out and rehearse at the MB Club because Minnie would come. And Sidney would come. Marshall would just barge in there with the entire integrated group. The owner would grind his teeth and hope to make some money out of it."

On Chicago's North Side, Barnes experienced an immersion in the burgeoning psychedelic rock clubs. "I never saw nothing like that before in my life," Barnes said. "They had balls turning on the ceiling with the lights and the iridescence and girls floating. I felt like the dude from *Midnight Cowboy* walking in there. I dug the shit out of it because by that time I was into the Beatles. When I went to Marshall, he said 'What do you got?' And I played a song, 'Turn Me On,' that was inspired by the Beatles and he said, 'You got the job.' As a writer, and to be an R&B writer for all these years, I was taken aback by the lyrical content, the subject content, the lyrics these young white kids were doing, it was blowing my mind."

During the sessions for Rotary Connection's eponymous first album, Hauff said that everyone was open-minded. Reworking group harmony took precedence over star solo spots. Drawing on her background singing in a Roman Catholic church choir, Hauff added Gregorian chant to an elegiac interpretation of the Rolling Stones' "Ruby Tuesday." Stepney combined organ and sitar to rework the hymn "Amen," and he arranged dissonances in the strings throughout the LP—notably on "Memory Band." On that track, wordless vocals form the melody, under which are layered sitar, theremin, and a phantasmagoric string section that defies common structure. "Turn Me On" reflects English folk strains. The album ends with the kind of experimentation that Stepney referred to in the *DownBeat* interview—a sonic collage that manipulated the previous songs' tapes.

Marshall Chess fondly remembered the classical aspect of the recording session as its high point. "I had all the ingredients and the key to the studio," Chess said. "And all of our string players were from the Chicago symphony. They were all Jewish men from the Chicago symphony string section. Charles had never heard his own charts played by strings. It was a great experience for both of us."

Chicago Tribune pop music critic Robb Baker became the group's most consistent media champion. He hailed the debut LP in a March 10, 1968, review, especially citing Riperton, whom he referred to only as "the soprano." He also praised Stepney's take on "Amen" as it "starts out in high church and ends up Negro spiritual."[30] Baker overlooked the marijuana in the LP's back cover artwork.

Presenting the music in concert posed a daunting challenge. Initially this assemblage was more of a studio construct than a live performing band. Combining its string section with tape manipulations was not feasible onstage. Producer Richard Evans brought his Chess studio ensemble, the Soulful Strings, with its dozen violins, guitars, and sitar to the downtown London House to interpret the Rolling Stones, but that entailed less technological maneuvering.[31] So Chess relied on Barnes's extensive touring background to rework Rotary Connection for its performance at the new Uptown neighborhood rock venue, the Electric Theater (later renamed the Kinetic Playground). "Minnie and I had never done this kind of shit before," Barnes said:

> But we learned it. I was on the road with Little Richard, I was out there a long time on the chitlin' circuit. Marshall rented a little club to rehearse for a week. We went out there, and when we did the show at the Kinetic Playground we couldn't leave the stage because there were so many encores. The only thing was, Minnie was such a hit on the record and people were expecting to see that, and she didn't want to [sing in an upper register] on the first gig. That puzzled everybody. Because if she had tried to do that in the R&B clubs before Rotary Connection, they booed her offstage. She was doing all that high thing, and black folks weren't ready for that in their clubs. They wanted Aretha Franklin up in there.

Marshall Chess played the theremin at about eight concerts, but those were his only performances with the group outside the studio. The debut album sold modestly, with strength in the Midwest. Chess claimed it "sold a couple hundred thousand" units. Members would come and go during the next two years, including guitarist-songwriter Jon Stocklin.

Hauff left the group after singing on its second album, *Aladdin*, but she remembered helping Riperton become more aware of her own capabilities. "I took over the piano one day," Hauff said. "I said, 'Minnie, how many octaves do you have?' She said, 'I don't know.' I said, 'Come here.' So I went down until I hit the lowest note she could hit. I think she could sing lower than I could. I have about an octave and a half range. Then I went up. She kept going. She went with me, and she went with me again. She had almost five octaves."

Rotary Connection recorded *Peace*, its next album, in summer 1968 while, just up the street, riots surrounded the Democratic Convention.[32] A year earlier, the radical underground newspaper *Chicago Seed* had begun, and it covered the antiwar movement, police brutality, gay liberation, student activism, and prices of street drugs. In October 1968 the group performed at a benefit for the *Seed* in front of a small audience at Uptown's Aragon Ballroom.[33] *Peace* was intended to be released as a Christmas tie-in, even as it linked to increasingly heated domestic and international conflicts. Some of the album's comments are musical, such as electric guitar feedback contrasting with strings and bells on "Silent Night." Barnes's lyrics criticize consumerism on "Sidewalk Santa" and "Shopping Bag Menagerie." ("The holidays are different and their meanings, I'm not sure / I've worked so hard the whole year long to purchase happiness" is a sample of Barnes's take on the season.)

"To an R&B guy like me, I had never heard the word menagerie," Barnes said. "I'm a country boy and all that shit. But I understood, when I sang around these white people, they were saying shit like that. I remember being in a store and people were going crazy, day before Christmas getting shit for people that don't mean shit, and I haven't bought anything for anybody for years. How would a black Paul Simon say that? I wrote that at a special time, too, because we weren't making that much money and working our butts off. That's why those tunes are kind of sad. I wasn't in a happy mood, although the group was going good."

Rotary Connection further challenged commercial aspirations at a time of an unjust war and championed leftist ideals with a volatile advertisement in Billboard's December 7, 1968, issue to promote Peace. The image depicted Santa Claus lying dead, arms spread out, on a smoky battlefield. A week later the magazine reported that the Chicago-based major retail chain Montgomery Ward boycotted the album. Other distributors and stores shrugged off complaints. Chess advertising director Dick LaPalm articulated in Billboard that more than shock value was behind the artwork.

"When we chose to illustrate our Christmas album with the traditional Santa Claus, we had to ask ourselves some pointed questions," LaPalm told Billboard. "How can Santa be fat when millions of innocent children are starving to death in Biafra? How can Santa be jolly when our nation is torn with racial strife and persecution? How can Santa remain unscathed when thousands lie dead and wounded in Vietnam? Santa, like all of us, must feel the shame and torment of a world that needs healing."[34]

Such messaging was fleeting while Rotary Connection itself neared the end of its run. In 1969 the band released Dinner Music, which highlighted Stocklin's compositions, including his lovely ballad "Want You to Know." Songs came out a few months later, although without as much creative input from the group. That one featured new arrangements of rock and R&B hits heard on AM radio. The band's star voice also began looking toward other opportunities: in November, Stepney began orchestrating and producing Riperton's moving solo debut, Come to My Garden. That LP boasted a consummate supporting crew of jazz pianist Ramsey Lewis's trio with bassist Cleveland Eaton and drummer Maurice White. This album came out in 1970 on GRT, which had purchased Chess Records a few months earlier.[35]

After more shakeups, Stepney led a final album released as the New Rotary Connection's *"Hey, Love."* The added voices included soprano and alto Kitty Haywood and contralto Shirley Wahls, both veterans of commercial sessions as well as R&B recordings. Wahls came to the group with the deep gospel background that her friend Riperton lacked. That was one way Riperton and Wahls complemented each other. "The contrast between us was that on the high she had a lot of octaves, and on the low I had a lot," Wahls said. "I could go higher than most people would expect and lower than most people would expect. And [Riperton] could go higher than most people would expect and, with a soprano voice, lower."

This combination became crucial as Stepney kept reworking the album over several months. Everyone's versatility became layered into "I Am the Black Gold of the Sun," which Stepney wrote with Riperton's husband, Richard Rudolph. Lyrically, the song echoes sentiments of the nationwide black arts movement. Yet the piece also echoes the beginning of the group as it draws on the kind of Gregorian chant that Hauff had introduced and mostly adheres to an unorthodox D-flat minor key groove with some modulation. British journalist Kevin Le Gendre is enthusiastic about the track in his 2012 book *Soul Unsung*: "Perceptions of time are scrambled here. The eldritch character of the piece derives from its juxtaposition of eras: the acoustic-guitar prelude is so close to a mandolin that it evokes a Middle Ages ballad, one abruptly shattered by a belligerent fuzz guitar pulled straight from 1960s psychedelia."[36]

Not that contemporary musicians noticed how Stepney's scores were supposed to work, according to Wahls. "Charles was very, very astute in mixing voices with instruments," Wahls said. "And way before his time. Some musicians are beginning now to play the chords that he played on the piano and chords that he heard in his mind. They were hard to sing, and they sounded like, 'Oh, that don't go together, what is he doing now?' But you put them all together, you say, 'Wow! How did he do that?' Each time he did something, you had to learn four or five different parts. And you were down in your lower register—this was every singer—and then he would pile on a little bit higher, then a little bit higher, and when it came together, it was dynamite."

All of this took well over a year, at which point the members of the group had to devote their full energies to finally recording *"Hey, Love."* Wahls said that the New Rotary Connection rarely performed during this period, but that they were financially compensated for their dedication. Terry Callier's

"Song for Everyman," which appears on *"Hey, Love,"* fascinated Wahls, who said it offered a deep reflection of his experiences growing up in Cabrini-Green. Still, the group did not continue. *Come to My Garden* helped to establish Riperton's solo career. She and Rudolph settled in California, where she would become an international star later in the 1970s. Wahls suggested continuing Rotary Connection with Haywood, but every musician had just moved on. Along with being an early showcase for Riperton, however, the group's impact exceeded its slight record sales. For a while it reaffirmed that a thoroughly mixed ensemble that took all kinds of chances could find an audience, even within divided Chicago.

Baby Huey and the Babysitters Blend Garage Rock with Rhythm and Blues

During Rotary Connection's three years performing throughout the Midwest, the band frequently shared billings with Baby Huey and the Babysitters. While both groups found more enthusiastic crowds in North Side rock clubs than in South Side R&B venues, Rotary Connection developed experimental concepts, while the Babysitters were there for the party. Rotary Connection highlighted Riperton's soprano. The Babysitters' lead singer, Baby Huey, had little vocal range, but he compensated with other capacities. Although he weighed more than 350 pounds, it was said he could dance like James Brown.

Baby Huey's journey began in Richmond, Indiana, 250 miles southeast of Chicago. He was born James T. Ramey, and early on he made the most of his unusual size and tenor voice, playing tackle on the Richmond High School varsity football team as well as singing in the school's choir.[37] During the early 1960s rock 'n' roll wave, he began performing with a local band, Richmond's Own Vets. He took his onstage name from an oversized comic book character. Melvyn "Deacon" Jones, a high school trumpeter, got the job as the group's keyboardist. Jones went the extra mile to keep the band together; he was the only one who didn't worry that Huey's weight might damage his car's springs.

At that time the historic Gennett recording studio still existed in Richmond, and Jones recalled playing trumpet at that site of early twentieth-century jazz dates. Other legacies were not so benevolent. In one of Huey's last recordings, an inward-looking interpretation of Sam Cooke's "A Change Is Gonna Come," he alludes to Richmond's backwardness (specifically to outhouses) and racial divisions (enigmatically noting "three kinds of people: white people, black people, and my people").

Jones reflected more directly on its entrenched segregation. "By growing up under the conditions there, we thought the whole world was like that," Jones said. "We didn't know any better. We could only sit in a certain section in the movie theater, we could only go to the skating rink on one night, Tuesday nights, we could not swim at the YMCA. And you know what YMCA stands for? Young Men's *Christian* Association! It was just that South thing was in Richmond."

So in 1963 Huey and a group of Babysitters left for Chicago, where Jones's brother Harold Jones was an accomplished jazz drummer. At least comparatively, the city proved less divisive than eastern Indiana. "We could go in the movie theater in Chicago and sit anywhere," Jones said. "When we got to Chicago, there were blacks and whites dating; it was completely different. It's like we got off a spaceship in a whole other world."

The African American group did have to navigate the city's ongoing boundaries. Baby Huey and the Babysitters included rock songs in their repertoire, which did not sit well with black audiences at the Regal Theater on the South Side, even though Jones said that was the part of town where they lived. So most of their performances were at such venues as Uptown's the Cheetah (as the Aragon Ballroom called itself for a couple of years), where a *Chicago Tribune* reviewer mentioned their widening appeal to teens.[38] In the mid-1960s the Babysitters found a regular home base at the Thumbs Up in what was becoming Chicago's newly hip—some would say gentrified— Lincoln Park–Lakeview area, about a ten-minute drive north of Old Town. As Jones related, "There was a line around the corner to see this 320-pound man onstage who could dance on his toes."

A couple of small labels in Chicago recorded the Babysitters during the mid-1960s, including St. Lawrence, which released the novelty rock single "Monkey Man," written by the Babysitters' trumpeter and cofounder John Ross. That song garnered some airplay on WVON, perhaps because, as Jones said, DJ Herb Kent was friendly with them. Constant gigging built the band's reputation. Jones recalls performing at Trude Heller's, a club in New York's Greenwich Village, when Miles Davis guested on trumpet. As described in the newspaper clippings that make up most of the liner notes to its sole LP, *The Living Legend*, the band also played at the Baron de Rothschild's daughter's debutante party in Paris. After it returned, the group went through lineup changes. Jones said that about early 1968 a power struggle had forced him out of the band, but Huey reinstated his childhood friend a few months later. Another shift came just after bassist Dan Alfano went to see them at the Aragon in mid-1968. Alfano remembers Huey as "four hundred pounds of dynamite" when he auditioned to join the group. "We were definitely soul brothers," Alfano said. "There wasn't anything prejudicial within the band. There were times when I was the only white guy in the band, but I felt I was part of the band, that's all."

In 1967 Marv Heiman (then going by Marv Stuart) had become their manager. He was twenty years old at the time and booked Chicago rock bands on the college circuit. These tours included a Babysitters concert in Madison, Wisconsin, during the tumultuous August 1968 Democratic Convention in Chicago. The riot that night took place just across the street from the band's Lincoln Park rehearsal space, and Alfano remembers watching that melee unfold on television in his hotel room. Heiman also sought another record deal for the group, and he approached Curtom Records, which would release *The Living Legend*.[39] The firm had hired Donny Hathaway to serve as director of artists and repertoire, among his other duties. After Hathaway and Curtis Mayfield checked out the group, they signed them up, although their deal was with Baby Huey, the star, instead of the group as a whole. Then Heiman took them to Los Angeles and, he said, a week of concerts at the trend-setting Whiskey a Go Go club led to appearances on such television programs as *The Merv Griffin Show*, even though Baby Huey did not yet have an album out.

Despite these high-profile opportunities, Baby Huey and the Babysitters primarily toured the Midwest. Echoes of his blend of psychedelic rock guitars and soul vocals reverberated on songs like the Bobby Franklin's Insanity 1969 maxi-single *Bring It on down to Me (Part I and Part II)*, which was released on Curtom's affiliated label, Thomas. No doubt aware of fashions changing as much as music, Baby Huey let his afro grow out and took to wearing dashikis or overalls and performing barefoot. Audiences of all kinds clamored for him. As Alfano said, "We would do sometimes three jobs in one night: a high school prom, then we would do a set at the teenage nightclub, and then we'd finish the third set at Barnaby's [a pizza pub] in downtown Chicago."

So in 1969 and 1970, despite racial tensions and widespread societal unrest, Baby Huey and the Babysitters could perform charismatic R&B-inflected rock at a clean-cut student dance held at the decorous and Catholic Gordon Technical High School on Chicago's white Northwest Side.[40] A year later, they enlivened the Sound Storm rock festival in rural Wisconsin. *Chicago Tribune* critic Robb Baker attended the latter event and wrote that Baby Huey, "sparked things up considerably with his 300 pounds of funk and fun." But the article also hinted that Huey was dabbling in illicit substances, quoting him saying onstage, "'Just imagine there are about 500 Indians up in those hills, swooping down on us all, bringing mushrooms and peyote.'"[41]

Despite Huey's actual heroin addiction, his generous spirit remained. Gavin Christopher had taken only a few saxophone lessons when he briefly became a Babysitter (Christopher's saxophone teacher was composer Anthony Braxton). "This guy was so beautiful on his feet, and so beautiful in controlling a band," Christopher said. "He taught me how to break, stop, turnaround, and bring the band down. He taught me how to segue in between tunes, and all those things I hadn't learned to do in a band, I learned to do in Baby Huey's band. I joined the band as a saxophone player, and I had only been playing saxophone for two weeks. He said, 'I don't care, they'll teach you how to play.'"

That freedom to take chances, combined with the group's firm rhythmic foundation, shaped Baby Huey and the Babysitters' *Living Legend*. Consider Baby Huey's take on Mayfield's "Mighty Mighty (Spade and Whitey)," from February 1969, renamed "Mighty Mighty Children." Like many R&B tunes from that era, it's presented in two parts, the A and B sides of a 45 rpm record. Oddly, only part two appears on the record. The A side is a straightforward rendition of Mayfield's plea for racial harmony ("Your black and white power / is gonna be a crumbling tower"). But while Mayfield's high tenor eased into a falsetto, Baby Huey delivers a husky call-and-response with the horn section. The guitar features Mayfield's open tuning and wah-wah effects, but it's not certain who is playing (it likely was Phil Upchurch). Baby Huey then tears into the second part. He free-associates with signifiers familiar to anyone who'd lived on Chicago's South Side: turkey dinners at Walgreens drugstore in the Bronzeville neighborhood, Lou Rawls, and a street rhyme about Thunderbird wine. Neither Mayfield nor Baby Huey had any use for racial supremacy or separatism, but they knew how to promote their culture not just through words, but through their delivery: presciently, Huey was rapping.

While the names of most personnel are listed on the album's sleeve, it remains unclear who played what. Also, *The Living Legend* was recorded in different places: Alfano remembers that part of it was taped in Colorado while the band was on tour and the rest in a Chicago studio, though he does not recall which one. Huey died before the album's completion, so instrumental tracks like "One Dragon Two Dragon" fill out the LP (the horn lines on that tune resemble arrangements by the band Chicago, a group that grew from another Heiman client called the Big Thing). Some Babysitters bristled that Heiman's deal was for Huey, not the band, and they left at various times. Alfano remembers that Hathaway also had a creative role in the recording. Neither Hathaway nor Upchurch, both on the Curtom staff, was cited on *The Living Legend* album, but Alfano felt that Hathaway should be credited for the way the bassist's lines accentuate Huey's sense of paranoia on Mayfield's "Hard Times" and for an inspired idea that the future soul star applied to another Mayfield-written track, "Running."

"On 'Hard Times' [Donny] looked at me and said, 'Bass man, play this over here.'" Alfano said before singing the song's line about "'having hard times in this crazy town.'" "That little [musical] phrase is what he gave me. And the beginning of 'Running,' if you listen, that was him on a Fender Rhodes piano, which he ran through a wah-wah pedal. I never saw anybody do that like that before. He gave us so much flavor doing that."

Hathaway's inventive effects, Huey's screams, and the band's emphatic attack on the first beat of each measure have helped make the album a staple for hip-hop DJs years later. But the emotional centerpiece of *The Living Legend* is Huey's nine-and-a-half-minute version of "A Change Is Gonna Come." Alfano said that when the group performed it live, the piece crescendoed after its studio fadeout. Whereas Sam Cooke framed his original with orchestral strings and a smooth delivery, the Babysitters accentuated horn lines and Huey's higher-register screams. While some of producer Mayfield's musical choices are misguided (an unnecessary echo effect), Huey's poignancy remains vivid. Sadly, within his midsong rap, he delivers a rambling autobiographical talk describing substance abuse. Shortly after this recording, on October 28, 1970, he died in Chicago's Roberts Motel, most likely from a heroin overdose combined with pressure on his heart.

Melvyn Jones played on some of *The Living Legend* but had not worked with Baby Huey for a couple of months before that. He relayed strong, but despairing, insights into the singer's final moments, although he was not actually nearby. "When he started shooting dope, I couldn't sit around watching my best friend deteriorate, so I joined the Impressions," Jones said. "Baby Huey knew the promise he made Curtis to stop, so he did one last hit, and that's what it was. He snuck away from the band and went with two teenagers who came by saying, 'I got this real good hit for you.' He decided to give himself that little extra: he fell off the toilet seat, and those youngsters got so scared they ran off and left him there."

Huey then returned home: his funeral was held three days later in Richmond's Bethel AME church.[42] Jones, after serving as the musical director for the Impressions, later worked with blues legends Freddie King and John Lee Hooker. Alfano played with another regionally popular rock musician, Wayne Cochran. Heiman bought out Eddie Thomas's share in Curtom and took over his position in the company. Although Heiman and Thomas do not agree on much, they share a bittersweet affection for Baby Huey.

Upon its release, *The Living Legend* had slim sales and received scant media attention. The LP reached only number thirty-eight on the *Billboard* soul charts.[43] But Lenny Kaye wrote an enthusiastic review in a 1971 edition of *Rolling Stone*, about four years before the critic-musician became renowned as lead guitarist in the Patti Smith Group. Calling Huey "this amazing man-mountain," Kaye refers to the Babysitters as "all rhythmic interplays and wailing brass and when they would lay back, content to ride the song for a while, they sent out a heartbeat which stirred movement in even the least likeliest of places."[44]

The Babysitters carried on for about a year with Chaka Khan singing lead and performed at Nero's Pit on Rush Street. Close to the posh Gold Coast, this stretch of Chicago's Near North Side had been home to upscale clubs, bars, and restaurants such as the jazz venue Mister Kelly's, which hosted Mayfield in October 1971 (other kinds of spots touting "Authentic Oriental Belly Dancers" and "Go-Go Revues" also lined the area). Marty Feldman had established the state-of-the-art Paragon Recording Studios nearby in 1969, and artists would record there before or after nearby gigs. These artists included Ask Rufus in October 1970, a group that would become famous four years later simply as Rufus, with Khan as its focus.[45] Khan also sang in the rock bands Lock and Chain as well as Lyfe with Gavin Christopher. "Once You Get Started," which Christopher wrote, would become a hit for Rufus in 1974. These were integrated groups, and Khan said she did not face much discrimination in that neighborhood, perhaps because her career was ascending at that point, her band provided protection, or comfortable audiences did not perceive her as a threat. Also, as she notes, artists enter strata that others cannot. "We did experience some racism, but not in Chicago," Khan said. "It's interesting that the world of art sort of floats above a lot of stuff, above a lot of social crap, because of what we're doing."

But Christopher saw the Rush Street scene differently. His observations echoed those of future television journalist Warner Saunders, who said that although there were no "for whites only" signs at Near North Side bars, bouncers frequently turned away young blacks.[46] Also, Chris James of the Natural Four recounted hearing derogatory comments from the staff at Mr. Kelly's during his group's week-long stint.[47] "There was a lot of segregation in the clubs," Christopher said. "A lot of times they wouldn't let black people in the clubs. I remember a couple of times I would threaten the doorman that I wouldn't do the gig. There would be black people at the door wanting to get in, and he would tell them no. And I would say, 'If you don't let these people in, then we're not going to play.'"

Paul Coleman, keyboardist and cofounder of the soul-rock band Rasputin's Stash, has another recollection of the exchange between his group and venue management. "Club owners would always say, 'Don't mess with the white women,'" Coleman said. "We heard it a few times. We totally ignored that, of course."

Rasputin's Stash also ignored any outside directives when it came to music. As a child growing up in the Park Manor neighborhood of Chicago, Coleman could access a piano only by crawling through the basement window of a closed church. "Every day I would sneak in that church and play," Coleman said. "I didn't know what I was doing, I would groove to the tones, the chords, even the clashes and dissonance were grooving me."

Coleman attended Chicago Vocational High School, where he joined doo-wop groups. He recalls singing in vestibules, underpasses, and onstage with the Chi-Lites in the housing projects around Wabash and Sixty-Third Street. Then he became a part of the Fantastic Epics with singer Jimmy Burns and guitarist Martin Dumas. After army service, Coleman toured with vocalist Vince Willis, Dumas, and drummer Frank Donaldson. On the road they experienced typical setbacks such as stolen money and equipment, so Coleman's girlfriend suggested his band be named after Rasputin, the early twentieth-century Russian mystic and faith healer, "because of the negativity we had encountered." Rasputin's esoteric aura would counteract adverse forces. A drug reference in the "Stash" part of the name also seems possible.

Rasputin's Stash, an eight-piece band with a horn section, signed on to Atlantic's Cotillion imprint. In contrast to Rotary Connection's layered orchestral charts, this band's panoply on its eponymous debut album flowed casually. Country-tinged acoustic slide guitar streamed across the album; so did flamenco. Relaxed, midtempo extended jams switched into tightly arranged horn passages. A love ballad preceded another piece that parodied the talk of street pimps. *Billboard* praised the mixture (in questionable terms) as "a soul-jazz-rock sound distinctly ghetto, distinctly soul." Atlantic did not encourage the release.[48]

"We came there with an album's worth of material, recorded it, and they said, 'Wow every tune is in a different direction,'" Coleman said. "And they want a band to be one direction. We were young and didn't know what direction—all we knew was we were full of music. Everyone wants to be a creator. I'm a writer, Vince is a writer, Martin is a writer. Whatever the hell we felt. Martin sat playing on the side of the pool to come up with that folk song on the first album. We had an opportunity to just express ourselves." Rasputin's Stash continued to tour and became a four-piece band after returning to Chicago, when it signed with Gemigo, an imprint of Curtom. Even with reduced numbers, it recorded another loose blend on *Devil Made Me Do It* in 1974. Extensive rock jams morphed into traditional soul beats, a combination the band's appearances reflected. Earl Calloway in the *Chicago Defender* mentioned that Rasputin's Stash appeared at the South Side's Bud Billiken Parade and the Soul Explosion '75 sales event at the Carson Pirie Scott department store downtown.[49] The group could also fit in with the counterculture when it performed at Alice's Revisited, a folk-blues club in Lincoln Park that had shared its building with the *Chicago Seed*.[50] After a questionable name change to r-Stash for a couple of disco singles and a few initially unreleased recordings, by the late 1970s the group dissolved.[51] Coleman then formed the band Crystal Winds, but he claims he actually supported himself as a card shark. He added that while gang members were frequent opponents, they were allowed to win their money back.

The legacy of all of these groups proved more lasting than sales figures suggest. Locally they show that, at least on an artistic front, social divisions were not impenetrable in the post–civil rights era. But these musicians fought uphill battles in a city where even well-intentioned progressive whites and black talent still overlooked each other. For instance, a *Chicago Seed* ad for a Fred Hampton Memorial Concert in Grant Park on June 28, 1970, listed a number of folk and rock artists—Spirit, Leo Kottke—but no African Americans.[52] Such lingering social disconnection helps show why many talents moved away. A Grant Park riot in July 1970 at an aborted Sly and the Family Stone concert likely further alienated the counterculture from the wider city.[53] Still, for some, transcending divisions within the city prepared them for overcoming similar gulfs nationwide.

Minnie Riperton and Chaka Khan drew on Chicago's convergence of R&B, folk, and rock as they launched successful careers in the 1970s. Other global impacts came through in different ways. Stepney's arrangements were exalted in England: Elton John remarked to *Billboard* editor Timothy White, "I was very influenced by people like Charles Stepney with Rotary Connection. . . . Charles was a big influence; I thought you should be able to do funky rock music with great string arrangements and brass arrangements, as he did."[54] Records by Chicago groups, moreover, contributed significantly to hip-hop and other genres through sampling. Whosampled.com, the primary website that demonstrates which records have been used where, lists at least ninety-eight samples from Rotary Connection and eighty-four from Baby Huey.[55] These are respectable numbers, even if not the massive totals of Lyn Collins's "Think (About It)" (sampled in 2,086 tracks) or the Incredible Bongo Band's "Apache" (which turns up in 534 tracks). The tunes have also been reworked in some interesting, and surprising, places. For instance, unconventional rocker Beck used Rasputin Stash's lighthearted "Dookey Shoe" as the core of his "Hotwax" in 1995.

What all these late 1960s and early 1970s musicians also share is that they were indeed groups. George Clinton's Funkadelic and Sly and the Family Stone are rightfully credited with bringing full bands to the forefront in R&B, not just having instrumentalists serve as backdrops to singers. Soul guitarists—like Funkadelic's Eddie Hazel—would be applauded for stretching out into rock hero excursions. But Chicago-based artists from that time deserve more credit for boosting this process. Also, these groups represented colorfully mismatched origins, whether as a studio construct (Rotary Connection), a dance band (Baby Huey and the Babysitters), or an outgrowth of an R&B unit (Rasputin's Stash). By the 1980s and 1990s, Prince and the Revolution and groups affiliated with the Black Rock Coalition would expound on how these electric and underground groups were part of a broad African American pop tradition.

Other ripples cannot be easily quantified. Dan Alfano and Sidney Barnes recount how Barnes's former partner Clinton showed up at both of their groups' performances and adopting their multiracial influences to his Parliament-Funkadelic juggernaut in the 1970s. Funkadelic also shared a bill with Rasputin's Stash at Chicago's Arie Crown Theater in January 1973.[56] Clinton and Barnes retained similar futuristic musical visions and still collaborate. Barnes cowrote such romantic—in their own way—Funkadelic tracks as "I'll Bet You" (1969), "You Can't Miss What You Can't Measure" (on *Cosmic Slop*, 1973), and "That Was My Girl" (on *America Eats Its Young*, 1972). Barnes described the moment when he realized that the times might be catching up to them.

"When George [Clinton] and I parted ways in Detroit, we said we're going to meet up one day," Barnes said. "We don't know where the music is going, but we're going to meet up and that's where it's going. Next time we met up in New York, I had a cape and boots on with a big ol' black hat with a feather in it, and George had a sheet on and a mohawk, and I said, 'Yeah, man, we got there.'"

FIVE

A New Day:
Afrocentric Philosophy and Sharp
Statements Answer 1960s Challenges

In 1968 the lobby of the Affro-Arts Theater in the Oakland neighborhood on the South Side doubled as a bridge. More than four decades later Phil Cohran, who converted this former movie theater into a cultural wellspring, recalled the wall paintings that joined ancient Egypt and modern Chicago. His eyes brightened when he talked about the conical African heads hanging from the ceiling. Cohran's Artistic Heritage Ensemble performed there regularly, and Chicago-born University of Ghana alumna Darlene Blackburn offered dance classes. Poet Gwendolyn Brooks recited her verses at the Affro-Arts, including one she wrote in Cohran's honor.[1] The theater's name combined the word "Africa" with "fro" to signify "from," in reference to the roots of black people worldwide.[2] This theater stood out while it connected with the city that surrounded it. "The whole community was bursting to celebrate Africanness," Cohran said. "Children that didn't have access to information, we'd get it out there for everybody."

Getting these messages out to eager soul musicians proved to be a legacy that lasted long after the Affro-Arts Theater closed its doors. The venue's revolutionary act was in affirming that African consciousness did not have to be esoteric—that black Chicagoans could adapt it to their daily lives. Cohran's artistic and musical philosophies derived from his lifetime study of traditions from within Chicago and from far away. As the late 1960s turned into the early 1970s, artists, activists, and street gangs encountered each other and occasionally shared agendas. This all proved challenging, but the music attests to its creators' resilience.

While the Affro-Arts Theater offered positive responses to situations young African Americans faced in late 1960s Chicago, Syl Johnson presented a different vision through his 1970 album *Is It Because I'm Black*. Written and recorded after Martin Luther King's assassination, this record eschewed spiritual rumination for confronting contemporary crises. Sparse arrangements contained blues, soul, and rock as Johnson and his group perceived them. The album's genesis also derived from artists' continuing to seek self-determination for themselves within the larger R&B industry. But for those musicians and their associates at the Affro-Arts, a drive for personal autonomy combined with community engagement, even when their approaches diverged.

Freedom Road: Rise of the Affro-Arts Theater and the Pharaohs

In *The Black Atlantic*, sociologist Paul Gilroy cites gospel groups, rappers, and the Impressions as among those who crafted and challenged concepts of racial and national authenticity. He writes about how organic intellectuals bring forward traditions without benefiting from wider institutional support. They communicate all this through a premodern system—in this case, music—that transcends verbal language. Using African-derived terminology, Gilroy refers to such people as being of a "priestly caste."[3] That is how many Chicagoans saw Cohran during his lifetime and after his death on June 28, 2017, at age ninety.[4] One singer in the 1960s, then called Yvette Stevens, envisioned Cohran as more than a priest when he fulfilled Gilroy's description; she remembers that "there was something very kingly" about him. Stevens participated in myriad programs at the Affro-Arts. There, as part of an African naming ceremony, she became Chaka. Later, after a marriage to musician Hassan Khan, she achieved worldwide fame as Chaka Khan. As she described it almost forty-five years later, her time at Affro-Arts during the 1960s was foundational:

> I remember how happy I felt at the Affro-Arts. It was a great institution in the community. Once you stepped inside the theater it took you into another place, to a place that was spiritually a really high place. I felt like I was in the presence of royalty with these guys. My philosophy was being formed in that place: a lot of things I learned and I did in the way of living that I've applied throughout my lifetime—like trying to keep myself together in an herbal way. That was a special time for man on the planet, man in America, a special time in Chicago. Chicago has always been a very racist city, but it was a time when self-expression was cool.

Maurice White, then the drummer with Ramsey Lewis's trio, also frequented the Affro-Arts Theater, and he focused on how Cohran played his invented instrument, the frankiphone, an adaptation of the southern African kalimba. The name derived from Cohran's mother, Frankie Mae Ragland.

By the early 1970s, White felt comfortable enough with his version of the kalimba to feature it in Earth, Wind, and Fire. In his memoir, White mentions that the theater represented "not a militant black power thing, but a place of black awareness, teaching us to fall in love with our culture, giving us an understanding of our rightful place on the planet and of ourselves."[5]

The theater also became a forum for black American activists. Their worldview reverberated through the music that Cohran and his adherents created, such as on his 1968 Artistic Heritage Ensemble album, *The Malcolm X Memorial (A Tribute in Music)* (Zulu). Their presence at the Affro-Arts also represented a strategy that had been developing in Chicago for a number of years. But in the late 1960s community-based organizations intersected with performers and other young people to reach a wider audiences. Illinois Black Panther Party (IBPP) chairman Fred Hampton spoke at the Affro-Arts Theater. His supporters included Khan, who distributed the party's newspapers and volunteered at the free breakfast program that became a core Panther initiative. Although pronounced African connections had been prominent in jazz for decades, Cohran's institution blended them with his own cosmology and warmth that won over youths in a way his predecessors and musical contemporaries might not have been able to accomplish.[6]

Nonetheless, the Affro-Arts Theater's precursors set the stage for these transactions. The American Negro Exposition, which opened at the Chicago Coliseum on July 4, 1940, exhibited works by accomplished black musicians and painters such as Archibald Motley.[7] About one year later, the South Side Community Arts Center, which proposed to bring "cultural and political radicalism into public space," was dedicated in a Bronzeville brownstone mansion.[8] Both these endeavors received government funding—the Illinois legislature helped with the former, and President Franklin D. Roosevelt's Works Progress Administration supported the latter. But not all such efforts at exploring African culture came from established institutions.

In 1946 Herman Blount, a jazz pianist from Alabama, landed in Chicago. Like Phil Cohran, he immersed himself in ancient Ethiopian and Egyptian lore. He changed his name a few times, ultimately performing and recording as Sun Ra.[9] During the middle to late 1950s, Sun Ra and his Myth Science Arkestra big band brought their interpretations of African melodies and instruments, as well as his theses about astronomy, onto such albums as *Angels and Demons at Play* and *The Nubians of Plutonia*. Cohran played trumpet and zither for the Arkestra during these years. But Sun Ra also had an ear toward the R&B that could be heard more locally: in 1954 and 1955, he recorded a few ebullient doo-wop singles as the producer of a harmony group called the Cosmic Rays, which included bassist and future Chess arranger Richard Evans.[10] But even with Sun Ra's mind traveling across time, continents, and planets, he and business partner Alton Abraham remained grounded enough to release these 45s through their own company, Saturn Records.

Many Chicagoans also joined in a wider movement that saw African and Eastern concepts as imperative. Nation of Islam leader Elijah Muhammad, who was based on the South Side, drew about five thousand people when he spoke at the Coliseum in 1960.[11] In spring 1961, opera star Etta Moten Barnett brought African art, handcrafted furniture, and rugs to decorate her Victorian-style Chicago home.[12] Later in 1961, pianist Ahmad Jamal opened his 200–seat Alhambra supper club, just south of the Loop, which reflected his own Islamic faith and connected consciousness. The restaurant, modeled after a Moorish palace in Spain, served mostly Middle Eastern and Indian food and no alcohol.[13] Celebrating the opening of the Alhambra, *Ebony* described it (perhaps with no pun intended) as "designed as a mecca for entertainment" and noted that Jamal owned five businesses including Mazzan Music Publishers.[14]

Soon such explorations spread within the city. Two years later, Vee-Jay released *Africa Calling*, which contains the Dungill Family's interpretation of West African rhythms. These pieces include the Chicago group's adaptations of Watusi drumming and Christian pleas sung in Yoruba. By the middle 1960s Cohran—a friend of Elijah Muhammad's lieutenant Malcolm X— had wanted to create new South Side institutions based on his readings of African and Asian thoughts and practices. His goal was to help enrich people in the neighborhoods artistically, no matter their finances. Cohran said, "In the past, it had been well-to-do people, the upper class, involved in culture. They had enough money, I guess, to pursue it. But it was the time for masses to become cultured."

Cohran always had the initiative to charge this movement. He was born in Mississippi in 1927, played trumpet and sang spirituals as a child, then added other brass and percussion instruments to his toolbox.[15] After moving to St. Louis and attending Lincoln University Laboratory High School in the 1940s, he studied at Lincoln University for a year. He later served in the army, learning more about classical composers at the Naval School of Music at Anacostia, in Washington, DC, and then relocated to Chicago.[16] But he read more about Europe, Africa, and Asia on his own after he worked with Sun Ra. Like Charles Stepney, he looked into the Schillinger system but became disenchanted with what he saw as its clinical approach.

I had read that in Hollywood the composers had to learn the Schillinger system because there were so many melodies [there] they couldn't produce those kinds of melodies. So they'd get unlimited extensions—that's for me! It would go in directions you wouldn't expect it to go in because of the mathematics. If you're writing from feeling, you'll go this way or that way, but the Schillinger system will take another direction. Well, I noticed it didn't have any spirit in it. When I got [to Chicago], I started going to the Chicago Symphony every week. I would take my score down there, and that irritated people—reading the score and because I was black, anyway.

Although Cohran worked in Red Saunders's house band at the Regal Theater during the mid-1960s, he also wanted to present his own music. He absorbed seemingly everything from Ravi Shankar albums to birds chirping in Douglas Park on the West Side. Cohran also pondered chromatic scales. In early 1965 he cofounded the Association for the Advancement of Creative Musicians (AACM), holding meetings at his home on East Seventy-Fifth Street.[17] None of this brought him much financial recompense. The city's Urban Gateways program hired Cohran to lecture to children about African instruments and their relevance for American music. The other boost came from Oscar Brown Jr. After Cohran saw Brown perform at the Happy Medium, they discussed an idea to create a musical based on the poems of Paul Lawrence Dunbar, whose verses had also influenced a young Curtis Mayfield. Cohran said he wrote the production's twenty-three songs in three weeks.

After touring the city with this production, Cohran formed the Artistic Heritage Ensemble. The large group of Chicago's R&B session musicians began seeking alternative paradigms on such self-released albums as *Armageddon*, recorded in 1968. Gospel plays a part, as do the advanced tonal conceptions of free jazz. Cohran's Afrofuturism never left the church. The liner notes on *Armageddon* state how the title piece drew on his "focus on cosmology and culture" after his performing with Sun Ra and learning from Elijah Muhammad's teachings. According to that album's back cover essay, one instrumental track, "The Window," envisions extraterrestrials peering down at Earth's major population centers to determine what should be altered. At that time the group combined Chess session guitarist Pete Cosey with alumni from James Mack's Crane classes, including bassist Louis Satterfield, saxophonist Don Myrick, and trumpeter Charles Handy. While percussionist "Master" Henry Gibson would become better recognized in the 1970s for his work with Mayfield, his initial immersion in African rhythms began when Cohran recruited him for the Artistic Heritage Ensemble about 1966. Another former Mack student, trombonist Willie Woods, also joined this group.

"It was an awakening, especially the kind of music he was playing," Woods said. "I was used to playing with Red [Saunders], but this thing was all spiritual. He wrote a lot of stuff that was dealing with the modal system; you had to play within that modal system. It was a new way of playing and understanding the music."

Cohran expounded on how to understand both the music and the musicians who play it in a manuscript he wrote in 1965. The manifesto includes his views on healthy diet and yoga training, which Chaka Khan mentioned. He also discusses the importance of studying "the movements and relationships of celestial bodies" about twelve years before Maurice White drew on that imagery for such Earth, Wind, and Fire albums as *All 'n All*. Crucially, Cohran urges musicians to look toward the East for philosophical guidance. He approached music scientifically but through the light of ancient knowledge. With such thoughts, Cosey moved from playing electric guitar as he had on most Chess sessions to doubling on sitar and drawing on aspects of the Indian instrument's tuning for other string instruments (which would become evident during Cosey's 1970s work with Miles Davis).[18] "A careful study of any or all of the great advanced cultures of the past will reveal a detailed use of music as a science," Cohran wrote. "This science is rooted in the mathematics of the open string (harps, zithers, tamburas, etc.). Only a fool or child would put pedals on harps. There are many instances we could cite to prove the importance of music to a people's strength and spirit."[19]

All the while, Cohran knew his programs should belong to everyone. A large photo spread in the *Chicago Defender* in August 1967 showcased regular Artistic Heritage Ensemble performances at the Sixty-Third Street beach and Cohran's work with the Washington Park YMCA summer program.[20] The article quotes his desire to build a "great civilization" based on African history; he remained visionary enough to expect a positive response. That sense was confirmed when the Affro-Arts Theater opened on December 1, 1967, largely because of South Siders who contributed money and material resources as well as their construction skills.[21]

Considering how sociologist Mary Pattillo describes the neighborhood in her study *Black on the Block: The Politics of Race and Class in the City*, the theater afforded a needed ray of optimism. Pattillo refers to a US Senate commission in 1969 that sent two physicians to learn about the public health needs of poor areas, who highlighted Kenwood-Oakland in their report. They mentioned unsanitary living conditions, tenements, and plywood sheets covering an elementary school's broken windows.[22] Pattillo also points to residents who stayed in the neighborhood not just for its low rents, but also because of family ties and a hope that the area would improve. The

Kenwood-Oakland Community Organization, formed in 1965, also advocated for political empowerment.[23]

Accordingly, the neighborhood possessed the kind of energy to place the Affro-Arts Theater within the sphere of what Larry Neal and other writers described as the black arts movement. This represented a drive for African American artists and their audiences that would "define the world of art and culture in its own terms."[24] Also in 1967, a mural was painted a few blocks southwest of the theater, at Forty-Third and Langley. This Wall of Respect lasted four years, concurrently with the theater.[25] The painters who designed the wall included founders of AFRI-COBRA (African Commune of Bad Relevant Artists) and OBAC (Organization of Black American Culture), which both sought to create a new black aesthetic based in part on what Neal identified as a collective identity.[26] This display featured musical, athletic, and religious heroes as well as activists who visited the theater, including Muhammad Ali.[27] Some, like poet Haki Madhubuti (Don L. Lee), spoke at both the Wall and the Affro-Arts Theater. On October 14, 1968, three thousand high school and college students who had walked out of their Monday classes attended a rally at the Affro-Arts Theater demanding more black teachers and an emphasis on African American issues in curricula.[28] A few months later, Neal would mention Cohran as an example of a musician who infused African American ideals with a sense of spirituality.[29]

Cohran and his co-organizers espoused a wide vision. In the performance space, plays, poetry recitations, and dance performances ran concurrently with concerts. Upstairs, the education center offered free classes in Arabic, Hebrew, French, and Swahili as well as discussions about such health concerns as diet and exercises for proper breathing. "All you had to do was show up every week," Cohran said. "The community was tired of crap, and we were offering substance."

Visiting musicians, from Sammy Davis Jr. to the Impressions, supported the venue through their performances. Resident groups included the Spencer Jackson Family gospel singers and Shades of Black, which included Chaka Khan and her sister Yvonne Stevens (later known as funk singer Taka Boom). But the Pharaohs made their name at the Affro-Arts. Although the group had a shifting lineup, the core members included Artistic Heritage Ensemble members (Woods, Myrick, Satterfield, and Handy) as well as other session players such as tuba player Aaron Dodd and trumpeter Rahmlee Michael Davis. Occasional Pharaohs guitarist Yehudah Ben Israel (Thomas Whitfield) had also been in the Soul Messengers, a band affiliated with the Black Hebrew Israelite movement. This faith, formed in Chicago about the late 1950s, merged African traditions with Old Testament theology and established a home base in Dimona, Israel.[30] The Black Hebrew tenets regarding diet, spirituality, and African connections overlapped with Cohran's precepts.

Derf Reklaw also joined the Pharaohs on percussion and flute. He had worked with African-inspired drumming groups as well as with such early AACM members as multireedist Joseph Jarman. For Reklaw, the African consciousness at the heart of the AACM and the Affro-Arts Theater influenced his shift from earlier in the decade when, as Fred Walker, his movements popularized a local teen dance, the woodbine twine.[31] While the Pharaohs started out playing covers of R&B hits, Reklaw said that Cohran's thinking and African influences in Shades of Black transformed its repertoire.

"Charles Handy had been engulfed in Egyptology," Reklaw said, "and we had to come up with some music that would be relevant to all the other kinds of things that were happening with what was going on. Because Phil had songs like 'Detroit Red,' which was a Malcolm X song, 'Unity,' and 'The Talking Drum.' And then you can't be putting all these acts on like Shades of Black and then have the Pharaohs going to play [the Four Tops'] 'I'll Be There.'"

The idea was not to duplicate African musical strains, but to combine them with what they heard on South Side streets. Just as Stepney showed how much Schillinger's system could be used in R&B, at the Affro-Arts Cohran and the Pharaohs demonstrated that African percussion belonged in soul.[32] This band mixed that continent's polyrhythms within familiar R&B melodic structures. They still covered Smokey Robinson's "Tracks of My Tears," which Reklaw mentioned was Satterfield's favorite song. Other tunes took different turns. Reklaw said his unrecorded "The Awakening" was a 6/8 piece that could stretch out for more than half an hour (the group kept the title for the only album it recorded). Handy's "Freedom Road" features staccato horn riffs and a medium-fast tempo in a song that urges enlightenment, while "Black Enuff" allows humor and blues guitar to advocate for African American unity. On "Great House" Satterfield's extended bass lines become the bedrock. It's the sort of piece that would have fit with the Art Ensemble of Chicago's concepts of bold insurgent Great Black Music. That jazz group included Jarman as well as Myrick's lifelong friend Roscoe Mitchell and toured colleges with the Pharaohs. Once in a while percussionist Famoudou Don Moye performed with both groups.[33] These friendly South Side–based bands shared aesthetic premises that transcended any perceived incongruities between their stylistic idioms, which were not far apart at all. The Pharaohs' positive press included a four-star review in the jazz magazine *DownBeat*.[34] But more than this numerical honor, critic Michael Bourne accurately captured, in his words, its "intense community of spirit" and "collective presence of energy" over a focus on soloists.[35] Bourne also picked up on the musical connections between the group and Sun Ra.

While cultural issues were Cohran's focus at the Affro-Arts Theater, he also invited political activists. When Fred Hampton spoke at the theater in 1968, his oratory propelled him into a leadership position in the Illinois Black Panther Party.[36] Stokely Carmichael also delivered a speech there, and Cohran said his rhetoric triggered unwelcome local and national government pressure. Cohran had solid reason to believe he was targeted, since the police killing of Hampton in 1969 illustrated that such baleful conspiracies did exist.[37] So Cohran left the theater that year, which Reklaw and Woods said caused the Pharaohs to step up as the Affro-Arts' main musical ensemble and to take on a bigger role in running the institution—another kind of territorial negotiation.

From the beginning, Cohran's outreach to young people also extended to gang members. He told the *Chicago Defender*, "These young men, so often labeled 'gang-banger' and 'criminal,' are in reality tomorrow's strength and leadership."[38] Cohran was not alone in proposing that these groups could become agents for positive change. Engagement between musician-activists, civic leaders and street organizations had been building throughout the 1960s. About 1966, folksinger James Collier connected with the Blackstone Rangers and Vice Lords to permit King's associates to bring their neighborhoods' young people into the Chicago Freedom Movement.[39] On the West Side, two days before Martin Luther King's assassination, the Vice Lords became the Conservative Vice Lords (CVL) to herald a new mission. The CVL opened Teen Town snack shop and the African Lion, which sold art and clothing. These ventures were funded through separate $15,000 grants, from the Rockefeller Foundation and from Operation Bootstrap.[40] Oscar Brown Jr. cast members of the Blackstone Rangers in his musical *Opportunity Please Knock* and believed the media's refusal to cover the production caused its demise.[41] Still, his daughter, vocalist Maggie Brown, told journalist Howard Reich that her father's efforts turned some "tough guys" into lighting designers, firemen, actors, and teachers.[42]

According to Woods, after Cohran left the theater, the Affro-Arts musicians maintained coexistence with the Blackstone Rangers and the gang's leader, Jeff Fort. "Jeff Fort was very respectful of what we were doing in the community, and he didn't give us any problems," Woods said. "In fact, he encouraged us to do what we were doing, and if we were having any problem in the community, he said he'd take care of it. But we would never, ever let him take care of anything! [Laughs]. All the other stuff they were doing, we weren't privy to that. They never came in and tried to push their will upon us or anything like that."

Throughout Chicago, musicians had varying interactions with different gangs. Marshall Thompson added that the Chi-Lites performed benefits for the Blackstone Rangers and their rivals, the Disciples, when these groups offered to help feed homeless people. "We weren't in the gangs, never in the gangs," Thompson said. "But they all loved the Chi-Lites." Other Chicago musical personalities had more dangerous encounters. In the early 1970s, the Blackstone Rangers reportedly demanded money from Curtis Mayfield. According to his son Todd, he refused but agreed to play a benefit concert for them.[43] That gang also tried to extort DJ Holmes "Daddy-O" Daylie into donating one of the gas stations he owned to the "youth of the area." After his rebuff, the stations were robbed. Battles ensued during which Daylie picked up a gun, hired a private security force, and urged merchants in the Woodlawn neighborhood to resist such shakedowns.[44]

Sidney Barnes's experiences with Chicago gangs could have happened only to a free spirit like him. After he'd lived in the Blackstone Rangers' territory on South Stony Island Avenue, the singer feared the Disciples would consider him a spy when he moved to their area around Sixty-Third Street and South Cottage Grove Avenue. On realizing his occupation, they persuaded him to coach their members to harmonize like the Temptations. But, Barnes added, "I had to do it because they'd kick my ass if I didn't." He proudly mentored Lou Bond, who in 1974 recorded a serene self-titled album for the We Produce subsidiary of the Memphis-based Stax Records. Bond's LP features his gentle tenor voice interwoven with acoustic guitar, horns, and a string section.

The songs are either inwardly reflective or his social commentary. Echoing Terry Callier, Bond's album might have been a quiet reaction to his harsh years on the South Side.[45] Barnes's input had a lot to do with that. "I'd talk to [gang members'] families, help them, take them out for picnics," Barnes said. "It changed their whole outlook. All the guys I'd meet were stuck in the ghetto rut. I'd introduce them to Simon and Garfunkel or Jimmy Webb, and I'd say, there's another world."

No absolutes can be stated regarding musicians' interactions with late 1960s–early 1970s gangs in Chicago, or whether the results were positive or negative. Even today, former gang leaders and law enforcement officers disagree on the sincerity of the Vice Lords' and Blackstone Rangers' outreach efforts. Also, looking backward, the societal awareness that some gangs expressed seems a world away from the nihilism that their factionalized descendants would demonstrate later. But one never knew how many potential artists were lost because of street violence in the late 1960s. The casualties included a seventeen-year-old aspiring singer who was stabbed to death just for refusing to join the Disciples.[46]

Is It Because I'm Black: Chicago Musicians Reflect on Martin Luther King

Martin Luther King's April 4, 1968, assassination had the potential to devastate his efforts along with the flames that engulfed much of the city. The bullet struck him as he stood on the balcony of the Lorraine Motel in Memphis, just after he shouted a request to Chicago saxophonist Ben Branch.[47] King had asked Branch to play "Precious Lord, Take My Hand," and the rifle shot that followed could have finished the civil rights movement.[48] Riots ensued in Chicago, where King's mission had taken him two years earlier, amid many roadblocks. Over the weekend, fires and looting tore apart the West Side's commercial stretches of Madison Street and Roosevelt Road, while snipers in Cabrini-Green and Englewood fired on police and firefighters. Mayor Richard J. Daley, who infamously ordered police to "shoot to kill" anyone with a suspected firebomb and "shoot to detain" suspected looters, called for reinforcements from the Illinois National Guard. By Sunday, when a semblance of quiet emerged, eleven people had been killed, hundreds were left homeless, and 2,900 black people had been arrested, most of them under eighteen.[49] Photographs from that time show enormous property damage: blocks resembled postwar ruins.

King's killing horrified Chicago musicians, as did the aftermath that seemed to repudiate his doctrine. Jerry Butler remembered that he was touring the South at the time, and he feared civil war. Larry Wade was sent home early from his job in a radio parts dealership and was "crying like mad" by the time he got home to Old Town Gardens. He thought of earlier days when he was growing up in nearby Cabrini-Green, when blacks and whites would celebrate together at neighborhood events such as the annual Italian festival. Nearby, on that night, saxophonist Willie Henderson was at Universal Studios with Billy Butler (Jerry Butler's brother) recording "Thank You Baby," with James Mack handling the arrangements. The news chilled them, but he did not find any long-term difference in collaborating with white musicians in the wake of King's death. Work and home lives were kept apart, and there was an understanding to emphasize the former. "The people you worked with, black and white, your relationship was basically the same," Henderson said. "Our neighborhoods were so separate anyway. We met a lot of white people when we were on sessions together, and if you have a good relationship with them, it's basically the same."

Bernard Reed also remembered that studio camaraderie when he became a session bassist at Brunswick. "In the recording studio we were integrated," Reed said. "The recording sessions were very integrated. Most of the string players were all white guys—Chicago Symphony guys. But we became like, 'Oh, here we are again, good to see you. OK, let's go make a hit!'"

These musicians, among many others in Chicago, were far from indifferent or immobilized. Immediately after King was killed, several Chicagoans did their best to quell the turmoil. Gospel historian Robert Marovich describes the first prayer vigil at Liberty Baptist Church, where minister and singer Rev. Clay Evans preached nonviolence to a crowd that shouted "Damn the honkies!"[50] The WVON staff tirelessly tried to keep the city peaceful. Retailer George Daniels, owner of George's Music Room on the West Side, told radio host Cliff Kelley in a 2015 memorial tribute to the station's former manager Lucky Cordell, "They [station staff] came out of the station, went to the 'hood, saw that Herb [Kent] was right there in front. There was no station that made that type of commitment to the community."[51] Kent adds in his memoir that the WVON team "got on the air twenty-four hours a day and all we did was talk to listeners and beg them, 'Please, please, stop burning and looting and destroying. This is not the way to do it!'" The station also had gang leaders call in to voice their opinions, and Kent hosted a special with civil rights leaders on the local ABC television affiliate (WLS) to discuss the situation.[52] Although the Affro-Arts Theater had been closed for spurious licensing violations after Stokely Carmichael spoke there on March 25, it was allowed to reopen after the riots (and then forced to shut its doors again on May 1 after what Cohran detailed as more ongoing police harassment).[53]

Less than two weeks after King's murder, Branch recorded *The Last Request* in Chess's Ter Mar Studios along with producer-arranger Gene Barge and the Operation Breadbasket Orchestra and Choir. The session included some of the company's top musicians—such as Morris Jennings on drums and Charles Stepney on organ—for instrumental takes on church standards with a focus on "Precious Lord, Take My Hand." The album's proceeds were to be donated to the Southern Christian Leadership Conference. Chess took the release seriously. Advertising director Dick LaPalm told *Billboard* that they produced 5,000 point-of-purchase dealer displays instead of the usual 2,000 to 2,500 for most Chess albums. Also, the company advertised *The Last Request* in publications affiliated with the Associated Negro Press.[54] Barge added that it also helped the musicians memorialize King in other ways. He said that Leonard Chess paid for him and his band to attend the civil rights leader's Atlanta funeral. Two years later, Barge produced and played saxophone on *On the Case*, a collaboration with the two-hundred-member Southern Christian Leadership Conference Operation Breadbasket Choir, with Donny Hathaway on keyboards. Like its predecessor, the album mixed jazz and gospel, and it included liner notes by SCLC president Ralph Abernathy about the endurance of black music "as a means of sustaining confidence and even as a weapon to show our solidarity and determination."

Two months after King's assassination, Swedish music journalist Jonas Bernholm visited the West and South Sides and wrote a report of his observations, which did not emphasize tumult. He kept a diary of his visits to concert venues, record company headquarters, and churches where he observed singers, entrepreneurs, and neighborhoods in transition.[55] Mostly, Bernholm remembered being treated warmly at such South Side clubs as the High Chaparral, Checkmate, and Pepper's Lounge. The Chaparral backing band, the Scott Brothers Orchestra, hoped to make a national name, while Syl Johnson worried about being washed up at the ripe old age of thirty. Ruby Andrews and Holly Maxwell eagerly worked to spark their own careers. Between club visits and interviews, Bernholm listened to WVON and WGRT. WVON's Ed Cook told him how he sought to increase opportunities for black people. Bernholm's strong imagery includes his noting the devastation on the West Side while riding in George Leaner's Cadillac (Leaner's wife would have preferred to look at the Civic Opera House). Meanwhile, veteran singer McKinley Mitchell retained his voice but became increasingly embittered. Mitchell dismissed militant currents with the declaration, "Don't talk about Black Power—give me Green Power instead!"

Those music clubs actually did produce instances of activism during the late 1960s, despite Mitchell's claims. Historian Jakobi Williams recounts how Tyrone Davis became enthralled when rising Illinois Black Panther Party leader Fred Hampton showed up to speak during the singer's performance at Mr. Ricky's on the South Side.[56] At first the usually apolitical Davis thought Hampton was crazy or a robber. But then he became impressed with Hampton's oratory and answered his call to become more involved.[57] Davis joined in a benefit for the Panther chair's family after his 1969 murder (this fund-raiser also included Garland Green and Syl Johnson at Roberts Lounge).[58] At the Pumpkin Room, a group of session and gigging musicians evolved into the sextet Boscoe. This band's sound and message could be compared to New York's militant nationalist Last Poets, yet with a tight brass section. In 1973 the group pressed five hundred copies of an LP on its own Kingdom of Chad imprint. One track, "Writin' on the Wall," decried the killing of Malcolm X and called for pan-African liberation, with Ron Harris's ominous bass line adding commentary. The group dissolved in the early 1970s, but its sole record became a sought-after collector's item and was reissued thirty-four years later.[59]

King's warnings against an economic system that left many in Chicago impoverished reverberated through Marlena Shaw's observations of on-going inequalities to generate "Woman of the Ghetto," which led off the singer's *The Spice of Life* album on Chess. She recorded the LP in February and July 1969, with Richard Evans and Stepney arranging and producing. The track blends African mbira with funk guitar. Shaw, a jazz vocalist with a regular gig at Chicago's Playboy Club, draws on her affinity for chants and modal scales. She sings "How does your heart feel late at night / Does it beat with shame or does it beat with pride? / Won't you tell me, legislators?" This was recorded four years after sociologist Mitchell Duneier reported that the word ghetto had become "inextricably associated with blacks."[60] But Shaw thought globally when she wrote the lyrics in one sitting on a flight from New York. "It was just what was going on in our world and in the United States," Shaw said. "I just wrote it down as I saw it. I remember still writing it on the plane going to Chicago to record it. I had brought my lunch. What was left of the brown paper bag, I wrote the rest of the lyrics on the bag. There was just a lot going on, and I was absorbing it all."

Other Chicago recordings that paid tribute to King's legacy included Mayfield's "They Don't Know," which opened the Impressions' defiantly titled November 1968 album *This Is My Country*. After declaring, "We have lost another leader," the track takes on a stridently optimistic tone—reminding listeners that organization (to "keep every brother on the case") and a new generation of activists will take over for whoever is lost. Terry Callier and Larry Wade turned their solemnity into the song "Martin St. Martin." That piece appeared on Callier's 1978 album *Fire on Ice* (Elektra). Shirley Wahls returned to her religious roots for the single "We've Got to Keep On Movin' On" and donated the proceeds to Operation Breadbasket.[61] She refused to just mourn, as the brisk up-tempo beat recalls gospel rockers such as Clara Ward's "How I Got Over." Wahls—who once met King and surprised him with a hug—said she wanted to write a song that captured the spirit of his life, not the violence of his death. Not long afterward, the Notations brought out the endearing "A New Day," written by group member Brad Bobo and released as the B-side on a single in 1971. Bobo and Cliff Curry overlap voices as they express confidence that their children's generation will play together without prejudice. Curry said that Mayfield's example inspired his group's songwriting.

The Notations' labelmate at Twinight, Syl Johnson, also felt the shock when King was assassinated. Before April 1968, Johnson would not have identified as an activist. But his thoughts on the killing and the violence that followed came through on the stark "Is It Because I'm Black." He wrote the song with Glenn Watts and guitarist Jimmy Jones, recorded it in July 1969, and released it toward the end of the year. A few months into the new decade, the song became the title track to a Twinight album that sounded and looked like a bleak indictment yet ultimately delivered a hopeful tone.

More than forty years later, the song remains striking. Stretching just longer than seven minutes, this minor-key lament moves at a deliberate tempo and addresses unfulfilled dreams, unseen obstacles, blight, and personal failures, ending with an entreaty for African American solidarity. The piece has a thirty-two-bar structure, yet it's also a minor blues in A-flat that hints at, but never quite gets to, the V^7 dominant. An eight-bar guitar solo in the middle of the seven-minute track leads into its second half, which repeats a series of two-bar phrases underpinning Johnson's improvised half-spoken testimonial. Instead of offering uplifting horns and harmonies, the instrumental focus is on that single electric guitar line. Urbane soul singers at that time leaned away from revealing much of rough origins in their vocal sound, but Johnson does not hide his Mississippi-rooted twang. Unlike Mayfield's songs celebrating the civil rights movement, this was no anthem. With a slightly nasal intonation, Johnson's urgency comes through his consternation.

"I wrote this song when they killed Dr. King," Johnson said. "That was a tragedy, but I'd been playing for a lot of white clubs, so my thought was that this is not a militant song. It's a song about reality. I'm just asking a question: 'Why did you kill him? Was it because he was black and wanted to help the black union, the garbage workers?' He was just there because he wanted to get a decent salary for the black garbage workers. I never did picket, I never did march, nothing. But naturally it was in my heart. I'm not completely black, but I'm black, too."

Johnson was far from alone in asking if racism was blocking his achievement. Sociologist Doug McAdam addressed pessimism among African Americans nationwide about the time "Is It Because I'm Black" was released. He concluded, "The proportion of blacks reporting that they 'usually get to carry things out the way they planned' declined from 45 percent in 1964 to just 23 percent in 1970."[62]

When Johnson talked about seeing the events surrounding King's assassination unfold, he linked them to other memories. Some of the singer's associates have said his tales should be carefully vetted—even the record company Numero Group titled its 2010 Johnson collection *Complete Mythology*. But that caveat does not make his stories any less poignant. Johnson mentioned one incident that he said occurred when he was driving a truck just before "Come On Sock It to Me" became a hit in 1967. The anecdote reveals much about the lingering institutional racism that existed in Chicago and how altruistic action could cut across it. In other words, this is the kind of story one just hopes is true:

You know glaziers—they install glass and they're the highest paid union. And I was driving a glass truck. It was a very racist thing, no blacks could install glass. But the rack boss would have me help install the glass. I wasn't making as much as $2.50 an hour and they were making $10. One day I stepped on some glass on this wood floor and [raised] hell. So they rushed me to the hospital and got the glass out. I wound up saving that same guy's life on Eighty-Seventh Street. A piece of glass hit him right here [points to his arm]. I had my belt doubled on his arm, drove that truck and shifted gears, and saved him. Everyone else was freaked out, the other glaziers freaked out. I didn't care about racism, I saved his life. He would've bled to death. Got in there, boom, down Eighty-Seventh Street, didn't stop for no lights when I drove him to the hospital. Kept holding him like that with it on his left arm.

Johnson never joined Elijah Muhammad's Nation of Islam, but he says that message of self-reliance influenced him throughout the ensuing years more than what he remembered as King's calls for integration.

I liked Elijah Muhammad's philosophy of quit begging white folks for what you can get up and do on your own. He had lots of Jewish friends right around him, right there on the podium with him. He said, "These are my friends just as much as you are. I didn't call them white devils because all of them are. But I called them that to make you understand who you are." He told them that when the Jews came here and couldn't get jobs, they made their own jobs. He wasn't as militant as anyone thought. He talked about the Irish, how they were kicked in the ass by the British. Martin Luther King wasn't completely wise: Quit begging for crumbs, man! Just look at this world wide open for you. Elijah said get up and do for yourself. A guy who believed in his philosophy could have a wife and kids and make $150 a week and beat the guy who made $400 a week.

Johnson personified these precepts through his production role at Twinight, ownership of his masters, and whatever percentage of the company he maintained. He also followed them in his positions outside the music business. In the August 1970 issue of *Ebony*, Hans J. Massaquoi wrote a respectful, if detached, feature about Elijah Muhammad's self-help initiatives.[63] Massaquoi described the Nation's farming operations in Michigan, Georgia, and Alabama, and Johnson discussed the importance of his family's historic farm in Mississippi as well as his extensive backyard vegetable garden. Muhammad's operation also ran the Salaam Restaurant on the South Side; years later Johnson owned Solomon's Fishery restaurants and managed them on similar principles.

During summer 1969, similar issues of ownership, control, and self-preservation became contentious at Carl Davis's Brunswick-Dakar-Jalynne offices. The result would shape the overall sound of *Is It Because I'm Black*. Bassist Bernard Reed had been fuming over the "Soulful Strut" slight and said things came to a head when Davis wanted to change the makeup of his group.

> Carl came into the office a bit upset. The first thing he did is say, "I'm getting rid of the horns. No more horns, we can do without them. I'm paying for an arranger to be here. I got arrangers over here on salary, no, I don't need the horns," Reed recalled. I said, "We built the group here and you want to break this up? We're gearing up toward this and you're tearing it apart." He said, "I don't want to talk any more about it." I said, "Well, hey, what do you have planned for me, Bernard Reed? I'm up against a brick wall. There's nothing I can do." He said, "I'm getting ready bust a hole in that wall." I told him, "You know what, I'm just going to go on through," and I walked out.

Guitarist John Bishop, drummer Hal Nesbitt, and saxophonist Jerry Wilson walked out with Reed. Wilson heard that Johnson was looking for a band, so they headed up Michigan Avenue to meet him. Taking a cue from the times, the group renamed itself the Pieces of Peace. At Johnson's studio, Reed recognized multi-instrumentalist Byron Bowie, who was working on instrumental arrangements there. He knew Bowie from jobs around town and conducting for singer Fontella Bass, who was married to Art Ensemble of Chicago trumpeter Lester Bowie (Byron's brother). Reed described Byron Bowie by saying, "He carried himself like John Coltrane. He could play the alto and tenor, the flute. Carrying all these horns around like Rahsaan Roland Kirk. Talking jazz, he's a hip cat."

The group convened at Chess Records' Studio A, and Johnson said they cut the "Is It Because I'm Black" single at 9:00 or 10:00 at night. After a few months away from the studio, the group reconvened in January 1970 to record "Concrete Reservation" and its flip side, "Together Forever." Both would appear on the *Is It Because I'm Black* LP. The A-side, written by Jimmy Jones, is essentially a twelve-bar A-flat minor blues with the strings responding ominously, first with a stabbing three-note ostinato to wordless vocals and then pentatonically, as if to emphasize the "reservation" in the chorus. That ominous musical tone echoed the song's lyrics. "Concrete Reservation" describes living in poorly designed housing projects that towered over Chicago—such as the Robert Taylor Homes, about a ten-minute drive from where the album was recorded.[64] Martin Luther King used "cement reservations" to describe such oppressive Chicago Housing Authority (CHA) buildings.[65] This was when more than 90 percent of the CHA's newly built low-income family apartments would have been in such high-rises.[66] By this time the progressive policies of early 1950s CHA administrators had become no more than a memory among remaining older tenants. The year 1970 was also the last time a sizable public housing development would be constructed in the city: Madden Park Homes, not far east of the first such project, the Ida B. Wells Homes, near Bronzeville and practically next door to the Affro-Arts Theater.[67] Many commentators have since detailed the drugs, crime, construction failings, and feelings of hopelessness within these buildings.[68] But looking back forty years later, Johnson almost regretted voicing these issues. He recalled a conversation with his sister, who was living in the projects with their mother, and they felt his song belittled African Americans' quotidian struggles. It's a surprising statement, since the song's sense of humanity remains manifest.

Bernard Reed feels differently about the song, applauding the "misterioso" parts within the music and the way Johnson was "hitting it hard." Reed wrote "Together Forever" after an incident when, while he was riding a Michigan Avenue bus with the other members of Pieces of Peace, a white passenger assumed he was a thug. Turning the incident around, Reed evokes a mood that is lyrical and hopeful, if initially plaintive. Reflecting on that encounter, Reed said, "I started coming up with the words, went on and put it together—the music itself. A little happy groove of a bass line I had. Looking for melody is how I found the other chords. It's meditative and it sails out smoothly."

Bowie cowrote the equally idealistic "Everybody Needs Love" and "Talking about Freedom," both with William Keys. The latter song fits into the overall political theme of the album, but he said he wrote it thinking matter-of-factly rather than philosophically. They had intended the song for Gene Chandler, but once he heard it Johnson decided to record it himself.

Experienced as a workshop ensemble, the Pieces of Peace interpret the Beatles' "Come Together" as well as Joe South's "Walk a Mile in My Shoes" to suit Johnson's delivery on *Is It Because I'm Black*. Oscar Brown Jr. had been composing socially conscious songs for more than a decade when his "Black Balloons" appeared here. For that track Johnson opted for jaunty strings to complement and even sweeten Brown's already buoyant writing. The largely instrumental funk jams "Soul Heaven" and "Right On" closed the two sides of the LP. Their messages of solidarity and pride do not require words—although Johnson's high-pitched shout-outs to his band had echoes of James Brown and may have been helpful to the Pieces of Peace a year later when they embarked on their own musical journey.

Black lettering that looked as if it was spray painted on a brick wall (actually done with finger paint) defined the front cover of the LP. Along with a back cover photo of Johnson standing in a graffiti-defaced South Side alley, the record looked as unadorned as it sounded. *Is It Because I'm Black* became one of the first concept albums in R&B, appearing about a year before Marvin Gaye's *What's Going On* and Sly and the Family Stone's *There's a Riot Going On*.[69] While the Impressions strongly addressed issues like discrimination and crime on *This Is My Country* and *The Young Mod's Forgotten Story*, Mayfield included such odes as "My Woman's Love" and "Love's Miracle." The Temptations sang "Message from a Black Man" on *Puzzle People*, but also "That's the Way Love Is." On *Is It Because I'm Black* no song describes love other than in a humanitarian sense.

Johnson said he did not care whether these songs would reach a substantial crossover audience. White radio reaction was, if anything, muted. Although the Impressions may have been banned on a handful of white pop radio stations in 1967 because of the misconception that "We're a Winner" was a call to militancy, "Is It Because I'm Black" did not spark such a reaction from any corner of the mainstream media. Maybe that's because Curtis Mayfield's trio opened that door for them or because, since Johnson's record was an independent release, Twinight may have simply been below the radar for most AM radio. Nonetheless, Johnson had his own working relationship with puissant black DJs like E. Rodney Jones at WVON. The title track reached number eleven on the *Billboard* R&B charts and even crossed over to number sixty-eight on the pop charts, making it the biggest hit in Johnson's career. "Concrete Reservation" also attained a respectable number twenty-nine on the R&B rankings. The record's appeal went beyond US borders: Jamaican singer Ken Boothe recorded a version of "Is It Because I'm Black" in 1973. Indeed, the loping beat of Johnson's song made it an easy fit for the slow tempos of rocksteady and early reggae.

Johnson and Reed's challenging their social and political predicaments while avoiding militancy mirrored a consensus across black media in Chicago. Harold M. Barger, a political science graduate student at Northwestern University, studied black newspapers in 1969 and 1970 for his dissertation. He looked at established black newspapers such as the *Chicago Defender* and neighborhood publications like the *Chatham Citizen*, along with *Muhammad Speaks* and the *Black Panther*. His finding was that the African American media in Chicago sought inclusion. So too did songs like "Black Balloons" and "Together Forever." As Barger wrote, "Blacks <u>do</u> believe in democracy [his emphasis], even when it hasn't worked."[70]

In the years immediately following the release of *Is It Because I'm Black*, some progress was made toward confronting the issues Johnson addressed. These advances included the Coalition of Black Trade Unionists' (CBTU), founded in 1972 to fight discrimination and push the state for full employment. The CBTU also sought to support independent black institutions as well as express solidarity with "Mother Africa and Caribbean nations." It set out to "buy and bank black" and to register African American voters.[71] Johnson's hope for a unified front reflected the inclusive nature of other activists who emerged in Chicago at this time. One of them, Illinois state legislator Harold Washington, started making waves as he called for a full investigation into the police murder of Fred Hampton.[72] What Johnson had hoped to see may have begun to materialize.

The Pieces of Peace then detoured in unexpected directions. As proficient as the band sounded on *Is It Because I'm Black*, it became stronger when organist Benjamin Wright joined shortly afterward. Eventually Wright would become one of the most accomplished arrangers in R&B, but back then he was just an ambitious working musician. Bernard Reed remembered that saxophonist Jerry Wilson thought the group needed keyboards for a fuller sound. Wilson recommended Wright, whom he knew from Greenville, Mississippi. The twenty-five-year-old Wright was in an integrated group called the Men from Soul, based in Charlotte, North Carolina.[73] Wright eagerly moved to Chicago, where he was sure he could write charts and record. But when he arrived with his organ, Fender Rhodes piano, and amplifiers, the situation was not what he expected. He was told there was no spot for him in the group. The band members changed their minds once he started playing.

Wright also wanted a more formal education in music theory to supplement his practical experience. He intended to enroll at the Chicago Conservatory of Music, which was downtown next to Orchestra Hall, where the Chicago Symphony performed. The school counted Maurice White among its alumni.[74] But this path remained no sure thing for a black artist. Prejudice still ran throughout the local classical realm despite the success African American composers and producers had achieved in adapting such techniques. For example, George Lewis described how racism blocked the aspirations of violinist Ann Ward, who became a jazz singer.[75] Wright's take on his experience warrants telling in full.

Well, I didn't have that classical training, I was a street guy. My situation was very unique. The Pieces of Peace and I had often talked about going to school. "We're going to do this, we're going to that," but school is a major situation, especially for me. Months and months go by, finally I decided I'm doing it. I went to the Chicago Conservatory on a Thursday afternoon, had to be around 1970. I went in there, saw a lady, told her I wanted to go to school. She said, "This is a music school." I said, "Yes ma'am, I understand." "Do you have a degree?" "No, ma'am." "Have you ever done music before?" "Yes ma'am." "What kind of experience do you have in music?" "Well, I played in quite a few bands."

And that was the funniest shit she ever heard in her life. She just laughed at me and just really made me small. OK? So, no problem. Only thing I could do was just stand there. She stopped laughing and said, "Do you think you can pass an entrance exam?" It almost broke my confidence. I said, "I'd be happy to take it." So in my mind, it's like, "OK, you're going to go back home, you're going to take out all the new books you got, study your ass off, come back here and take that entrance exam." She said, "Come with me." She took me to the library and pulled out a test. I was just scared. I began to look at it and started answering the questions, and I think I did it in record time. Monday morning, I started school. Now, this is where the real prejudice part came in: When I showed up at the Chicago Conservatory, everybody knew who I was. As the weeks proceeded, class and the whole bit, some teachers would say something and then, "Isn't that right, Mr. Benjamin?" It was some unnecessary pressure. I was not being glorified, I was to some degree being mocked. But no problem, I handled it well. I remember I got into an argument with a teacher, he marked my paper wrong. And the teacher was wrong. He used the word inharmonic. It's a B-flat. The note is a B-flat. If you write A-sharp and it's a flat key, technically that's wrong, but it's the same note. At the time, I'm writing charts. So he says, "This is what it has to be in my class." Here's a cat, graduated from high school, got his BS, took a vacation, got his master's, took a few days off and then worked on his doctorate. And before he gets his doctorate the school offers him a job. Excuse the expression, but this motherfucker never made it work. He just got book, book, book. But I knew how to go on the bandstand and make it work.

Because Wright had these skills as an arranger and composer, he wrote the charts for sessions that were intended to constitute the Pieces of Peace's first album. They saw how their friends, the Pharaohs, had released *Awakening* on their own Scarab label and were about to become independent players in the field. The versatile band had also produced the smooth vocal group the Conservatives, whose members had day jobs as Chicago public school teachers.[76] So Willie Woods and his group recorded the *Pieces of Peace*, which sounds unlike their other productions. Instead of the sharp horn lines (characteristic of the Pharaohs) or polished harmonies (like the Conservatives), Wright's group favored more relaxed tempos and interwoven guitars. King Johnson sang such desperate-sounding ballads as "I Still Care." After making the recording, the group toured Southeast Asia. Wright describes the sojourn as entwined with the plight of American troops of all colors during the late stage of the Vietnam War and with a scourge that would follow the soldiers home. Once more Wright's account deserves his own words.

We decided we'd go to Asia and get our shit together and come back and kill the Chicago town. Our music was coming together, but everything else was falling apart. Let me just put it in its proper perspective: all the druggies were happy as hell. Listen: "It's time for us to hit. Where are the guys?" I had a relationship with most of the little rickshaw drivers. "You see the band?" "Yes, I take you." Jump on the rickshaw and opium dens were legal. Can you imagine cats from Chicago coming to Asia and can sit in an opium den all day long? And then I had to worry about cats bringing opium to the hotel. They're deporting people! I don't smoke, and most of the shit is in my room. Oh my God! That part was bad. The music, great. We ran into a lot of Asian players, and they were excited about us. That part was OK. Cats were high 24/7. And don't let the ships come in, because the people from Vietnam, Singapore was an R&R place. Ships come in, Oh my God, because all the GIs were druggies. I'm a GI too but I had to go to survival training because of my job. They'll teach you how to eat snakes and shit. My weapon was a .45 and teletype machine. They weren't concerned about me protecting myself—just type this shit up in the field. The military was providing these cats with drugs. Because these cats were mostly kids. The first time they see someone's head blown off and shit, "How do we control them?" "Fuck it, get 'em high." And that's what was happening. But we loved Asia, we learned a lot there.

The experience shattered the group, and on returning to Chicago they went their separate ways. The Pieces of Peace album would not be released until 2007 (on Cali-Tex). Wright had become increasingly active with arranging for the Dells and leading the house band at the 1,300-seat High Chaparral. Soon he took on more roles, an experience that became crucial years later when he worked on top-selling pop albums for the likes of Michael Jackson.

"There was something happening every night," Wright said. "When I got the band there, I wouldn't go to the club until midnight. Most time when acts would come in, I was indoctrinated enough that the DJs would come and say 'We need another $1,500 for this act to come in.' So a lot of times I could come up with the money and help bring in Harold Melvin and the Blue Notes when Teddy Pendergrass was playing drums. A lot of the acts would come in, didn't have charts, didn't have a band. So that was another opportunity for me to shine, write the charts and let the big band play. It was a glorious time for me."

During the early 1970s, Pieces of Peace and the Pharaohs broke apart, but individual members moved on to new realms, sometimes on larger stages. The Affro-Arts Theater had disbanded by the end of 1970, which Woods attributed to a lack of funds. Today he believes the Pharaohs should have taken the landlord's advice and installed a candy machine for revenue. Ironically, the Black P Stone Nation's descendants, the El Rukns, acquired the building about eight years later and turned it into their headquarters.[77] That gang took a more nefarious and bizarre path, which extended to devising a terrorist plot with Libya.[78] Among the Pharaohs, Satterfield would move from bass to trombone. He and Myrick relocated to California a few years later to be part of Maurice White's Earth, Wind, and Fire. Woods ran a series of clubs during the 1970s while also playing sessions. Meanwhile, former Pieces of Peace members Bernard Reed and John Bishop looked at their options and returned to Brunswick, where Carl Davis welcomed them back. The company had bigger plans.

Although many of these groups and organizations may have been short-lived, taken together they attest to the complex responses that Chicago's R&B communities formulated to address social ills. And they did so outside any well-funded oversight. While Syl Johnson asked "Is It Because I'm Black," others turned that question around and responded differently: Phil Cohran and the Affro-Arts Theater's artists said to their audiences, "This Is What It Means to Be Black." They triumphed because they showed the city, and their followers showed the world, that interpretations of African thought proved to be personal and responsive to the neighborhood. Although Johnson and Cohran's musical approaches differed, both had drawn inspiration from Elijah Muhammad's call for African American self-sufficiency. Benjamin Wright combined his playing in clubs with conservatory training in the classical model. He incurred condescension from music professors, but he negotiated musical demarcations—reflective of social divides that also concerned the Association for the Advancement of Creative Musicians. That experimental bastion proved a retort to cultural nationalists of the time, who felt that black art must be isolated from European influences.[79] Wright chose to take that European model head-on and on his own terms. Ultimately the Pharaohs turned such issues of identity and inclusivity into a party on "Black Enuff." Unity prevailed, and such motivation would remain essential.

All this was shown throughout Curtis Mayfield's work in the early 1970s, when he captured much of its visionaries' idealism as an artist and entrepreneur. As noted earlier, he also brought Affro-Arts percussionist "Master" Henry Gibson into his own band. The potent wordplay on his 1970 solo debut *Curtis* would have thrilled Chicago's emerging black advertisers with the inviting song and slogan "Move On Up." The extended LP version of that song features a quick-tempo percussion solo from Gibson. While the song maintains a standard 4/4 time throughout its eight and a half minutes, Gibson's propulsive attack makes an instrumental break feel like it's adding a contrasting tempo. The percussionist makes a quietly assertive statement on a concert album that Mayfield recorded at New York's Bitter End and released in May 1971 as *Curtis/Live!* On "Mighty Mighty (Spade and Whitey)," Gibson upends Western ideals that had prioritized melody over rhythm while Mayfield sings to the audience and to him, "We don't need no music, we've got conga."[80] Some of the songs Mayfield performed at the Bitter End could have been comments on his hometown's rising murder rate, which coincided with its high unemployment ("We the People Who Are Darker Than Blue"). Others decried the drug abuse that destroyed such promising singers as Baby Huey ("Stone Junkie"). It's just as likely the audience went away humming his anthems "People Get Ready" and "We're a Winner." On the latter song he had reintroduced a radical verse decrying Uncle Tom servitude that had been cut from the single at the record company's behest. The crowd's appreciation is audible. If the coming decade represented continuing transition, Mayfield's audience back home had prepared for those changes.

SIX

Rhythm Ain't All We Got: Organizational Drive Shapes 1970s Black Music, Commerce, and Politics

Sometime in spring 1967, Marshall Thompson rode a Michigan Avenue bus heading toward the Brunswick Records office. He had a lot on his mind. His group, the Chi-Lites, had been together since 1960, under slightly varying names, yet none of their singles had caught fire.[1] That outcome did not reflect their abilities. Singer Eugene Record wrote a number of endearing songs, but he made ends meet by driving a taxicab. Creadel "Red" Jones's bass voice and Robert "Squirrel" Lester's second tenor added the right kind of harmonies, though they seemed unusual to some. Thompson could have been recollecting how a couple of years earlier the Chi-Lites had performed a show in Altgeld Gardens, hoping to raise money for new uniforms; they netted five dollars apiece.[2] So he took singer Major Lance's advice and headed toward Brunswick to meet another singer, Otis Leavill, who also worked in the company's artists and repertoire department.

"I was on the bus, got off at Twelfth Street, and Otis said, 'I've got you now!'" Thompson recalled. "He said, 'I've been trying to get you to come down here for a long time—the record company is right upstairs. Go up there and see Carl Davis.' I knew he was a big-time guy in the record business. I knew I wouldn't have to worry about getting a record played—that much I did know."

Thompson was right about what Carl Davis could do, as Earl Calloway of the *Chicago Defender* would observe not long afterward. Within five years, the Chi-Lites would enjoy international hits as the most visible group on Brunswick's accomplished roster. String arrangements and layered vocal combinations made its yearning ballad "Have You Seen Her" fit with the forceful "(For God's Sake) Give More Power to the People." Davis and the Chi-Lites were not quite anomalies. Talent thrived across Chicago during the late 1960s and early 1970s through individual achievements and cooperatives. Large businesses did not merely coexist with an underground economy, the two frequently depended on each other. Richard Nixon was president, the Vietnam War dragged on, and Mayor Richard J. Daley's white political machine held tight control all over the city. So both artists and activists tried new means to convey their messages.

Soul musicians as well as their political and commercial associates in Chicago recrafted organizational models while advocating for self-sufficiency in the face of external challenges. That internal cohesion played out in studios and stages as popular records adapted Afrocentric influences or advanced musical theories derived from the city's neighborhoods and schools. Others made sure that venerable traditions like gospel did not disappear within a modern secular context. Performers and activists also worked closer together and on larger platforms as they shared agendas. Elective office and entrepreneurialism had become priorities. Artists who had achieved financial autonomy fit right in with this direction. These messages were carried through a combination of media that had ties to Chicago. Television programming featuring black perspectives hit the airwaves with a reach beyond niche audiences. Likewise, as radio stations still broadcast voices from the neighborhoods, so did stages that lined the South and West Sides. Some venues fell victim to a changing economy, but others grew to become vital bonding centers. Meanwhile, jukeboxes continued to spread new black music to white neighborhoods and suburbs, and not just in areas where African American families had started to live. While sharp rivalries did exist among performers and industry leaders, perhaps such competition fueled a movement that seemed to be going forward.

Chicago artists saw their methods as key to these musical and social movements. So did their audiences. In 1969 Jerry Butler conceived of his Songwriters Workshop, a collective initiative and business venture that supported new material from such writers as Terry Callier and Larry Wade. Callier and the Dells' innovative albums sometimes expressed the results of Butler's workshop, as did the Independents, a vocal group that emerged in 1972. Some musicians, like Curtis Mayfield and Gene Chandler, firmed up their control over the way they operated; other entrepreneurs and artists dealt with limited budgets to achieve their visions. And in a small studio in the Chicago Board of Trade Building, former WVON reporter Don Cornelius showcased these acts on a television dance program called *Soul Train*. Commercials on *Soul Train* included—among many other ads—contributions from many of those same players who cut the records that energized the show's dancers. These musicians proved crucial for the black-owned advertising agencies that arose in Chicago during the 1960s and early 1970s (such as Burrell McBain Advertising and Proctor and Gardner). R&B was key to how these firms called on cultural identity to sell products. The commercials became about more than just hyping soft drinks and hair care products. In their own way, advertisers promoted a sense of inclusion. Unmistakably black music in these jingles reached homes whether or not listeners had tuned in to African American radio stations.

As more musicians started to enjoy the benefits of such autonomy, bonds with political advocates followed. Local activists had become increasingly focused on running for office. They also began looking toward bringing the assertive philosophies of Fred Hampton and Stokely Carmichael into more corporate models. Performers remained natural allies. Not only had artists built up recognition within and outside black communities, they had also gained significant experience within an industry that ranged from independent operators to large companies. Since R&B had become established within this midwestern city that had been a focal point for civil rights struggles, such pacts made perfect sense. This was a time when the black population in Chicago increased from 22.9 percent in 1960 to 32.7 percent in 1970.[3] Meanwhile, African American economic focus made sense on a national level: by 1972, 195,000 black-owned businesses operated across America, with receipts totaling $7.2 million.[4] Popular R&B artists and their producers had connected with these audiences in ways that politicians and marketers could only dream of achieving.

Donny Hathaway's LP debut exemplified these meetings of pride and tenacity. Hathaway had spent about three years in Chicago employed, and sometimes volunteering, as an arranger, copyist, singer, session keyboard-ist, and creator of ad jingles when he released that hopeful 1970 album *Everything Is Everything* (Atlantic).[5] Even though the meaning of his and Le-roy Hutson's "The Ghetto" could be interpreted in different ways, Henry Gibson's congas in tandem with Hathaway's Fender piano lines generate a sturdy groove that leaves no doubt how these musicians feel about the sounds coming out of such a neighborhood. A similar spirit shows through his religious declaration "Thank You Master (for My Soul)" and his inter-pretation of Nina Simone's "Young, Gifted, and Black." Hathaway called in local favors for his recording sessions (though mostly in New York). He recruited a mixture of Chess players, Affro-Arts alumni, and other profes-sionals like Willie Henderson, baritone saxophonist and Brunswick musical director. Asserting artistic control on a major label, Hathaway and drummer Ric Powell produced the album themselves.[6]

The annual Operation PUSH Expos provide another example where cul-tural affirmations combined with entrepreneurial resourcefulness and embraced urban politics. This event started as the Black Expo sponsored by SCLC's Operation Breadbasket at the International Amphitheatre on October 3, 1969, which drew 100,000 people.[7] Organizer Jesse Jackson emphasized "turning 'protest into progress'" as he stood among three hundred exhibits of black-owned companies and of corporations that promoted their involvement in African American communities.[8] But though this was a vanguard event, it had precedents in Chicago. The same number of people attended the Negro Business Exposition at the Eighth Regiment Armory in Bronzeville in April 1938. Business and religious leaders organized that Depression-era gathering, which included church choirs and what were described as "hot bands."[9]

When Black Expo was held again the following November, it drew 600,000 visitors over five days and, like its predecessors, spotlighted gospel and R&B. Artists at this iteration of the Black and Minorities Business and Cultural Exposition (its official designation) included Syl Johnson, the Emotions, Hathaway, the Dells, and gospel singer Albertina Walker. Tellingly, the theme of the 1970 Expo was "Rhythm Ain't All We Got."[10] While President Nixon and others advocated for "black capitalism," this event represented a more complex call to action. The participants understood that the economy might be stacked against them, but they still sought to participate on their own terms. Nor were they emphasizing such typical conservative mantras as lessening government regulations or decreasing spending on such essential functions as public schools. Essentially, *Jet* writer Chester Higgins raved that it showed that "Black money must finance the Black movement if Black people are going to maintain their integrity."[11] Despite—or because of—that success, the SCLC leadership in Atlanta was displeased that Jackson had cast the event as its own entity with Chicago sponsors as the governing board. So Jackson quit the SCLC and formed Operation PUSH (originally standing for People United to Save Humanity).[12] Not that this harmed the event's popularity. The PUSH Expo continued into the mid-1970s.

Musicians and black radio stations remained integral to the PUSH Expo mission. Hathaway occasionally performed on its stages. The Affro-Arts Theater and WVON exhibited at the first event, as did large musical entities from out of town, such as Motown and Stax.[13] Saxophonist Gene Barge, who worked with Operation Breadbasket, noted that "they got black products on the shelves of some stores for the very first time,"[14] citing Ultra Sheen and Soft Sheen hair care products as two of them.[15] Recurring performers like Jerry Butler, who served as coordinator for entertainment in 1971, helped attract visitors.

Butler commented on the significance of the Expos for *Ebony*: "People think of performers as not having any interest in business other than show business. But I've learned that we have black entrepreneurs in Chicago who could be able to help me and whom I can help. . . . I took all of my money out of the white bank downtown and put in one of the two black banks here. It's a much better situation. The president of the bank and I know that we need each other desperately."[16]

The 1970 Expo also embedded workshops run by arranger Quincy Jones and saxophonist Julian "Cannonball" Adderley, which were held at Dunbar High School in Bronzeville to "initiate and encourage the study of Black music from its African roots to its current status as a major contributor to world culture," according to the *Chicago Defender*.[17] Gene Chandler and Carl Davis were listed as consultants to that workshop. Butler and Mayfield, along with a host of R&B, gospel, jazz, and pop acts at the 1972 Expo, performed in the well-received documentary *Save the Children*, which was filmed at the event.[18] Offstage, the Expo also provided a space for artists and others in the entertainment business to converse.

Musicians had myriad reasons for participating in the Expos. For some, it was attachment to the organization. By the early 1970s, artists and activists had spent time together, attended the same venues (such as the High Chaparral), and advocated for shared interests. Bassist Bernard Reed performed as part of the house band at the 1971 Expo and believed it evinced wider aspirations. Although he received no immediate financial compensation for his services, Reed asserted that not only did he benefit down the line, but so did young and future musicians.

> I think all blacks wanted to do something. After King's death we all wanted to do something to try to make it better, anything you could do to feel good about seeing something happen. There was no money, but we were looking at the opportunity, and the opportunity can bring money. So we see those strides, OK, we're being noticed, what did it do? Programs have developed out of things that happened back then. Ben Branch came to Chicago with Martin Luther King, and he became political with [Illinois governor] Jim Thompson and got a lot of funding through Governor Thompson and opened up a school for teenagers through the summer program to give them something to do. You want to learn an instrument? We've got the greatest musicians in Chicago as instructors.

The Black Expo/PUSH Expos were not the only events of this kind in the Chicago area. Nearby Gary, Indiana, hosted its Black Business Festival in September 1970, and performers included singer Renaldo Domino.[19]

A couple of years later Hathaway helped raise funds for the much larger National Black Political Convention in that city.[20] African American elected officials and activists from across the country met at the Gary conference to establish common goals.[21] That Chicago soul musicians were highlighted in both of these political and commercial campaigns contrasts with their absence at the Soldier Field rally in 1966. Historian Brian Ward contends that although earlier civil rights activists had little interest in employing soul performers, "a torrent of treatises" on black aesthetics in the late 1960s and early 1970s meant that black power advocates "began to curry the support of soul stars and black music entrepreneurs in a far more systematic and sometimes highly aggressive manner."[22] Or, possibly, with early 1960s teenage R&B fans growing into young adulthood by the end of the decade, the music followed the audience and its increasing seriousness.

Many of these developments were chronicled in a soul-themed section of the August 22, 1970, issue of *Billboard*. The articles had a national scope, as did an opinion piece by Bernard E. Garnett, head of an organization called the Race Relations Information Center, urging black radio DJs to speak more articulately and "seek relevant and progressive programming and fair employment."[23] Even though just a handful of the city's artists appeared on that issue's chart of top-selling soul acts, Chicago loomed large in its longer news stories and opinion pieces, including an account of Butler's Songwriters Workshop.[24] On the other hand, Curtis Mayfield announced that he intended to move to Atlanta, calling it "a very progressive city for the Black man."[25] He said nothing in that article about the progressive political and cultural movements that had been expanding in his own hometown.

Jerry Butler's Ideals and Financial Need
Become Creative Collaboration

Jerry Butler also wrote an article in that issue headlined "Black Music Is Getting Intellectually Involved," in which he mentioned that soul music was now "getting into things that really touch people," becoming more socially conscious.[26] He observed that R&B artists no longer felt compelled to make simple pop records, in part because of the "advent of the acid rock and the stuff coming back from Europe." Butler used Sly Stone as an example; Rotary Connection would have been just as illustrative. With barriers to airplay on white radio stations tumbling, Butler said, "the music itself is becoming more honest." Although the short article did not reveal his political leanings, it reflected Butler's integrity and his sharper awareness of racial issues inherent in, and outside, the music industry. After Vee-Jay put that white couple on the cover of Butler's *Aware of Love* album in 1961, he insisted that black artists must be depicted in such artwork. The company's sales department objected, but he held firm, and by 1965 he prevailed. His principles continued to override purely commercial limitations, as he recalled in 2016.

"By 1968 I was a real militant," Butler said. "My militant thing was just based on the fact that there were certain engagements I wouldn't perform in, certain places I wouldn't play. As a matter of fact, there was an opportunity to go to [apartheid-era] South Africa and to perform, and the South African people had asked us not to come because the government would use it as propaganda to show how they're treating blacks in South Africa. So I decided I wouldn't go."

Butler's Songwriters Workshop started as a means of self-preservation. He was signed to Mercury and benefited from the composing-producing team of Kenny Gamble and Leon Huff, who crafted such songs as "Only the Strong Survive," an enduring proclamation of fortitude. The pair left the company in 1969 and went on to become moguls with Philadelphia International Records.[27] Butler got stuck with three years left on his contract and a need for new material, so he approached Mercury president Irving Steinberg, who contacted the New York publishing firm Chappell Music. They all struck a deal, and in January 1970 Butler established the Songwriters Workshop at 1402 South Michigan Avenue, which also housed his Fountain Productions. By March 1971 Chappell supported the new enterprise at a rate of $55,000 a year.[28] The *Chicago Defender* noted that one year later the Workshop had become responsible for about $4 million in record sales, and by the middle of 1974 it had produced seventeen albums.[29] The success achieved by the songwriting teams of Terry Callier and Larry Wade and of Chuck Jackson and Marvin Yancy was an unexpected result of his initial necessity.

"I had a contract with Mercury Records that required four albums a year, which was probably more than I could produce out of my own head," Butler said. "So here was an opportunity. Plus we were chasing Motown, and Philly International came later, but all of that was spawned by the way [Motown founder] Berry Gordy had his company structured [so that] the artists were the company and the company was the artists. And he promoted them simultaneously. We did the same kind of things with our workshop to help us create enough good music to fill up those albums we were required to deliver. I was the coach, facilitator, recipient, and all of that."

As a talent scout, Butler did not have to look far to build his team. Former Vee-Jay vice president Calvin Carter helped with the organization.[30] His brother, talented singer Billy Butler, brought on Wade. Because Billy Butler always coaxed Wade's composing, he extended the invitation to include joining his own group, Infinity. The songwriter remembers that the Workshop pay was a weekly advance of $100, to be counted against future royalties. Wade then recruited Callier. Although Callier performed at folk spots, the Workshop provided a regular, and less stressful, daytime gig, as he described it in 1997.

> I was still playing local clubs around Chicago, and I was walking down the street one day and a friend of mine [Wade] comes running up to me and said, "Terry, Terry, Terry! Jerry Butler is starting a songwriters workshop and wants you to be a part of it." I didn't know what to make of that. I thought maybe he had gotten the information confused. I knew Jerry because we had been in the same grammar school and had a couple musical exchanges, but nothing really permanent or lasting enough to give me the idea he wanted me to work on this project. However, I did go down and talk to him. This was spring 1970, and sure enough he was starting the Songwriters Workshop and wanted me to be a part of it. So I started working for Jerry, and our assignment was to write as much as we could. There was no real time limit or pressure or anything. We'd just show up every day and if we finished a song, OK. If we didn't, we'll finish one tomorrow, and if not, then the day after.

The workshop shared some attributes of other artists cooperatives at that time—for example, the Association for the Advancement of Creative Musicians. Both of these predominantly African American organizations required original compositions and sought self-sufficiency. Butler discussed copyright ownership with songwriters and explained how to work with such publishing entities such as ASCAP and BMI, while musical education of all kinds was pivotal to the AACM. But Chappell's corporate oversight and the obligations that went with it were indispensable. W. Yale Matheson, an attorney who helped set up the workshop, speculated in *Billboard* that Chicago musicians could take advantage of the relative lack of an entrenched class structure. He reasoned that, without a rigid show business hierarchy in the city, fresh talent faced fewer hurdles.[31] Callier questioned whether such institutions shared a locally specific organizational philosophy. "I don't know if it's strictly a Chicago phenomenon, but it's definitely a part of the Chicago scene," Callier said. "That type of cooperative endeavor has been here since King Oliver and Louis Armstrong."

Lacy Banks described in *Black Stars* magazine how the eight-room, 2,000-square-foot suite that housed the workshop started getting busy in the early afternoon. Work went on into the night, punctuated by dinner deliveries from nearby Chinatown.[32] A few of the results appeared on Jerry Butler albums including the aptly titled *Jerry Butler Sings Assorted Sounds with the Aid of Assorted Friends and Relatives* and *Sagittarius Movement* (both Mercury, 1971). Although the writing sessions may have been loose, Gerald Sims, James Mack, and Hathaway crafted sharp arrangements. On *Assorted Friends and Relatives*, Butler's baritone and recurring incisive electric guitar lines make the bricolage of ideas into a warm, cohesive statement.

Hathaway also recorded the perennial holiday favorite "This Christmas" in 1970. Thirty-four years later, ASCAP listed it as the thirtieth most played holiday song in the publishing organization's history, and *Pitchfork* proclaimed it one of the best such seasonal odes of all time.[33] But Butler did not see such a future for the single when cowriter Nadine McKinnor showed it to him. He recalled, "I thought, 'Who needs another Christmas carol?' They already have them. But Hathaway introduced the 6/8 feel inside, and it was fresh."

Although McKinnor added that she wrote the song away from Butler's workshop, she appreciated the experience of being part of Butler's team. She treasured its mix of musical personalities. While McKinnor's own training in songwriting had just been "singing to the trees," the polish of songwriters Chuck Jackson and Marvin Yancy impressed her. So did the warmth she felt from Wade and Callier.

Wade said that his first big collaboration with Callier, a lament in A-flat called "The Love We Had (Stays on My Mind)," came about through shared disappointment. Their way of crafting the piece illuminates both their method and their affinity. "I had been going back and forth to the Workshop, and I was riding a bike and had my guitar in a bag," Wade said.

> I came up through the stairs in the back way and got my guitar out and asked Terry, "What are you playing there, buddy?" He was sitting at the piano, and I said, "It sounds pretty decent." He said, "It's just some notes here." He was in a somber mood, and I said, "What's wrong with you?" He said, "Well, I don't know, I'm just thinking about old times and all of that." I said, "It's funny that you say that. Because, I don't know, man, I left my wife and I'm trying to get something together here." He said, "Well, let's stop talking about all this and try to finish this song." So we went into the song and I got into a collaboration with him, going verse by verse, note by note, and finally it started to get pretty colorful. Eventually he stopped and said, "We're just going into it, but we don't have a title." So I came up with a title. Terry said, "That's going to be too long!" And I said, "No, we said all of that to say that." He thought about it briefly, we didn't even ponder too long, and he said, "OK, that does make sense."

Butler thought the song needed revising. Callier had mentioned Chess producers Charles Stepney and Esmond Edwards. So they took "The Love We Had" one mile down Michigan Avenue, where the company had moved. They had a feeling someone would interpret it.

Chess was a changed company. Leonard and Phil Chess had announced in 1969 that they would sell their family operation to General Recorded Tape, mostly a manufacturer of music duplicated on tape.[34] Leonard Chess had died of a heart attack on October 16 that year, at age fifty-two. Yet in 1970 Marshall Chess carried on and determined to release multiple albums in numerous genres.[35] The label had also opened offices in New York and Los Angeles.[36] His ambitions kindled the ideal environment for conceptualists such as Stepney, even in a time of uncertainty.

One prominent Chess group, the Dells, had collaborated with producer Bobby Miller and Stepney since the group returned to the company to record *There Is* in January 1968. As opposed to Stepney's productions with the youthful Rotary Connection, the Dells had been together for several years. Their match was equally ideal: after spending a few years touring with Dinah Washington, the Dells had widened their repertoire into jazz harmony. That fluidity and discipline blended with Stepney's ideas and everyone's openness toward improvisation. You can hear all this on the group's popular 1968 version of "Stay in My Corner" when Marvin Junior extends the *a* in "baby" for four measures.

Chuck Barksdale also remembered others of Stepney's ideas that he found intriguing. One was the prepared piano introduction (à la Henry Cowell) to the Miller-written 1968 single "Wear It on Our Face." "Step went down to the studio, picked up the leaf on the piano, put the stick under it, took some screws and screwed the strings inside," Barksdale said. "I turned around because I didn't want him to see me looking like, 'This man here is crazy.' Got ready to put it on a record—perfect."

The Dells, Stepney, and Edwards made the most of Callier and Wade's song. Perhaps not coincidentally, the group had been wanting to interpret more African American composers when they heard Callier and Wade's work (although they had emphasized earlier black songwriters like W. C. Handy and Andy Razaf). Barksdale told *Soul* magazine, "In this day and age when President Nixon is talking about black capitalism, we can make a small contribution in our way toward this goal for our black brothers."[37] Along with a pronouncement of black unity in Barksdale's vision, the Dells' performance of this song spoke to everyone. As the internal voices of the group, they embody the conflicting feelings in looking back and wondering how finite a romance truly was. Soon "The Love We Had" became one of the Dells' biggest hits, reaching number thirty on the *Billboard* pop list on October 16, 1971, and charted for twelve weeks.[38] "I think it would have went further [up the charts], but it was almost five minutes long," Callier said. "The people at Chess kept asking for an edited version, and it just never happened."

This song was part of the Dells' landmark *Freedom Means*, which had been released in August 1971. Callier and Wade wrote six of the ten tracks, including the title piece, in collaboration with Stepney.[39] Such conflicting visions of romance make up the bulk of the album, but the title track is a plea for racial harmony. Musically, *Freedom Means* also reflects some of the advances from Rotary Connection, including polyphonic choral writing. The background voices, at first almost ethereal, grow more substantial and combine with the strong voices of the Dells. A staccato three-note motif from trumpeters Art Hoyle and Murray Watson provides contrast and a sense of resolution—not only harmonically, but by suggesting the trait of being resolute. "Freedom Means" coalesces from diverse musical cultures: funk, gospel, and classical being three. Indeed, while its lyrics describe a hopeful future, the music adheres to time-honored traditions. Like that of Mayfield, Cohran, and Syl Johnson, the Dells' agenda promoted liberation and uplift, and they would never have been considered firebrands. As Wade said, "This is going to be something we're going to talk about—how people should come together to make the right change for the world instead of going out there with guns and stuff. We thought that would change that perspective."

Callier's success with the Dells contributed to his record deal with Chess. He was more than prepared. During the late 1960s and early 1970s, he continued singing in clubs, usually with his acoustic guitar as the sole instrumental accompaniment. He modestly said that his playing was "just trying to cover all the spaces on the up-tempo things and trying to do something tasteful on the slower tunes." On songs like "Dancing Girl" (on *What Color Is Love*, 1972) he fashioned a signature as an exemplar of the burgeoning folk-jazz subgenre.

But Callier did not come up with its name. "[Jazz club impresario] Joe Segal asked me if I would do some opening sets at the Jazz Showcase when they were on Rush Street," Callier said. "That was just the guitar and me. I opened for Diz [Gillespie], Rahsaan [Roland Kirk], Elvin Jones, and all the people, I can't remember them all now. Joe was the first person to say, 'What you're doing is folk jazz,' and I thought, yeah, that's it. It's never the same way twice."

Spontaneity became key when Callier collaborated with Stepney. So did spoken and intuitive communication as they worked in different scales.

Recording with Charles Stepney, we tried a number of approaches. We tried just myself and the guitar doing things and then writing arrangements around that. We tried doing just myself and the rhythm section, and *Occasional Rain* [1972] is that taken to its logical extreme—guitar, piano, bass, drums, voice, and background vocals and other keyboards are overdubbed. *What Color Is Love,* some things were done by themselves and orchestration was added. Some other things were done with twenty-five musicians in place at the same time, like "Sing Me a Song of the Sun," "You Don't Care," "Just as Long as We're in Love." They were done in the studio with musicians everywhere. I've found that it's best to have everybody in the studio at the same time and have everything go down, for good or ill. Because when you come back and start trying to layer stuff on, for one thing, you lose stuff. There's that feeling of having everybody there, you just can't beat that.

Derf Reklaw of the Pharaohs played percussion on these sessions (under his original name, Fred Walker). Callier's dates alternated with other Dells recordings, which Reklaw said were all completed during a busy series of eight-hour days within a short period.[40] Other Pharaohs, like Don Myrick, were on hand, as was Phil Upchurch. Reklaw added that the foundation to the producer's artistry derived from his rhythmic concepts. While Stepney continues to be touted for postromantic classical elements blended with electronics, these records were different. The arrangements foregrounded Callier's voice against subtly shifting beats. Although Stepney did not promote an outwardly Afrocentric vision to the extent that Phil Cohran did, according to Reklaw such ideas permeated his music. They were just cast in a more populist musical arena. "What he did was he understood a lot of rhythms are not on one," Reklaw said, referring to the first beat of a musical measure.

A lot of things anticipate one or come after one. Let's say, in the case of the Brazilian rhythm. So if a person is thinking of one, they're already off. [Laughs.] They're off the beat because it's not one. You know, it's anticipating one. And a lot of Cuban music and a lot of West African music, they anticipate one with the low drum. Whereas in a lot of American music, they hear one as the bass drum, as the low drum. That's kind of the difference. And [Stepney] would bring that. So that gave so much freedom and space to go somewhere else. He would do that and then he would take a clave and give the clave maybe to the piano. So he put that from being just a stick of wood and putting it at the piano for this song, maybe put it on guitar for the next song. Then changing it up, and then that opens it up for that to be something and to make it on the and-one. Nobody was playing like that. So that just cut through and became the thing. With him playing the vibes, you got the four mallets, he can come up with those inversions and other kind of stuff that would be where they could hear that. I mean, he had it together.

One critic who noticed Callier's records was New York–based writer Vernon Gibbs, who had called for new approaches to R&B in such rock publications as *Creem* and *Crawdaddy*. He asserted that black music does not need to be tied in with the traditional template familiarized by, say, popular harmony groups but should include sounds from all over, chiefly progressive rock (Gibbs later became an early proponent for Prince). Gibbs claimed that Callier's Cadet albums stood apart because of their focus on his acoustic guitar and the "almost hymn-like structure" of the songs themselves. Meanwhile, as Gibbs stated, the production "enhanced his ability to sing on a folk jazz level, to scat and to create a natural sound that really complemented his writing." He had hoped such records would create a groundswell for an alternative soul music, but that revolution took a few years to be realized globally.

While Callier, the Dells, Stepney, and their collaborators infused jazz and classical music into their recordings, Butler dissuaded another Workshop member from doing something similar. South Carolina native Chuck Jackson—whose older half-brother is Jesse Jackson—had been an art director at *Playboy* when he switched careers and joined Butler's organization about 1970.[41] Reportedly, by 1971 he had written 135 songs.[42] Early on, Chuck Jackson wrote such pieces for Butler as "If It's Real What I Feel," but the singer thought this songwriter should team up with a gospel traditionalist. "When Chuck came and showed me the first batch of songs he had written, he had an arranger who was more interested in jazz than he was in rhythm and blues," Butler said. "And so he would turn them more into jazz-oriented kind of songs. I told Chuck, 'What you need to do is find yourself a good church organist or pianist, because the way your stories flow, the music is not matching what the story is about.'"

To find that match, Chuck Jackson took advantage of a talented field, as Butler did in gathering writers. Marvin Yancy played organ for his parents' Fountain of Life Missionary Baptist Church choir in 1964 and received attention for his skills in the *Chicago Defender* when he was thirteen years old.[43] Seven years later Yancy was the pianist for popular gospel singer Albertina Walker at the PUSH Expo, where he met Jackson.[44] Jackson brought Yancy into the Workshop and thought their songs and voices would be ideal for a group. When Jackson and Yancy saw Maurice Jackson (no relation to

Chuck) and Helen Curry perform at the Pumpkin Room on the South Side in 1972, they invited them to join the Independents.

Both Curry and Maurice Jackson had come up as solo artists, and initially they wanted to maintain their autonomy. In 1969 Curry released the quietly moving "A Prayer for My Soldier," which addresses lovers' separation during the Vietnam War. Maurice Jackson's "Step by Step" benefited from Donny Hathaway's tight string arrangements. While Maurice Jackson felt his own career was gaining traction, he also realized that Chuck Jackson's connections with the Operation PUSH leader could prove beneficial. But Curry added that Chuck Jackson actually wanted to make a name for himself without relying on his brother's fame. A more hands-on ally was Eddie Thomas, who had left Curtom in 1970 to become a freelance promotional agent. He got the group signed up to the New York–based Scepter/Wand Records, which two years later released the Independents' first album, *The First Time We Met*.[45] Thomas also interceded with his friend Don Cornelius for the group to perform on *Soul Train*.[46] Still, Jesse Jackson's organization did provide some help: the Independents performed at the 1973 PUSH Expo, and after Yancy decided to serve in the background, PUSH Choir singer Eric Thomas was hired to tour and sing on the second album (*Chuck, Helen, Eric, Maurice*, 1974).

From its first single, the ballad "Leaving Me" (1972), the Independents established their approach: Chuck Jackson's pleading voice lifts into near falsetto in a call-and-response that engages the backing voices, who state the chorus—strings, occasional brass, and Yancy's church-derived chords. Similarly styled, the driving "Arise and Shine (Let's Get It On)" from 1974 is a persuasive call for collective action to save the world's future. The Independents made a direct case to the dance floor with the proto-disco "Show Me How" (1974). Curry's range also added considerably to the Independents' unique texture—few R&B vocal groups at that time claimed both multiple male leads and a female background singer who could easily shift to the front (as she does on "Let This Be a Lesson to You," 1974). Curry also fit in with the group's Sanctified-rooted gospel strand, even though she described herself as "Methodist—quiet, reserved, and all that stuff."

According to Maurice Jackson, that adherence to one of black American music's most venerated traditions during the early 1970s shaped the group's individuality. "The gospel sound made the Independents, period," Jackson said. "Marvin Yancy set the tone. He was a genius the way he did it, a great reader of music. Chuck put the lyrics on his music, and Marvin had the spiritual insight. Chuck has the southern feel with his voice, so it was a great match."

Although the group seemed to be on an upward trajectory, they broke up about 1975. Maurice Jackson experienced a religious epiphany onstage in Detroit and decided to follow a more spiritual path. Curry became suspicious about the Independents' questionable incoming cash flow—or lack thereof—despite the group's continuing presence on *Billboard*'s R&B and pop charts. Chuck Jackson and Yancy left Butler's workshop, but later in the decade this songwriting and production team would craft hits for Natalie Cole (to whom Yancy was married for a few years during the late 1970s) and many others. Veteran saxophonist Gene Barge frequently handled their rhythm arrangements on albums such as Ronnie Dyson's *Love in All Flavors* (CBS, 1977).

As they set up their operation, Jackson wanted to continue looking backward for inspiration. His statement echoed a nostalgia craze that had been growing across popular culture during that time.[47] "Of course there is nothing new in black music," Chuck Jackson told *Billboard* writer Jean Williams in 1976. "Everything is just reverting to the sounds of the '40s, when the sound was big and blasting but the vocals were mellow. The big sound is what's important today. I must tell you that we are not going that route. We are taking the simple mellow sound and expanding on that. We are going headlong into ballads."[48]

Veterans and New Players Reshape Chicago Records and Radio

Meanwhile, Gene Chandler tried something else, although he had a connection to the Workshop: Chandler was Butler's longtime friend and occasional duet partner at Mercury. But Chandler created a business for himself within Mercury's corporate structure. During the two years he was with the company (1970–72), the singer made a deal for it to distribute productions he made on his own Mister Chand label.[49] Mercury likely gave him this leeway because his "Groovy Situation" was a gold-certified record.[50] On that song, Richard Evans's bass lines never let Chandler leave their embrace as he repeats the phrase "Can you dig it," and the thrill is that they sound like they're always about to jump away.

The session also brought Evans back to his roots as a player. "R&B artists and pop artists would not hire or producers would not hire Richard Evans because he's a jazz bassist, upright bass," Chandler said. "Richard came to me and said, 'I'd like to arrange some of your stuff.' And I said, 'Okay, but you're jazz.' I was listening to everybody else. And Richard said, 'I can play anything. They just don't know. Give me a shot.' So I did."

On *The Gene Chandler Situation* (Mercury), which included "Groovy Situation," WBEE radio personality Merri Dee notes that the singer had begun presenting himself as a businessman. Chandler has said that his entrepreneurial skills came from reading books and interacting with record company executives. In that way he was as much an autodidact as Curtis Mayfield and Eddie Thomas.

The album featured arrangements from Thomas "Tom Tom" Washington. Chandler mentioned that he was "working him night and day" also for recordings on Mister Chand, and he described how they worked together.[51] "Whatever the writer wrote, I would take that tape and play that and give Tom the little stuff I wanted," Chandler said. "'Bip-Bip,' or 'I want the strings to say Yop-Yop here,' whatever. And then Tom would take it and refine it and make it beautiful."

Washington had already built up a track record since his time studying with James Mack. In 1967 he arranged the Esquires' hit "Get On Up," which the Milwaukee-Chicago vocalists recorded for Bill "Bunky" Sheppard's Bunky Records. On the liner notes to that group's album, *Get On Up and Get Away*, WVON host E. Rodney Jones declared, "This group mixes bluesy cascades of notes with rhythmic patterns which blend tones into mellow dissonances. You will find a sensitivity and sense of structure that's hard to find today." While that verbiage may be a bit overstated, the Esquires did stand apart from other groups that emerged in the earlier doo-wop era. Millard Edwards, who sang with the group, credits Washington for smoothing off their rough edges. Edwards said, "I was more of a blaster, and he was the only one who told me you don't have to sing that hard."

As Carl Davis consolidated his place at Brunswick, Washington, along with arrangers Willie Henderson and Sonny Sanders, became pivotal to the music he produced. Bernard Reed said that when the Pieces of Peace broke up in 1972, a phone call to Davis was all it took for him to be invited back. Guitarist Gerald Sims, formerly at Chess, also came onboard as a musical director. Their confluence of experience gave rise to the multifaceted and robust variety of the company's early 1970s records.

Singer-songwriter Marvin Smith of the Artistics said his group worked with all these musicians at Brunswick. Like Bernard Reed, he left the company for a while in the late 1960s but returned in the early 1970s. He and Reed also wrote the group's "Trouble, Heartaches, and Pain." While he credited Davis for coaching him as a singer—persuading him not to imitate Sam Cooke but to cultivate his own high tenor—Smith touched on how each staffer had a specific role.

"I felt that Tom Tom was pretty much up-tempo and Sonny was more melody," Smith said. "Like on the [Sanders-arranged] 'I'm Gonna Miss You,' that's a perfectly written song for us when you look at the changes, the flow, and the way my voice went. I could just get to a false tenor. Gerald was a a take-your-time kind of guy, just take your time and you'll get it right. He was patient and had a really good ear."

Davis's continued ascent would have felt right in step with a PUSH Expo agenda. In late 1971 he had made a deal to merge his own Dakar label into the larger company and his Julio-Brian publishing operation (named after his sons, Julio and Brian) into BRC (Brunswick Record Company) publishing.[52] Davis wound up running the artists and repertoire division of Brunswick from Chicago and owned 10 percent of the company.[53] He also hired his brother, George Davis, in 1971 to manage the office. George had just been discharged after serving in the US Air Force for twenty-two years, and he brought stronger discipline to Brunswick. At first he oversaw work flows and schedules and instilled the kind of order that led his staff to nickname him the Sergeant. He then organized publishing—coordinating between the company's Chicago and New York offices. Knowing that he needed to acquire more business skills, George concurrently turned to the City Colleges of Chicago. This was the same route many musicians took, and he encountered some of the same teachers. One was James Mack at Loop College.[54] What George Davis learned from him—and what he imparted to others, was similar to what Butler told members of his Workshop.

> I used to tell the guys about going with advances. In the way back, BMI and ASCAP were very liberal on giving advances. They're not as liberal today. As long as they had a tune published, writers could call up and ask for $500 and they would advance them way back then. If the record hardly sold, they were in debt for I don't know how long. They would never earn any money. Yes, you had to get a statement. But I used to tell them, "If you can avoid it, don't get advances. When you finally accrue something, boom, you go, Oh my God!" It's a lot of paperwork involved in publishing. That's the only thing.

Writers affiliated with Brunswick handled those business aspects in mixed ways. During the 1960s, for example, Jack Daniels had moved from distributing records to producing to songwriting with a partner, Johnny Moore. They composed Tyrone Davis's 1970 hit "Turn Back the Hands of Time," which was based on Daniels's tangled romantic misadventures.[55] Daniels said that, unlike other writers connected to Carl Davis, he insisted on owning his publishing rights.

Sometimes musical and commercial strategies complemented each other, especially in the case of the Chi-Lites. During the late 1960s and early 1970s, the group's international sales came from a format that was recognizable but uncanny. Their close harmony emphasized ballads, some of them stretched out and interspersed with spoken interludes. The Eugene Record/Barbara Acklin-written 1971 pop hit in E, "Have You Seen Her," is the most notable example. Rather than eschewing the doo-wop tradition, they extended it. But within this framework the group and the company's arrangers, producers, and engineers created a variation of that sound. Meanwhile, as the market for R&B, like the market for rock, had shifted from emphasizing singles to full-length LPs, Brunswick sought to fill the album sides by capitalizing on the Chi-Lites' elongated songs. The company initially held off on releasing "Have You Seen Her" because it wanted to push the entire album, *(For God's Sake) Give More Power to the People*.[56] That LP showed off the group's wide musical and thematic reach.

Give More Power to the People, the group's third album, cemented the core team approach at Brunswick as well as the Chi-Lites' autonomy within the company. Record wrote, or cowrote, all of its tracks. Along with singing, he also produced and arranged the album with Washington and Sanders. Willie Henderson and drummer Quinton Joseph codirected the session. Henderson said their position meant contacting the right musicians and making sure that sessions flowed well. Bruce Swedien came on board as recording engineer. For "Have You Seen Her," the team inserted relaxed fuzztone guitar and, when the chorus begins, concise cymbal strikes (likely from Joseph, who sometimes preferred to play while standing).[57] Still, the group's vocalizing commanded the most attention. According to Marshall Thompson, that emanated from the Chi-Lites' religious upbringing.

> We would always go with the Catholic church. We wanted to bring the choir sound. You got first, second, third and they got a fourth note, and that's what we based our harmony around. A lot of groups just got first tenor, second tenor, baritone, bass. It's natural for anybody. But we did first, second, baritone, bass, plus a middle voice. The only person who knew how to do that was Red [Creadel Jones]. We didn't know how to do that. We used to get at Tom Tom, "Tom Tom, get on the piano and find that chord for us!" Red said, "I'm a-tell you, it's right." Tom Tom would get on the piano, and it was right. We didn't know. But Red knew.

With advanced multitracking, the Chi-Lites and Swedien discovered novel twists to layering vocal harmonies.

> Gene did the writing and lead vocals, but Red controlled that background, very strong. We came up with all that together with Bruce. We had some very,

very tight harmonies, and with stacking. Squirrel [Robert Lester] had to almost go outside because he was louder than all of us. We started stacking the harmonies. For "Have You Seen Her," we must have stacked the harmonies about eight times. We started baritones, second tenor, first tenor, soprano because we had Barbara Acklin on there. Then we did that to make the first layer. After we did the first layer, Bruce would say, "Layer another one over that." So we did it again. And we said, "Wow, look at that." Because it got thicker. Then he said, "We're gonna layer another stack, and another stack." Dang, look at that! And then another! That man was amazing.

The album also mixes romance and social consciousness. "We Are Neighbors" is an earnest plea for racial understanding, while "Love Uprising" could be about a couple until it reveals itself as possibly more spiritually concerned and declares, "The Ten Commandments have been cast aside / So the devil gives orders."[58] The title track is the most anthemic. From a synthesized introduction that may be emulating a warning siren, the song sequences into a give-and-take among the vocalists before Jones's baritone intones repeatedly, "Why don't you give more power to the people?" Although "Power to The People" has come to signify black militancy, the lyrics focus on income and political inequality above purely racial issues ("If you don't have enough to eat, how can you think of love? / You don't have time to care, so it's crime you're guilty of"). This perspective echoed Illinois Black Panther Party (IBPP) chairman Fred Hampton's call for unity based on shared economic and social concerns. Thompson said the Chi-Lites knew Hampton and appreciated his organization's support.

"We were out singing a lot, and we had to get something dealing with what was happening that day, so we decided to do 'Power to the People,'" Thompson said. "The Black Panthers took it up and ran with it. Everywhere we'd go, the Black Panthers were there. Me and the Black Panther leaders would talk. We'd go to Cleveland, and it would be full of Panthers. [IBPP cofounder and future congressman] Bobby Rush was right there behind us."

The Brunswick production team also crafted two compelling albums from a group called the Lost Generation, *The Sly, Slick and the Wicked* (1970), and *Young, Tough and Terrible* (1972). Eugene Record had a hand in producing here too. The Lost Generation shared surface similarities to the Chi-Lites. Both hewed to an earlier style of harmony, which they adapted to Washington's intricate arrangements. Just as the Chi-Lites prided themselves on their own lead singer's remarkable songs, the Lost Generation's main voice was the equally consummate Lowrell Simon. But the Chi-Lites' voices were intricately orchestrated, whereas the Lost Generation took an almost conversational tack. In terms of the dynamic between the two groups, Simon said, "What I did for Record was make a bad dude badder. When he came and saw me, that's when you heard, 'Power to the People.' We gave him more of the competition to outwrite, even though there was no jealousy."

Simon backed up this claim. He formed the Lost Generation with tenor Jesse Dean, who was also a member of his earlier group, the Vondells. Dean had convinced Simon that if Smokey Robinson could write his own tunes, he could too. Simon also recruited his brother, Fred Simon, and singer Larry Brownlee, who could transpose and structure Lowrell's hummed melodic phrases into finished songs. Gus Redmond, a promotions staffer at Brunswick and a friend of Dean's, signed them to the label. In exchange for Redmond's managerial role, the group gave him partial composing credit along with the Simon brothers and Brownlee.

Everyone relied on Lowrell Simon's ability to quickly turn extemporaneous ideas into knockout songs. On the Lost Generation's first and biggest hit, "The Sly, Slick and the Wicked," Simon just wanted to play on the title of the film *The Good, the Bad, and the Ugly* and mess around with an echo effect that an earlier Chicago group, the Sheppards, used on its "Tragic" from 1961. Fred Simon said that was his typical method. "He would just be sitting there and all of a sudden say, 'Fred come here, check this out.' Everything would come to his head, and he didn't play an instrument. He would have a piano player or guitar player interpret the riffs he wanted. He was very spontaneous and very aware of the times."

Bernard Reed, who played bass on the Lost Generation's albums, said it got to the point where Lowrell Simon's quick-thinking method turned into an office game. That also shows how Carl Davis's firm managerial approach did not always extend to the company's creative side. "I remember hanging out with Lowrell," Reed said. "There was nothing going on that day, and we were downstairs under the offices, and he had his pencil and paper, and his cigarette in hand, and he'd always be thumping the fiery end of the cigarette on his thumb. That was a habit he had, and while he's thinking, he's writing. I asked, 'How fast can you write this song?' He said, 'I don't know, let's see.' Lowrell could write a song in twenty minutes—and that's how I found that out. Today people ad lib, like the rappers—freestyle. So I guess that was a form of freestyle writing, that's how fast he could put together a song."

Like Mayfield and Record, and not unlike the rappers who came later, Lowrell Simon alternated between individual narratives and broader social themes. But whereas his contemporaries wrote anthems—"Move On Up" or "Give More Power to the People"—Simon preferred dialogues. On the pensive "This Is the Lost Generation," he addresses his grandmother's apprehension about contemporary youths' increasing militancy. The sense is that he is listening to her experiences even as he's defending his own. Obstacles in communication become the theme. (Simon had proposed naming his group the Generation Gap, but entrepreneur Mel Collins convinced him that the Lost Generation sounded better.) The outwardly easygoing melodic feel offered a fascinating contrast to the lyrics, as with "Young, Tough and Terrible." While the words center on alienation, the tune conveys a medium tempo sway (punctuated with finger snaps) and accentuated through Washington's string arrangements.

"Young, Tough and Terrible" encapsulates what made the Lost Generation and its arranging and production team at Brunswick so exceptional. Simon said he wanted to write a tune similar to the Temptations' "Just My Imagination." But then it got transformed. The tune is in G, but it shifts surprisingly: Bernard Reed's bass line (about fifty seconds in) that moves to B-flat alongside the string section's B-flat arpeggio in the strings before returning to the original key.[59] Reed said this melodic ease came about because he did not use a pick and tried to emulate jazz bassists like Richard Davis and Ron Carter. The later instrumental interlude implies a D scale, but it also omits a few notes to make it fit with G without musical awkwardness. Essentially, the string interlude plays on the two keys—G and D—without committing to either one, yet it also makes the piece as a whole seem unified. Even if the song and production has more sophisticated key changes than Chicago R&B of a decade earlier, songs from the Lost Generation and the Chi-Lites shared a foundation, and heart, with their predecessors.

The Young, Tough and Terrible album indicated another shift with a cover photo of the group, dressed sharp and gazing seriously into the horizon. When Fred Simon discusses the previous LP, The Sly, Slick and the Wicked, his remarks about that album's graphics could have described Jerry Butler's experiences with the white couple on Aware of Love in 1961. He said the group turned the slight into a joke. "We were in Washington, DC, when it came out and went to the local record store," Fred Simon said. "It came out with all these white people, these hippies, on the front and then our photo on the back because they marketed it toward a pop audience. It was so funny, we were just laughing. It did help sales. Once that white young lady, white young man, bought the album it was about the song, not race."

New Media Players Deliver the Sounds

Selling these records also meant contending with changing media across Chicago. Globetrotter Communications purchased WVON in 1970 for

$9 million.[60] While this remained the city's commanding R&B station, during the late 1960s it shared the dial with three others.[61] Competition did not hurt WVON on-air personalities. A pact signed early in 1971 gave the staff pay increases (Jesse Jackson and Operation Breadbasket mediated the agreement).[62] The deal formalized plans to air salutes to deserving black high school students and business owners, as well as tributes to Martin Luther King.[63] Cecil Hale, WVON assistant programming director in the early 1970s, adds that while the pop station WLS remained the largest music station, its limited playlist helped his company's bottom line. WVON benefited from WLS's overall dismissal of R&B and its audience (although WLS did take a step toward internal integration when it hired Yvonne Daniels to play records overnight in 1973; she also became the station's first woman DJ).[64]

"In Chicago, WLS was the big dog, everybody wanted to be WLS because they had the big numbers, they had the big cash flow, they had everything going for them," Hale said. "But the thing they didn't have that worked for us was there was a certain segment of music they would not play because they made the same assumption that had been made in the 1950s in terms of how music was played, by whom, and who was consuming that music. Because WLS didn't play a lot of black music, that meant that for us there was an audience who liked that music who would come to us. So our ratings would improve and continue to stay high."

WVON staffers also had their hands in record production and artist representation during the early 1970s. E. Rodney Jones managed singer Bobby Hutton, and his position on the radio secured Hutton a major label contract. Hutton recalled, "He told people at ABC, 'You don't treat Bobby right, I'm taking the Four Tops off the air.'" In 1972, WVON's Lucky Cordell partnered with independent entrepreneur Clarence Johnson to start General Entertainment Company (GEC). Their artists included the vocal groups Brighter Side of Darkness, Heaven and Earth, and Cordell's daughters, who performed under the name Pat and Pam.[65] Larry Blasingaine arranged the rhythm on the youthful Brighter Side of Darkness's album *Love Jones*, while Tom Tom Washington coarranged its strings and horns. The sound echoed the wildly popular Jackson Five. GEC also had its offices on Record Row, and Blasingaine recalls that its composing and production methods followed a collaborative model like Butler's Songwriters Workshop.

Chicago's other major black-oriented radio station at the time, WGRT (950 AM), offered the most competition to WVON, according to longtime DJ and journalist Richard Steele. Steele had sung doo-wop with WVON's Richard Pegue in the late 1950s when they were students at Hirsch High School. After moving to the East Coast, Steele returned to his hometown in

1970 and became an afternoon DJ at WGRT. Steele said that whereas WVON featured outsized characters, his station was "more format-oriented, more Top 40-oriented." Like its counterpart, WGRT engaged in public forums, including airing the late-1960s Youth Action Program that allowed teenagers to voice their grievances.[66] Although WVON DJs made fun of WGRT's limited daytime hours, Steele said his show reached farther north, including Evanston, where he hosted record hops. In any case, all these radio luminaries convened at clubs like the High Chaparral, as the *Chicago Defender*'s "Charlie Cherokee" gossip column regularly reported.[67]

Steele stressed their congeniality. "We all knew each other well," he said. "When I came to town I was at something and Rodney Jones introduced me and said, 'There's a new guy in town from our competition. We're going to beat him to death, but this is Richard Steele and we love him.' We used to do that and it was fine, so we were very, very close and hung out in the same places, all of that."

As with WVON, Jesse Jackson claimed that Atlas Communications, which owned WGRT, paid its black on-air staff unfairly.[68] He pointed out that experienced personnel at WGRT earned less than $80 a week more than starting announcers at WGN, the larger AM station.[69] WGN's greater resources and reach did not seem to factor into Jackson's calculations. But these disputes highlight how the financial status of Chicago's African American media remained precarious. This issue would be taken in a different direction in October 1972 when John Johnson, owner of Johnson Publishing, bought WGRT for $1.8 million and it became WJPC, Chicago's only black-owned radio station.[70] Jackson immediately transferred his weekly radio show to WJPC. Not long afterward, the competition among black-oriented radio stations in Chicago intensified.

Soul records also continued to reach different demographics through jukeboxes. Twenty years after the Chess brothers used nationwide jukebox networks to circumvent radio stations that would not play Muddy Waters, these machines not only endured as beneficial sales agents but could reach neighborhoods beyond the range of radio stations' signals.[71] *Billboard* reported in 1972 that the presence of black music had been growing on the playlists of the estimated 500,000 jukeboxes nationwide. "Clearly, soul is pop," wrote jukebox editor Earl Paige.[72] Chicago proved central to the article, since the city was home to at least eight black-owned firms operating jukeboxes. Moses Proffitt, the first black member and officer of the trade organization Music Operators of America, noted that although urban renewal had removed "whole sections" of the city, his routes had adjusted. He branched out south along Lake Michigan, and many operators were following African Americans who were moving to the suburbs.[73] In the article, R&B records are mentioned as being on the playlists of jukeboxes in white suburbs and farther afield, a Chi-Lites hit being an example. Betty Schott, who ran Western Automatic Music, said, "We used 'Have You Seen Her' on every location except our country stops."[74]

These points come with a disclaimer. As a trade magazine that depended for advertising revenue on companies that included jukebox distributors, *Billboard* conceivably could have run an article that magnified their actual status. Nor did the issue deeply consider the shadowy connections between organized crime and the jukebox industry that had existed for decades.[75] Kerry Segrave's social history of jukeboxes reports that they had been declining since the 1950s and that the industry tended to overstate its importance.[76] Nevertheless, Segrave adds that jukeboxes did "help music outside the mainstream" and cites black (and country) artists as examples.[77] Gus Redmond agreed that when he promoted Brunswick acts, the city's jukebox distributors remained a pivotal stop on his rounds. This was a form of direct marketing that he said could outdo seemingly dominant radio stations. But the jukebox industry also had its own set of rules to be navigated, aside from its murkier aspects. Redmond said it was up to individuals to gauge and build connections with distributors, then to use those sales to spark interest from radio stations.

As Chicago families began moving to the suburbs, the city experienced what was charted as a decline. Some of this movement came about because the 1968 Fair Housing Act prohibited discrimination in the sale and rental of dwellings based on race, making more housing available for black families who could afford it. The number of African Americans living in suburban neighborhoods rose from 4.2 million in 1970 to 6 million by the end of the decade.[78] An editorial in the July 1971 issue of *Ebony* stated that with large and small factories relocating to outlying industrial parks, black employees moved along with them.[79] But these demographic changes and ongoing municipal neglect contributed to the city's tribulations. Crime had increased, reaching 862 murders during 1973, a higher total than the statistics that raised the alarm forty years later.[80] As the overall black percentage of the Chicago population continued to grow during the decade, new political and cultural campaigns would be launched and sometimes combined.

Songs Move Stages to Small Screens

All these factors affected community centers such as live music rooms. The Regal Theater's closing and its eventual—inexcusable—demolition in 1973 marked an era's demise.[81] But a number of smaller venues managed to thrive into the 1970s on the South and West Sides, providing entertainment and serving as oases for cultural survival. Historian Clovis Semmes has written that the Regal met the "aesthetic demands and norms of Black audiences"; the same applies to those clubs that endured.[82] For some, visiting remaining clubs meant journeying back to a foundational source.[83] They were part of a culture that could not be transferred as easily as records. Other people across the Chicago area seemed to be seeking them out as well. Addressing a readership that included suburbanites who may have been more familiar with Near North venues, journalist Angela Parker's enthusiastic *Chicago Tribune* feature on August 13, 1971, mentions more than twenty-five bars, clubs, and lounges on Halsted Street between Sixtieth and Eightieth Streets, such as the 650-seat Green Bunny.[84] This report noted that their function transcended outward appearances. Parker stated, "Though there may be a dearth of first-class, extra-plush places, the spots are comfortable, intimate, and give the folks an opportunity to dance and rap."[85] The *Chicago Defender* spotlighted the High Chaparral for its variety of performers—from Duke Ellington and Count Basie to Jackie Ross and the Impressions—a year after Mayfield's last performance with that group occurred there.[86] Carl Davis ran his Carl Davis Palace farther south and for a while showcased Larry Blasingaine's group, Larry and the Hippies, as the house band. On the West Side, Herb Kent and Chicago police officer William "Chico" Freeman spun records between live soul and blues sets at Barbara's Peppermint Lounge.[87] Years later, Freeman recalled that Peppermint Lounge proprietor Barbara Trent Balin's welcoming yet tough spirit kept her club thriving from the mid-1960s into the 1970s—though she broke from her otherwise strict compliance with the Illinois drinking age when she gave a gig to the Jackson Five.[88]

Clarence Ludd, who managed the High Chaparral, strove to maintain a family-oriented atmosphere, even though the place could hold 1,300 patrons. Ludd (a former Harlem Globetrotters basketball player) attested that while he had no formal business education, he insisted that performers always be paid even if the club lost money. His generous nature included hosting an all-star benefit for the Guys and Gals Club when that competitor was shuttered in 1973 for not paying its federal taxes.[89] Singer Holly "Holle Thee" Maxwell recalled that even as a teenager she felt safe at the club. Another vocalist, Reginald Torian, added that not only did Ludd lend him $750, he also arranged his audition to join the Impressions. Although the venue attracted mostly black audiences, that changed when more widely popular performers were onstage.

Benjamin Wright led the High Chaparral's house orchestras in the early

1970s. This ensemble residency replicated the role of the Red Saunders orchestra at the Regal a dozen years earlier. The High Chaparral served a similar aesthetic, even if it was not part of the densely packed and intense Bronzeville scene of decades earlier. Musicians also supported events featuring WVON personalities (such as during Al Benson's time at the Regal). For instance, Cecil Hale hosted a regular party called "All Hale Breaks Loose." Yet the biggest outgrowth of DJ-hosted shindigs was Don Cornelius's regular Wednesday night set.

Cornelius turned the dances he saw at venues such as the High Chaparral into the long-running television program *Soul Train*, but his reconnaissance was not limited to clubs. He drew from dance moves and styles across black Chicago during the late 1960s and early 1970s. Gregory Moore, who grew up in the Harold Ickes Housing Development on the South Side, remembered a line dance at the project's Henry Booth House in 1968 that would later be famously replicated on Cornelius's show. Whereas the music, fashions, and dances of an earlier group of Chicagoans—the gousters—filtered through pop culture gradually, *Soul Train* would become a direct pipeline into American households. Media activists and emerging trends within the city made possible the show's launch on August 14, 1970, on local channel WCIU (channel 26 on the UHF frequency).

WCIU instituted new outreach efforts three years before *Soul Train* debuted. The station had restructured itself to target a new generation of viewers. Station president Bill O'Connor told the *Chicago Defender* in 1967 that his goal was to present a mix of show business names and discussions of controversial issues.[90] His plans would take a couple of years to develop, but R&B singer McKinley Mitchell performed on the station's *Show Biz* program.[91] And in 1968 African American meteorologist Jim Tilmon began hosting "Our People" on the public television affiliate WTTW (channel 11). This black-oriented program began with a focus on entertainment but then introduced more thoughtful political and cultural content. Although *Our People* ran for four years, the only known surviving episode presented legislator and future Chicago mayor Harold Washington along with jazz singer Johnny Hartman.[92]

Cornelius's career in broadcasting began serendipitously. While on duty as a policeman in the mid-1960s, Cornelius pulled over WVON news director Roy Wood to write a ticket, and the radio host suggested he consider joining the station's staff.[93] Early on he held various jobs—reporting, filling in for DJs, and answering the telephone, and in 1967 he completed a three-month broadcasting course. E. Rodney Jones persuaded him to include political activism in what he covered.[94] Wood brought Cornelius to WCIU to comment on sports for his program *A Black's View of the News*.[95] That opened doors for Cornelius, but he also gained notoriety for his outspoken remarks. The *Chicago Defender* noted that at a party hosted by Western Electric for *A Black's View of the News* in 1969, Cornelius "was controversial, as usual, in his comments about Leo Durocher and black athletes who are superstars."[96]

In 1967 Cornelius devised *Soul Train* and lined up Sears as a sponsor.[97] His earlier experiences with Martin Luther King and Sears executive George O'Hare had built up goodwill. In *The Hippest Trip in America*, Cornelius claimed to its author Nelson George that persuading WCIU to go along with his concept was easy enough because, he said, television is a medium where good ideas can easily find a footing.[98] The *Soul Train* creator sells himself short. He had to forge connections among the musicians who appeared on the first show—including Jerry Butler and the Chi-Lites.

Soul Train also included political activists within this forum on a commercial channel. Cornelius did so with a plan. In 2011 he told *Chicago Tribune* journalist Andy Downing his method for structuring interviews with personalities like Bobby Rush and Jesse Jackson. "I felt like we could help people like Bobby and Jesse get people's attention if we didn't overplay it," Cornelius said to Downing. "I was always convinced that television was an entertainment medium as opposed to a talk medium. I was committed to keep talking to a minimum. That's why most of my interviews were so short; once we started talking the show kind of stopped. It was part of our mission to support these guys that were trying to make things better."[99]

Danae Williams, a Chicago teenager who danced on the initial episodes in 1970, was most excited about meeting the Chi-Lites and winning tickets to see the Jackson Five. But her resulting popularity created a bigger mission. Williams recalled being invited to Chicago Park District events intended to inspire young African Americans to realize their goals. As she got to know Cornelius, she understood that his agenda included speaking with, and listening to, young people in the city. In that way he resembled Herb Kent and his record hops. Cornelius also aligned with teachers such as James Mack: classical inclinations were encouraged as well as enthusiasm for pop. Williams said he endorsed her interest in ballet as part of his advocacy for young African American dancers and believed that "It's not just in the house. It's not just in the basement. But they've got talent that they can, you know, showcase, that everyone would love to see and mimic."

Williams performed on the national premiere of *Soul Train* in Hollywood on October 30, 1971.[100] Distinct choreography characterized the two cities. She recounted that Chicagoans did the bop, but in Los Angeles the sunset reigned. Chicago dance "was more or less like a swing," Williams said.

What Californians performed "was almost like a cha-cha—two steps up, two steps back." She was not the only midwesterner who accompanied Cornelius to California. Bobby Hutton sang "You're My Whole Reason," a ballad by Donny Hathaway that let the guests slow dance. The singer wore a tuxedo, and the *Chicago Defender* applauded the sophistication of the program's nonmusical segments, stating that "there wasn't any jive talk on 'Soul Train.' The conversation and dialogue was relevant, but intelligently projected and exceptionally articulated even to a crisp 't' and 's' in every word."[101]

Soul Train promoted black youth culture and stressed an uplifting worldview in a setting of discernible but unpretentious urbanity. This principle had run throughout the PUSH Expos. Although initially the show's national advertising marketers were frustrated at major research firms' inability to measure which demographic was watching, by early 1972 the producers directed its commercials toward the 53 percent of African American households that did tune in.[102] Chicago-based Johnson Products (maker of Afro Sheen) sponsored the early national broadcasts of *Soul Train* for a reported $600,000.[103] The advantage for a black hair care company targeting this show's audience was obvious. But the image Cornelius sought to present was intuitively connected to ideals that new black-owned advertising agencies in Chicago envisioned—whether or not they were his sponsors. Soul music catalyzed that connection.

The rise of Chicago-based African American advertising agencies coincided with the evolving civil rights movement and Operation Breadbasket–PUSH's entrepreneurial goals. Vince Cullers was a trailblazer: he started his Vince Cullers Advertising agency in 1956, Barbara Proctor established Proctor and Gardner in 1971, and Thomas Burrell and Emmett McBain founded Burrell McBain that year (it was later named Burrell Communications).[104] Like any such company, their agenda was to obtain clients and turn a profit. In that regard they were no different from white firms that started to use black imagery to seek more consumer dollars.[105] But these Chicago-based black companies also wanted to lead by example. All of them had to begin from scratch, cold-calling on corporations for their business, then appeal to African American consumers. They operated in a fiercely competitive domain in a city where whites had become entrenched in well-established sectors, ranging from industry leader Leo Burnett to jingle writer Dick Marx. For all of them, music remained crucial for any ad campaign, since it serves as a cultural identifier as much as—if not more than—the visuals. But doors started to open wider for black musicians to play on these sessions after the local musicians' unions integrated. Their essential struggle continued, however: Maurice White stated that discrimination prevented him from gaining a foothold just to play tunes for the city's established advertising agencies during the 1960s.[106]

Civil rights organizations expressed concerns similar to White's but focused on the images advertisers projected. Establishing identity within the medium and dismantling stereotypes became key for them along with jobs. By 1967 the Congress of Racial Equality and NAACP had started earnestly calling for boycotts if blacks were not totally incorporated into advertising.[107] Former Urban League director Whitney Young commented the following year, "It's important that blacks are used more frequently in ads because they serve to educate the masses of viewers that black people, like themselves, have an important role in American life. The situation was awful, is better and has to get better."[108]

Also by the early 1970s, just about all national companies knew they had to reach out to the growing African American consumer base. As advertising historian Jason Chambers noted, at this time the black buying market was approaching $30 billion annually.[109] Mainstream advertising agency executives were told that these shoppers wanted to see their lifestyle represented, but they had few staffers available to accommodate the demand.[110] Moreover, scant research had been done on strategies to reach these customers.[111] In 1972, according to the *Chicago Tribune*, out of the six to seven thousand advertising professionals in Chicago, only sixty were black.[112] None of this diminished the optimism of those comparative few who strove to influence black buying power.

Vince Cullers Advertising produced Johnson Products' Afro Sheen commercials that aired on *Soul Train* in the early 1970s.[113] These spots made a considerable impact for its client. Johnson's founder George Johnson had first wanted to concentrate his company's $2 million annual advertising budget on black-oriented radio and billboards instead of television.[114] To sell a hair care product purposed to make one look good, it's not hard to see how the commercials' stylish and effective images changed his mind (as did increasing sales).[115] How the ads sounded mattered. In these early television spots, segments embracing African American lineage and unity proved as significant as fashions and coiffures. Ads ended with a leitmotif of a one-line sung coda and an African-inspired drum ensemble. Its lyrics, "Watu-wasuri use Afro Sheen," was a Swahili-English mashup (Watu-wasuri translates roughly as beautiful people).[116] This dual language usage and instrumental arrangement had direct links to the Affro-Arts Theater: the Pharaohs wrote and performed the music.

Chicago's black-owned advertising agencies also did not pigeonhole themselves or musicians during the early 1970s. Willie Woods knew that their being a culturally conscious ensemble did not prevent Cullers from calling the group in to score advertisements for banks. "He had us in on a lot of stuff and people didn't know it," Woods said. "We had our dashikis on and we'd come in and cut, we'd rehearse it and get it down. When we went into the studio we were tight, laying down lots of tracks."

These agencies' founders also expressed an ideology of bringing positive images of African Americans into corporate marketing programs. Thomas Burrell became mindful of this after working in other firms throughout the 1960s. Burrell believed ads should also reflect a deeper understanding of identifiable qualities of black culture. He drew more inspiration from Stokely Carmichael's call for black power than from Martin Luther King's integrationist vision. By no means a militant—early clients included McDonald's and Coca-Cola—Burrell said that Carmichael's rhetoric necessitated asserting a genuine identity.

> We coined the term "positive realism." Our whole idea was to just show the kind of unvarnished positive side of black life. Up until that time, it was distorted either negatively or over-the-top positive—you know, acceptable exception kind of phenomenon where a black person would be shown as not like the rest of them, the Sidney Poitier kind of character. In order to be a businessman, he knows six languages and can play the violin and speaks perfect English and so forth. So we basically wanted to go right into that sweet spot area where people live, and it gave us an opportunity to do well by doing good in the sense of showing people in a way that they hadn't seen themselves before. We realized how hungry we were to see ourselves positively reflected in the major media. It was such a simple way to be great and to be revolutionary, just show people being real. And, man, it had such a profound impact on the black community.

Burrell knew the role for music in this mission. He was not a musician, although he sang in choirs and began performing as a jazz vocalist age sixty-three. But he always retained an interest in the sounds around him in Chicago, and he wrote the liner notes to Jerry Butler's 1967 *Soul Artistry*. As he started Burrell-McBain in 1971, his first account was a nightclub that paid $1,000 a month, although by the end of the year revenues rose to $500,000.[117] He knew his operation had to scale an intensely competitive market. Leo Burnett was the fifth-largest advertising firm in the country and had racked up more than $422 million in international billings by early 1972.[118] So Burrell's insider knowledge of contemporary black music, and of how to use it, was a needed advantage over the industry's behemoths.

As Burrell launched his firm, he met Charles Stepney, who must have understood that Chess's business moves meant a questionable future for himself and the company. Stepney brought other Chess session players with him to Burrell. Anna Morris, creative director at Burrell, remembered guitarist Phil Upchurch and drummer Morris Jennings at recording sessions, along with vocalist Kitty Haywood. Advertising jobs, moreover, provided musicians with solid paychecks more promptly than record sales royalties. Morris put Stepney's acumen to use when she devised a jingle for Carnation evaporated milk that sounded like the Hues Corporation hit "Rock the Boat." She said the idea was to sound similar without plagiarizing. Stepney's abilities would also enhance the raw talent that Burrell recruited off the street, where the company hoped to gain a sense of authenticity. Morris said, "We had a guy working for us, all he would do is go around and see people and say, 'You want to be in an ad?'"

But the company also emphasized older black popular music, including hiring singer Walter Jackson for a McDonald's spot that highlighted family. The big breakthrough for Burrell occurred when the company created "Street Song" for Coca-Cola in 1976. This joyful ad's black teenagers touted the drink by singing doo-wop on the steps of a brownstone. The thirty-second commercial was a hit, playing into the retro craze hitting mid-1970s America with a 1950s song form and singers who were unmistakably African American. Whereas Cullers's commercials for Afro Sheen had used African-inspired music to reinforce bonds among black consumers, Burrell's ad used a different strain of black pop to attract everyone.

Although the commercial was filmed in New York, the actors mimed to a jingle that Stepney's protégé Morris "Butch" Stewart recorded in Chicago. Stewart said coming up with the tune was simple for him, since his older brother Phillip had sung on street corners years earlier. "Having grown up black in a black neighborhood, it's just really easy once Tom opened the door for this to have exposure in the advertising realm. It was kind of easy for guys like me to come in and say, 'Here's who we are. Here's what we do. And here's how we sound.' And that was very different for downtown Michigan Avenue."

With "Street Song" winning a coveted Clio Award, the company had become more of a national player.[119] They also fought a bit of a backlash as the number of blacks in nationwide television advertisements dropped slightly, from 12.9 percent in 1974 to 7–10 percent in 1976, according to different studies.[120] As Anna Morris explained, "At the time it was difficult for Burrell to be taken seriously by production houses. Their attitude was, 'You're doing a black thing and maybe you need to go to black people.' Getting that Clio made a hell of a lot of difference. Then the top tiers listened and looked at our boards when we sent them in."

Once in a while commercial songs took on unexpected lives of their own. Sidney Barnes got into this venture during Rotary Connection's demise about 1970. At that time former WVON ad sales manager Don Jackson aspired to starting an advertising firm. An early account was a low-cost retail store, Ember Furniture, which had a few locations on the South and West Sides. So he approached Barnes. "Don Jackson didn't have a freakin' budget," Barnes said. "They were advertising furniture you could buy cheap that they could [put on] layaway. You know, selling shit. They had $250 to spend on the budget, and he put $250 to have his first account. I'm doing good, living high, so I put this together, it went on the air. And Don Cornelius was on it, and it was such a beautiful song, just a little short thing because it was a commercial, but it was so badass that the station got bombarded with calls saying, 'What the hell is that?'"

The song's melody made that cheap furniture sound inviting, though Jackson argued that Ember actually had a respectable business. Radio host Richard Pegue—who also worked in advertising and ran his own small record companies—produced it as a single. Initially given away at the stores, the 45 of the obliquely soothing "Ember Song" became a valued collector's item worldwide, and the Numero Group reissue company included it on a Pegue compilation album in 2011 (*Eccentric Soul: The Nickel and Penny Labels*). Jackson—whose other early clients included Illinois Bell and Jewel Food Stores—became considerably more successful as his Central City Productions went on to produce and market an array of black-oriented Chicago-based and national television programs. Jackson had turned down his WVON colleague Cornelius's invitation to collaborate on *Soul Train*, but he acknowledged that they shared a common intent.

Partly due to the economic growth, the buying power that advertisers were beginning to recognize, the tremendous concentration of African Americans in key cities like Chicago, the viewership that African Americans had, and acceptance they had on radio and television, they were the major audience. When WVON was the number one station in Chicago it was because of the crossover and success of its music in white America. The African American market was a trendsetter in music and fashion, and white America hadn't seen it. So this awakening came about when they saw this trendsetting among the African American community, and that spurred it and it hasn't stopped.

Cecil Hale saw this change happen while he was at WVON in the late 1960s and early 1970s. The key for advertisers, as he observed, was connecting social awareness with selling while retaining an overall respectful tone.

> If you look at the black power movement, what was happening during that period, and look at the advent of the Black Panther Party in the 1960s, what was happening with Martin Luther King and Malcolm X, and you think of black consciousness becoming a very big deal—an overt very big deal—you begin to see this whole new group of consumers that you can approach not only in terms of "my product is good" but you can tie ethnicity to it. Afro Sheen became more than stuff you put in your hair in terms of the campaign that was directed toward that community. It became part of the identity of that community. Same thing happened with manufacturers with Coke, with beers, you name it. Everyone was going after that marketplace because America suddenly became aware that you can make a whole lot of money focused on that demographic when you do it well.

Some have questioned what advances these advertisers formulated. Scholars and television series have also depicted the ways 1960s advertising agencies co-opted that decade's overall counterculture.[121] Some appropriations dug even further back: this was a time when an apparition of Frederick Douglass appeared in a commercial for Afro Sheen that aired on *Soul Train*.[122] In 2015, a series of articles in the *Atlantic* asked whether McDonald's ads in the early 1970s reinforced inner-city stereotypes. Both Burrell and Chicago ad man Lowell Thompson responded forcefully on the magazine's website, stressing the respectful nature of their efforts, which should be looked at in their historical context.[123] Separately, James Baldwin reacted with a derisive laugh when television host Dick Cavett mentioned to him in 1968 that blacks' appearing on commercials represented the "ultimate accolade."[124] But advertising firms did more than just stimulate revenue streams for themselves, their clients, and their musical employees. They provided another means for work by black artists to reach a mass audience when other media remained unstable or otherwise unreliable. Their images and sounds entered homes that may not have been tuned in to black radio stations. All of this exemplified the stated goals of the PUSH Expos and the musicians who supported them. Also, down the road, some of Chicago's African American advertisers would adapt their hard-earned experience to the political arena, which would promise significant change in the years to come.

1. Eddie Thomas (*left*) and Curtis Mayfield. Courtesy of Eddie Thomas.

2. Jackie Ross. From the Robert Pruter Collection.

3. Ruby Andrews. From the Robert Pruter Collection.

4. James Mack. Courtesy of Shelley Fisher.

5. The Chi-Lites. *From left:* Creadel "Red" Jones, Robert "Squirrel" Lester, Marshall Thompson, Eugene Record. Courtesy of Julio Davis.

6. The Lost Generation. *From left:* Larry Brownlee, Lowrell Simon, Jesse Dean, Fred Simon. From the Robert Pruter Collection.

7. Carl Davis at home. *Far left:* Johnny Collins (Carl Davis's accountant at Brunswick). *Front row:* Carl Davis, Walter Jackson, Dedra Davis. *Back row:* Gwendolyn Libscomb ("Pip," E. Rodney Jones's girlfriend), Gene Chandler. Courtesy of Julio Davis.

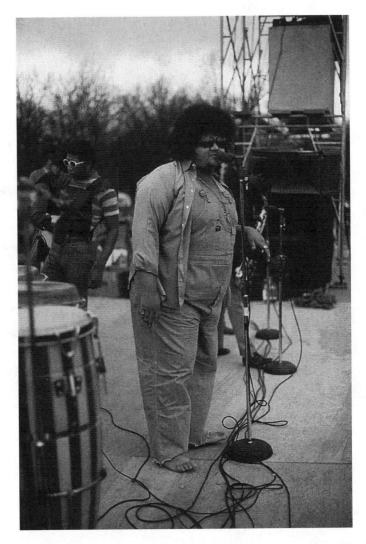

8. Baby Huey performing as leader of Baby Huey and the Babysitters at Sound Storm Festival, Poynette, Wisconsin, 1970. From the Wisconsin Historical Society, Madison, Wisconsin.

9. Minnie Riperton performing as part of Rotary Connection at Sound Storm Festival, Poynette, Wisconsin, 1970. From the Wisconsin Historical Society, Madison, Wisconsin.

10. The Independents. *From left:* Chuck Jackson, Helen Curry, Eric Thomas, Maurice Jackson. From the Gilles Petard Collection.

11. Radio group. *Seated (from left):* Cecil Holmes, Don Cornelius, Curtis Mayfield, Jay Johnson, Emmett Garner, Clinton Ghent. *Standing (from left):* Jack "The Rapper" Gibson, unknown, unknown, Sonny Taylor (WJPC program director), Richard Pegue, Richard Steele. Courtesy of Richard Steele.

12. Gene Barge in a production still from the film *Stony Island*. Photo courtesy of Andrew Davis/Chicago Pacific Entertainment.

13. Syl Johnson at home, 2010. Photo by Aaron Cohen.

SEVEN

Sound Power:
Funk and Disco Highlight Connections,
Divisions, and Aspirations

When Curtis Mayfield blew out the candles at his thirty-third birthday party at Chicago's Hyatt Regency hotel in summer 1975, he celebrated more than this milestone.[1] In the seventeen years since the Impressions first recorded, Curtom, the record company he co-owned, remained successful. Along with the triumphant soundtrack to the film *Super Fly* in 1972, his other early 1970s albums had achieved widespread acclaim.[2] As a *Black Stars* article stated, Mayfield also announced that Curtom had signed an international distribution, marketing, and promotion deal with Warner Brothers. That agreement promised to take those records worlds away from his office on the city's Northwest Side. A feature in the *New York Amsterdam News* applauded Mayfield for being a black artist who was able to attain financial stability while performing only when he wanted to.[3]

His Hyatt party featured an array of pacesetters. In one photo Mayfield led a three-way conversation with his mother Marion Jackson and Jesse Jackson (no relation). The Impressions performed, as did such affiliated artists as the Natural Four and the Jones Girls. WJPC program director Richard Steele was there, along with such business veterans as the High Chaparral's Clarence Ludd and Columbia Records' Granville White. In an instance of life imitating art imitating life, another guest, actress Esther Rolle, played Florida Evans in the hit television sitcom *Good Times*, which its co-creator Eric Monte set in the Cabrini-Green housing project fifteen years after he and Mayfield grew up there. At the same time, the gathering marked a transition.

As industries of all kinds faced formidable changes in the 1970s Midwest, Chicago's music field proved no exception. Along with affecting manufacturing as a whole, economic downturns challenged the ability to produce music at all. Although the city's R&B musicians released several fine recordings and venues continued hosting artists, many of these companies and clubs would close by the dawn of the 1980s. Yet black cultural producers continued to work within and rise above these difficult times. New technology helped African American radio stations maintain a discernible sound as they reached wider audiences. Station WJPC, owned by Johnson Publications, would challenge WVON, but both faced a new contender, WBMX, which broadcast on the expanding FM frequency. While soul singers and groups from the city would cross over to achieve greater popular heights after leaving the Midwest during the 1970s, they reached back to Chicago for musicians and musical ideas. Divisions among followers of specific kinds of popular music reflected tensions rising in the world outside concert halls and record stores. But some Chicagoans sought a diverse range of soul and rock influences to devise their own take on funk. Integration may have remained a dream deferred, but artists in the city continued to present that ideal in the underrated film *Stony Island*. After an intense racially tinged backlash against disco, another form of electronic-heavy black dance music—house—emerged within an infrastructure that had been established long before. So when Harold Washington, an African American congressman, ran for mayor in the early 1980s with a pledge to unite the city, musicians jumped on board.

Several of these cultural and political campaigns followed similar paths and faced related obstacles throughout the 1970s. Suburban home-ownership opened up a bit for any residents who could bear the expense of mortgages, yet historic neighborhoods within the city declined following a mid-decade recession and loss of manufacturing jobs. That downturn hurt laborers across color lines, and this economic pain exacerbated racial schisms. Even with the persistence of segregated schools, an increasing number of African Americans attended college and entered more professions, though not at the same rate as their white counterparts. Crime rates remained threatening. Another stabilizing force also diminished: the Black Economic Research Center revealed that, of the eight hundred black businesses operating in 1972, 40 percent had shut down by 1975.[4] The black population of Chicago continued increasing throughout the decade in numbers and as an overall percentage of the city: to 32.7 percent in 1970 and 39.8 percent ten years later.[5]

Ebony detailed this growth and these conflicts as they connected to the 1970s Midwest. In the February 1978 issue, Chicago was highlighted in an article titled "The Ten Best Cities for Blacks."[6] Despite a harsh climate and higher-than-average cost of living, it was cited for being home to more black banks (six) than any other city. More professional opportunities existed, yet the local black unemployment rate stood at 13 percent (compared with

4.7 percent for whites). Although the metropolitan area included ninety-three institutions of higher learning, the article bemoans the lack of quality education for black secondary school students.[7] Six months later the magazine ran a series of features in its August issue looking at the aspirations of eighteen- to thirty-year-old African Americans nationwide; Chicago remained pivotal. Career goals, economic hardships, and lifestyle choices were covered.

Sociologists also studied the industrial decline in Chicago, and this situation could have signaled a diminishing future for potential musicians. As William Julius Wilson wrote, between 1967 and 1987 Chicago lost 60 percent of its manufacturing jobs.[8] The West Side had taken strong hits with the closing of factories such as the International Harvester plant in the late 1960s and the subsequent loss of small businesses like retailers.[9] So the steel mills that employed singers Tyrone Davis and Otis Clay in the early 1960s would not have been there for budding performers living in the same neighborhoods ten years later. Still, singer Finis Henderson III said that his 1970s group, Weapons of Peace, acquired a cheap house in that part of the city and used it for living space and as an artistic base of operations.

Others on the West Side recognized the decay, but they also describe a complexity of vibrant, if smaller, music venues in the neighborhood, intertwined with less altruistic activities. One of these people was Benneth "Benny" Lee, a past chief of the Vice Lords, who went on to counsel the formerly incarcerated and help steer youths away from gang life. He remembered a string of clubs in the 1970s on a stretch of Cicero Avenue between Harrison and Lake Streets, including the Safari Room and the New Natural Club. Lee said upstart groups opened for established stars on their stages. Whereas competing sets of gousters and Ivy Leaguers squared off in 1960s teen dances, their successors would likely not have been in the same room a decade later; everyday social life took on a harder edge.

"You've got to look at the era," Lee said. "It was after the civil rights movement and black power movement when drugs flooded the community and *Super Fly* and *The Mack* hit the scene. That culture shifted from people wearing dashikis and afros to the seventies, when we started getting our perms. With the *Super Fly* look—the long collars, bell bottoms—everybody was into some type of hustle. We would play con games, we were influenced by reading [pimp-turned-author] Iceberg Slim. That had an impression on us young guys. That's who we wanted to become."

In that February 1978 "New Generation" issue, *Ebony* responded to the way earlier social and economic progress seemed to have derailed, yet it indicated new cultural possibilities. National Urban League president Vernon E. Jordan Jr. wrote that "back in 1950, two out of three Black male teenagers were in the labor force, a figure that has dropped to less than two out of five."[10] A photo of boarded-up storefronts in Chicago's once-thriving Wood-lawn neighborhood accompanied the piece. Alvin Poussaint lamented that while blacks could move more freely in white society, their political engagement had diminished.[11] Overall, these articles assayed mutual understanding in an evenhanded tenor that fit with the corporate ethos of the magazine's parent company, Johnson Publications. Bill Berry's feature "Beyond the Here and Now: New Generation Blacks Search for Religion" considered African Americans seeking new spiritual paths; it included a photo of Maurice White leading Earth, Wind, and Fire in meditation.[12] Other references to music pervaded the articles. Lerone Bennett Jr. described Stevie Wonder as "perhaps the nearest thing to a generational voice," yet he asserted that blacks who had not grown up under legal segregation were losing the connection to what he termed "the Negro Folk Tradition."[13] Somewhat ominously, Bennett added, "The generational progression from Funk to Soul to Rock to Rock-Jazz is a new line leading God knows where and with God knows what implications on the levels of consciousness and identity."[14]

Rather than completely breaking with the past, young Chicago-raised R&B musicians had stayed within established traditions during the late 1970s. But they formed their own identities, as singers in the preceding decades had done. Those voices included Minnie Riperton and Chaka Khan, who had drawn on psychedelic rock, jazz, and funk from their time in integrated bands in the city until they reached their artistic highs later in the decade. Riperton and Khan also defied any stereotypes of women soul singers' sound and appearance, especially in terms of sexuality.

Singer-songwriter Daryl Cameron embraced various avenues and crafted them into his own intergalactic fantasy, using Chicago as a launching pad. He had grown up on the Far South Side, including living in the privately owned Princeton Park Homes. With the help of his mentor Eddie Thomas, in 1978 he released an album that announced his conceptual persona, *The Adventures of Captain Sky*. Like George Clinton and Bootsy Collins with their conceptions of Afrofuturism, Cameron used comic books and science fiction to devise that Captain Sky alter ego. Playfulness runs throughout his music, as in the way he uses electronic effects to clown around with his vocals. That's on top of the quick stop-time rhythms that compel anyone's limbs to move. A cape, silver suits, and matching boots consolidated the look. The album garnered positive press in African American media, such as a review in *Black Radio Exclusive* magazine that stated, "The world of funk had better watch out, Captain Sky could well become its guiding head."[15]

For Cameron, listening to WVON and WJPC was just one foundation. Cameron's father, who bought him his first guitar, sent him to private institutions for his elementary and high school years in the late 1960s and early 1970s. He went to the Lutheran-run Luther South High School. Later alumni include the rapper Common (Lonnie Rashid Lynn Jr.), but at the time Cameron attended the Southwest Side school, he said it was, "15 percent African American and 85 percent otherwise. So that was a new experience for me."

A largely white school in this part of the city might have been a tinderbox of racial tensions, notwithstanding its religious affiliation, but Cameron recalled that such strife felt inconsequential, if it was there at all. Instead, he talked about playing soul and rock radio staples such as Led Zeppelin's "Stairway to Heaven" with other students in the school's stage band. He saw no reason to limit his musical boundaries. Nor, as with Lerone Bennett Jr., did his performing a white British band's signature song mean he was disconnected from his own traditions. Instead, Cameron personified sociologist Ellis Cashmore's statement that "what we popularly accept to be black culture is, on closer inspection, a product of blacks' and whites' collaborative efforts."[16] Cameron's experiences exemplified a wider movement. Finis Henderson III believed that nothing kept Weapons of Peace from adapting ideas from such white prog rock bands as Yes. About the same time in New York, young DJs sought out Rolling Stones and Steely Dan records as sample material during the early days of what became hip-hop.[17]

"This is what a lot of people don't understand—everything that we listen to, everything that we're introduced to, becomes a part of us," Cameron said. "Because it's in us, like Prego [pasta sauce]. Remember the Prego commercial 'It's in there'? It's in there. Music is universal. It really has no color. It doesn't have a gender, really, though some of it does. You can listen to some stuff, and it's kind of soft. And some other stuff is hard. But it's got a mixture."

Cameron's education continued in the city's R&B venues. For a while he worked with the soul group the South Side Movement, which would later release a series of LPs and singles on New York–based Wand Records. He sang at such South Side clubs as the Burning Spear and the High Chaparral, where he remembered proprietor Clarence Ludd as "one of the biggest teddy bears I met in my life." Mostly, though, he avoided clubs, since he did not care for that lifestyle and preferred to focus on recording. But Cameron—as Captain Sky—made inroads into other media, including a memorable 1979 performance of his "Wonder Worm" on *Soul Train*. His onstage props that day included a shield that looked like an oversized album.[18]

Those clubs that had been part of Cameron's development persevered throughout the decade. With Ludd continuing to personify the goodwill that Cameron and others mentioned, the High Chaparral hosted charitable events, including a December 1975 fund-raiser for legal fees on behalf of Al Bell, the besieged president of Memphis-based Stax Recording Company.[19] Former Staple Singer Pervis Staples parlayed his family's investment and connections to unveil Perv's Place on Halloween 1974.[20] Musicians and politicians alike made frequent appearances at the club. In addition, during the final years of the Affro-Arts Theater, Willie Woods put together money from his commercial sessions, his performances, and his day job as youth director of the federally funded Model Cities program to start hosting parties at his River's Edge, just north of downtown. Woods and his partner, James Christopher, ran such events throughout the city in the 1970s, including at the CopHerBox and CopHerBox II.[21] Despite economic woes such as the 1974 recession, Woods said his business did not decline, since people were always looking for fun. WVON's Cecil Hale agreed and put that belief in wider terms. He saw music and its extended social life as an expected release during any crises.

> Gerald Ford became president in 1974, and before that Nixon was president, so what you had was a deepening bifurcation of employment opportunities and poverty levels around the country. So you ended up with the black population on the short end of the stick again with all those economic indicators. There were more people out of work, and when people are out of work there are certain things they'll spend money on in different ways. In terms of young people, they had less disposable income, but the income they had, where did they spend it? They'd spend it on music and events.

Nonetheless, some African American Chicago club owners did show an altruistic streak that went beyond selling drinks. Nor were all patrons simply looking for an easy release. As Pervis Staples did with Perv's Place, Willie Woods made the CopHerBox available for political rallies. Sometimes these proprietors offered at least a local foothold within a larger market. In ways that were not obvious, the club scene encouraged entrepreneurial power citywide. For example, when Ludd let two start-up shoe merchants, Kham Beard and Nate Parker, sell their wares in the High Chaparral lobby, they leveraged that business to transform a deteriorating single shop into a small chain. By the end of the decade, they had hired thirty employees in five stores across the city.[22]

Beamin' Black: African American Radio Competition Builds as Artists Top Bigger Stages

Chicago radio personalities, who had made their club appearances part of their rounds, faced a changing terrain amid more pointed competitive strategies. New and veteran business executives targeted African Americans more aggressively. John H. Johnson's Johnson Publishing purchased WGRT and its 950 AM frequency in October 1972 for $1.8 million.[23] When the station relaunched as WJPC in 1973, its ownership became a selling point. An early *Chicago Defender* advertisement exclaimed "Sound Power!" and "Beamin' Black."[24] Its musical playlist, though similar to WVON's, reflected the latter slogan, as did its other programming. That included *The Ossie Davis and Ruby Dee* story hour, which presented dramatic readings of Paul Laurence Dunbar.[25] As I noted before, Operation PUSH brought its Saturday morning program from WVON to WJPC, a decision the older station could not effectively contest.[26] WVON's Lucky Cordell argued that Globetrotter Communications, which acquired his station, wanted to emulate what it perceived as WJPC's emphasis on music over public service.[27] But long-standing disputes by WVON employees over management styles caused its senior staff to leave the station, or get dismissed, throughout the decade.

Richard Steele, who became WJPC program director in March 1975, contended that his station's catchphrases for empowerment did not filter down to its treatment of its workers; labor and management coexisted uneasily. In the mid-1970s Steele led the Chicago chapter of the black media organization National Association of Television and Radio Announcers. Although Steele said the way the station owners treated staffers "was pretty awful" across the country, he wondered if Johnson actually wanted to devote resources to the broadcast industry. Also, as Steele said, Johnson did not look favorably on labor unions, including broadcasters' collectives.

While WJPC and WVON competed on the AM dial, FM transmission, with its improved sound quality, encroached on their territory.[28] Annual sales of FM radio sets doubled in the late 1950s, and they exploded throughout the 1970s. By mid-decade, with FM radios cheaper and more available in cars, in 1974 broadcasters anticipated that by 1981 this format would overtake AM.[29] *Black Radio Exclusive* writer Jerry Boulding saw African American radio stations moving into FM alongside the growth of black album sales (as opposed to singles) and "the mass appeal of much of the music we play."[30] This mattered because it meant R&B artists would come over the airwaves as clearly as their contemporaries in other idioms. In Chicago, from the late

1960s into the mid-1970s, commercial FM stations had tended to focus on classical, folk, and rock music.[31] Steele thought that would be all of it.

> Just the thought that there'd be FM coming in and end up being king of the hill, we just didn't see that. We were fighting it mentally but slowly as we began to look at FM, and FM began to have a real presence, and the sound was great and the reception in terms of where you happened to be was great. We were still holding on to the vestiges of AM radio, thinking it would never be replaced by something like FM radio. Unless you were a forward thinker, like programmers who did a lot of research, and saw that FM was going to be the next big thing. But we weren't on that page, at least not at my level.

Oak Park-based WBMX (102.7 FM), formerly WOPA, stepped into the breach in late 1973. Rather than promote personalities, the station made music a priority and restrained excessively ebullient DJs. According to Jerry Boulding this was part of a nationwide trend.[32] The call letters themselves marked a generational shift from what the initials VON stood for: supposedly BMX meant "Black Man Experience."[33] The station's urbane positioning connected to the rising number of African Americans entering higher professions. Despite which—and recalling the Chess brothers at WVON— German immigrant Egmont Sonderling founded WBMX. His Sonderling Radio Corporation owned black-oriented radio stations across the country from 1950 until 1987.[34]

The idea of a black-music FM station proved successful in Chicago. By 1977 WBMX had taken the lead over both WVON and WJPC in the ratings. An Arbitron ratings analysis in spring of that year showed that WBMX reached a market share of 2.9 among the total population, while WVON was at 2.5 and WJPC at 0.9.[35] Disco station WGCI stood at 3.8 and WLS at 8.3, although big promotional budgets played a part in the AM pop station's continued strength, according to *Black Radio Exclusive*: WLS gave away a Datsun each day for thirty days.[36] But at this time black listeners still preferred AM over FM: as reported in *Cash Box*, nationwide 27.6 percent of African Americans were tuning in to FM, as opposed to 40.1 percent of the general population.[37] In Chicago, where FM had a 23 percent market share among African Americans, AM was listed at 69.4 percent.[38] There were a few reasons for this disparity. Some may have been traditional, as AM stations remained entrenched in the West Side and South Side communities. Also, FM radios were not yet ubiquitous in cars. So WBMX's capture of this wide a segment of listeners despite its deep-seated competitors on AM attests to its programming.

Earnest L. James, WBMX program director in the 1970s, conveyed the quiet confidence designed to appeal to young professionals. In interviews, the Oklahoma native described the same kind of broadcast strategy that Boulding mentioned in *Black Radio Exclusive*. James also told *Chicago Tribune* reporter Gary Deeb, "We're going after adults, so our announcers speak clearly and intelligently—no broken English—because the level of our music is intelligent."[39] This statement represented a notable change from decades earlier, when Al Benson drew in Chicago's migrants through his southern-inflected speech. Deeb noted that the station was "heavy on the 'disco sound'—lushly orchestrated, danceable music that transcends the boundaries of soul, rock and easy listening."[40] If integration remained outside the city's grasp, it was within the scope of WBMX's demographic.

So WBMX continued to engage its black audience through music and community action. Along with its playlist, on-air personality LaDonna Tittle put together events such as a bike-a-thon in summer 1975 to raise money to fight sickle-cell anemia.[41] While these were smaller-scale and far less dramatic efforts than WVON DJs' serving on the front lines of the civil rights movement in Chicago eight years earlier, they did continue shared ideals. Even though Jesse Jackson decried what he described as overt sexuality in R&B and rock, he launched a weekly talk show on the station. This amused the *Chicago Defender*'s "Charlie Cherokee" gossip column, which remarked that Jackson had moved from WVON to WJPC because WJPC was black-owned, unlike WBMX.[42]

Some older artists benefited from the broadcasting trend. Gene Chandler said, "We didn't necessarily need [AM station] WLS because the whites could hear us on FM." The singer had a career comeback in 1978 with a disco song, "Get Down." Typical of its time, the track is fun: it's danceable, if at a somewhat relentless tempo, with an extensive synthesizer part responding to Chandler's voice. Nobody could equate it with the calmly confident delivery of "Duke of Earl" or the sway of "Groovy Situation," but after his recording at Mercury and other labels, the song marked Chandler's reunion with a few friends. Carl Davis produced it at Universal Studios, and the *Get Down* (Chi-Sound Records) album's personnel included such Brunswick veterans as musical director Sonny Sanders and arranger Tom Tom Washington. Davis was not a fan of disco, but he appreciated the revenue.[43] "If you don't have good artists and good writers, you're nothing," Chandler said. "So I went out and found my own people to write, and that's how it went down. A hit record is a hit record, no matter where it comes from. If you can get it promoted, get it played, and it's a hit, you got a hit."

All of this remains valid, yet so is the truism that there's always been more to producing and selling anything than hoping quality comes through. Those who left Chicago still knew that this city's talent could make individuals and groups stand out from other popular artists on the radio. These musicians and executives left for myriad causes: some for personal reasons, others to move up in bigger entertainment companies increasingly based on the East and West Coasts. But just as they took their artistry national, some media players discovered that local barriers to airplay also existed on a national level. One early corporate transplant, Ron Alexenburg, moved from his job at Chicago's Garmisa Distributors to join Columbia Records in 1965 and became vice president of its Epic subsidiary in 1972. This was at a time when his company responded to a 1971 Harvard University Business School report that advised it to get more invested with soul, which made up 10 percent of the $1.66 billion record industry in 1970.[44] He signed the Jacksons (formerly the Jackson Five) to the company in 1976 and saw Michael Jackson's meteoric rise a few years later. Alexenburg said the initial struggles in helping Jackson cross over to a wider audience were similar to the issues with AM pop radio stations he remembered from 1960s Chicago.

> When I was fortunate enough to get the big job at Columbia and signed a little kid named Michael Jackson, I saw MTV not really acquiescing to the black videos or the rhythm-and-blues videos. That pissed me off to no end. And I let it be known. Same thing to *Rolling Stone* magazine when I wanted artists like that on the cover. You know, being born and raised on the South Side of Chicago, hanging around Old Town, and going to Buddy Guy's club, music was never segregated by me. I believe that—and you can quote me—I believe that all music is good. Some is just better than others.[45]

Between the Jacksons' signing to Epic in 1976 and the emergence of MTV in 1981, Michael Jackson launched his solo career with the help of other former Chicagoans. Whether they brought a midwestern sound, aesthetic, or work ethic to these recordings may be debatable, but their combined extensive, and sometimes unusual, experiences proved invaluable. Engineer Bruce Swedien recorded and mixed Jackson's 1979 album *Off the Wall* (Epic) in Los Angeles. Former Pieces of Peace keyboardist and High Chaparral bandleader Benjamin Wright arranged the strings on three of its tracks.[46] Wright, who had moved to California in 1975, started collaborating with Earth, Wind, and Fire about three years later at the recommendation of Chicago recording studio owner Paul Serrano. Then producer Quincy "Q" Jones called Wright about Jackson. While Jones, like Charles Stepney, promoted the Schillinger system, Wright relied on a higher source of inspiration over what he saw as abstract mathematical theory. His account of his role on this album echoes the determination he showed when entering the Chicago Conservatory.

> Q [Jones] gives me this tape: Michael Jackson. I didn't know what to write. This is Quincy Jones. Then, what do you write for this cat? About three days before the session, the Lord said, "You have to put some notes on this paper." Finally put some notes on the paper. I get to the session. Mr. Extremely Confident Benjamin Wright—I didn't know what to do. I'm in the studio and somebody said, "Hey, Ben." I look around and it's Bruce Swedien. I knew him from Brunswick, all the sessions, and that made me feel a little better. Then Ben, with his untactful butt, said "Q, Ben's here, gonna be a piece of cake." Oh my God, I don't need that kind of pressure, I'm already scared to death! But once the sessions started, all the fright went away. But I didn't know how Quincy reacted. I'm in the control room and the cat is falling on his knees. Until we finish the take and Q is like, "Oh my God, this is it." That made me feel a little better. To confirm that Q was on the up and up in terms of his reaction, he gave me another song that day. First was "Don't Stop 'til You Get Enough." Second was "Rock with You." God helped me pass the test.

Relocated Californian Maurice White employed Tom Tom Washington after Stepney's death in 1976.[47] This was also about the time when White recruited Louis Satterfield and Don Myrick for the instrumental section that would perform under the Egyptology-inspired name Phenix Horns, sometimes with Chicago trumpeter Elmer Brown.[48] White had also become a major industry player in the decade since his days as a Chess session drummer. By 1977, CBS Records held 25 percent of the black music market, and Earth, Wind, and Fire was recognized as its most consistent act.[49] White's company, Kalimba Productions, had recently signed the Emotions, a vocal trio of Chicago natives.

Englewood sisters Wanda, Sheila, and Jeannette Hutchinson initially sang together as a gospel group, the Hutchinson Sunbeams, before becoming the Emotions.[50] When the trio turned secular, they did not abandon the affirmative spirit and three-part harmonies they had absorbed from the Presbyterian Church. After sealing a recording deal with Columbia Records, the Emotions used Stepney (on *Flowers*, 1976) and, after his death, Washington (on *Rejoice*, 1977). Wanda Hutchinson wrote several of the group's songs and, according to White, Stepney realized that flat fifths and minor sevenths formed most of the melodies.[51] These unusual intervals are not overt in the group's infectious tunes. Hutchinson added that the two Chicago-trained arrangers had contrasting methods.

You know how we see in one or two dimensions. Charles hears in three dimensions. [Laughs.] He can hear something—I mean, here I am at the piano
[at his home in Hyde Park], and he was already hearing the horns and strings.
And I couldn't hear any horns and strings. But as I was playing, he was humming something. And I was like, "That ain't my song." But it was the arrangement he was humming. Tom would have me come over just for the melodies.
He just needed one of the singers that knew all the parts of the song. And he
would have the radio playing—the soap operas on, because he loved his soap
operas—at the same time as he would be [arranging]. I was like, "How can
you do that?" He said he did that all the time. And then he had this guy that
was bringing him Famous Amos cookies. But it was, "How can he hear all this
with everything . . . ?" He said, "Everything is concert." I would be like, "What
is he talking about?" Yet it all worked out.

Indeed it did—for example, there are Washington's joyful horn lines in
the Emotions' hit "Best of My Love." Those short staccato bursts from the
brass alongside the sharp rhythm section accents are set against the sisters'
flowing shouts as Wanda Hutchinson soars above it all.

In the mid-1970s Washington's colleagues from Brunswick had gone in
other directions. Willie Henderson left the company in 1974 to establish
Willie Henderson Productions. There was no ill will between him and Carl
Davis; Henderson even set up his shop downstairs from Davis's office. And
Henderson went back to Malcolm X College (formerly Crane). This time it
was to write and direct a science fiction musical, "Music Magic Space Fantasy." When Henderson described the staging and storyline four decades
later, it sounded as if it was all of a piece with the Afrofuturism of George
Clinton and Captain Sky Cameron.

Davis left Brunswick after a distressing experience. In January 1976 he
and other company executives had faced extensive federal criminal charges,
including embezzlement and payola, at a trial in Newark, New Jersey.[52]
After he was found innocent, he told journalist Sidney Miller Jr. that all of
those alleged activities had taken place out of the New York office while he
was in Chicago.[53] So Davis stepped up that summer and started Chi-Sound
Records, with its new office on the city's Gold Coast.[54] The location north
of downtown near the new Water Tower Place shopping center made its
own kind of statement. Davis saw no reason to remain on what had been
Record Row on Michigan Avenue, and the upscale address echoed WBMX's
crossover perspective. It was also near Marty Feldman's Paragon Recording
Studio and not far from Universal Studios. All the same, Davis mentioned

to Miller that white radio stations would not play his records, even though they had been listed on their charts.[55]

Along with radio airplay, live performances, jukeboxes, and television, these artists were appearing on more film screens. A few movies offered their own takes on R&B in Chicago, even though none of them triumphed at the box office like *Super Fly*. Mayfield sought to repeat that success as he became a soundtrack industry almost unto himself. He wrote the songs for the *Sparkle* film, which became the foundation for Aretha Franklin's last great album in 1976.[56] The following year he served as composer, producer, and actor in the brutal 1977 prison drama *Short Eyes*. The Staple Singers and Gladys Knight and the Pips also used Mayfield's songs and his musicians for their cinematic entries.[57] Gordon Parks Jr., who directed *Super Fly*, included the Impressions singing Lowrell Simon's and Rich Tufo's songs on *Three the Hard Way* in 1974. Simon proved to be continually versatile as he wrote the ballad "Wendy" and the driving, consciousness-raising "Make a Resolution" on that Curtom-produced soundtrack. The storyline—partially filmed in Chicago—involved a white supremacist plot to poison an African American water supply; Jim Brown played a record producer who leads a trio that foils the attempt.[58] Charles Colbert Jr. wrote the songs and Richard Evans composed the score to Lawrence Anderson's *No Place to Run*, which was shot at the Roberts Motel on the South Side early in 1974.[59] Despite the names of other musicians as part of the project, that movie quickly vanished—if it was completed at all. Eric Monte scripted the semi-autobiographical *Cooley High* in 1975 based on his experiences growing up in Cabrini-Green in the mid-1960s, but no Chicago R&B songs were included despite the wealth of talent from that neighborhood. Motown's backing of the production would explain why that company's catalog was presented almost exclusively. Nevertheless, several Chicagoans, including musicians, who lived through Monte's experiences in those projects remain fond of the film.

Also filmed in Chicago, director Andrew Davis's *Stony Island* from 1978 tells a story about music making on the South Side and remains the most intriguing fictional account of this process. This was an independent production at a time when Davis said that American filmmakers "either worked for the studios or were Roger Corman." The story focuses on the efforts of guitarist Richie Bloom (Richie Davis, Andrew Davis's younger brother) to form an R&B band with singer Kevin Tucker (Edward "Stoney" Robinson), both of them actually musicians in the city at the time. In another bit of musical realism, their characters enlist as mentor Percy, played by saxophonist-arranger Gene Barge. Other musicians, like guitarist Phil Upchurch, show up briefly, and Clarence Ludd appears as a sympathetic venue owner. Oscar Brown Jr., in a wink at his real-world activism, plays an alderman. With Andrew Davis and coproducer-cowriter Tamar Hoffs's relative inexperience at that point and their reliance on nonactors, the film has an endearing rough and spontaneous quality. Part of its charm comes because they recorded all the music live owing to a mere $300,000 shooting budget.[60] David Matthews and pianist Tennyson Stephens composed most of the soundtrack's songs, which are lively but have a loose feeling that corroborates Richie Davis's description of a rushed process. The band came together and recorded in three weeks. Robinson's talents and spirit radiate throughout, but his bright promise was cut short when he died in April 1979 at twenty-six of unknown causes, possibly liver failure.[61]

While *Stony Island* presents an idealized vision of artistic collaboration in Chicago, it also reflects a progressive vision of social connections within the city. The film's narrative seems to argue against the idea British music critic Charles Shaar Murray and several other writers have noted, "the need to separate black music (which, by and large, white Americans love) from black people (who, by and large, they don't)."[62] Not only is the band integrated, but an Appalachian migrant from the Uptown neighborhood is the group's saxophonist. Racism becomes an overt issue only when Percy interacts with his nefarious boss. Poverty does not impede these musicians. Gangs are absent, and while musical instrument sellers are depicted as shady, they help more than they harm. When Andrew Davis was asked about his optimistic depiction, he replied, "I don't know if it was idealism, it was reality—you can't be a white guy playing that music and be racist. There's just no way."

Both Davis brothers grew up immersed in the city's political hotbed, and that environment emerged on-screen as it did in their values. The son of left-wing theater actors, Andrew Davis had been an assistant to director Haskell Wexler on the 1969 film *Medium Cool*, which wove footage of the 1968 Democratic convention riots into the narrative. *Stony Island* included shots of Mayor Daley's 1976 funeral; despite the mayor's authoritarianism, his passing is treated with mournful respect by all on-screen citizens. If this footage may seem incidental to the plot, as Andrew Davis said, the event was a changing of the guard that proved decisive for the city.

Stony Island opened to generally favorable reviews. But the release of the film on DVD in 2012 included a short documentary that describes its distribution problems, including an ill-advised attempt to remarket it as blaxploitation. Andrew Davis adds that white movie theater owners recoiled at having black youths as patrons. Overall, though, Barge, the Davis brothers, and other musicians who participated in the film justifiably contend that its vision remains valiant.

Despite this commercial failure, interviews included on the DVD release show that the film had an unexpected impact. One of its admirers, Chuck D of the rap group Public Enemy, stated, "The movie didn't talk about race, but it just shattered the myth of race" and "It's rarely told how people come together and drop their differences and line up with their similarities in music and culture."[63]

Disco Backlash and the Rise of House Echo History While Signaling Changes

At the time of *Stony Island*'s release, R&B shifted from the kind of cross-generational instrumental band depicted in the film to the ascendant disco. Chicago was prominent in that nationwide movement as well as in the back-lash against it after the "Disco Demolition Night" of public record burning. While this event highlighted racial divisions that ran throughout popular music audiences, the city's younger and veteran black artists held mixed attitudes toward this dance music. Some performers recognized openings, others saw larger obstacles. Meanwhile, collective action among disco DJs echoed collaborative efforts from a few years earlier. For many, the bigger white backlash came as no surprise.

Disco production and marketing in Chicago fit in with American trends: try out its beats and arrangements, hope for something big. Gene Chandler's *Get Down* (1978) succeeded; Curtis Mayfield's monotonous *Do It All Night* (1978) backfired.[64] But Curtom had better luck with producing Linda Clifford from New York. The singer moved around before settling in Chicago during the mid-1970s. She sang in suburban and North Side clubs such as Rush Up and Mother's. Clifford said that with her band performing a variety of music—from funk to Broadway standards—the small audiences were usually integrated. But Clifford sought more. So she took a cab to the Curtom office and invited company heads Marv Stuart (Marv Heiman) and Mayfield to see her set at the Playboy Club. They promptly signed her up. In the studio, Clifford started a free-association rap about her ex-husband, the band joined in with a disco groove, and the result became the highlight of her 1978 dance hit, "Runaway Love."[65]

While Clifford enjoyed a crossover appeal, she added that the disco era was initially liberating for black artists in terms of basic economics.

I think [disco] opened a lot of doors for people as far as performing. It opened clubs and gave more opportunities to singers to get out and to travel the world and do a lot of things that normally they wouldn't do because at that time you either worked what was called the chitlin' circuit, or you could work the pop clubs. And that was very difficult for an artist of color. You could not get into those clubs. They didn't want you there. It was no secret. So having the disco clubs really gave you avenues to work. Unfortunately, the problem with some of the disco songs was that a lot of the producers became greedy. There's no other way to put it. They thought, "Wow, I can just make these sounds on this machine and put a beat behind it, and people will dance to it, and I got a big record."

Club DJs also had a role in determining such hits, and at this time they had begun organizing themselves. In cities across America during the mid-1970s, these DJs began to collectivize to exchange information before such records became hits and to support each other. Frankie Knuckles, a DJ who helped launch the New York Record Pool in 1975, moved to Chicago's insurgent Warehouse club a couple of years later.[66] DJs in Chicago similarly empowered themselves to approach major record companies from a position of strength when they formed a collective organization called the Dogs of War in January 1977.[67] In its way, this group also acted as a DJ equivalent of Butler's Songwriters Workshop. The highly experienced Eddie Thomas led the organization. With its office at 2112 South Michigan Avenue, it was one of the street's last musical connections to the years of Record Row. Like their counterparts in other cities, the 150 Dogs of War members would obtain records from companies and rate them according to their own tastes and how clubgoers responded. Those record companies and retail stores received the reports; radio stations and other traditional media would be bypassed. One hit that resulted, Le Pamplemousse's "Le Spank" in 1978, took its name from a dance popular in local black clubs.[68] The Dogs of War record pool also made a million seller out of keyboardist-percussionist Peter Brown's 1977 "Do You Wanna Get Funky with Me," an early popular twelve-inch single.[69]

Thomas and the Dogs of War acted as more than just a commercial enterprise. The organization's newsletters dispensed organizational advice and pledged equal opportunity within the ranks, all without downplaying its observations about dances and fashions. Meanwhile, Thomas provided guidance to musician Larry Dixon, including helping get his songs into stores and on the radio.[70] Dixon had grown up in Englewood during the early 1970s and experienced those difficult early years that *Ebony* journalists and sociologists had described. He hung loosely with neighborhood gangs and landed a series of odd jobs when his band recorded the record *Star Time*, featuring a sparse keyboard line, at the CopHerBox in 1979 for his own LAD Productions. For decades afterward, Dixon continued composing and producing, primarily as a one-person operation.

Not that these trends appealed to some older Chicago musicians. Several black artists resented the changes it wreaked. For instrumentalists on the club circuit, the preference for DJs signaled an end to their own revenue streams. Bassist Bernard Reed had continued performing on recordings in the second half of the 1970s, such as an unfortunately overlooked Walter Jackson album, *Feeling Good*. But he argued that disco precipitated the downfall of small stages on the South and West Sides and took away jobs for musicians like him.

> Disco turned the turntables on, and turned the stage around from live music to records. That's what happened, and a lot of the artists weren't equipped well enough to handle that new form of expression. For a band to compete with a DJ is almost impossible. Most people would love to dance to a live band playing, jamming. The club owners could get away with paying the DJ less money than the band, but then it got to where they'd pay the DJ more money than for a band. The DJ would get people up in there, dancing, buying drinks. Disco was a rhythm to make people dance, then it got to a different thing.

Likewise, Captain Sky Cameron clarified that he was not a disco artist, even if his records seemed tailored toward dancers. For him there were aesthetic differences between that sound and the funk he declared as his own. "It should be against the law to use the words funk and disco in the same sentence," Cameron said. "Yeah, only because it's just so far away from each other. You're not going to hear that hi-hat [in funk]. You're going to hear [hums a couple of rhythmically annunciated notes]. I don't understand why they do it. But I'm here to correct anyone that tries to do it."

Such distinctions did not matter to several white radio station staffers and their audiences, who tended to lump much of black music into one category during the late 1970s. This was a time when Bobby Thomas of the Notations said his group received a less than welcome reaction in nearby Milwaukee, Wisconsin, since some in the city were aghast that their 1977 "Judy Blue Eyes" might be about a white woman. In turn, arguments about musical taste often metastasized into broader racial battles. In his *Stayin' Alive*, historian Jefferson Cowie mentioned that the decade's industrial fissures—inflation, labor struggles—heightened divides between working-class whites and blacks. Cowie mentions that those divisions fueled the antidisco back-lash. He observes that as disco became a craze, the studios diluted it into a more rhythmically dull corporate product.[71] But Cowie also describes "the white everyman" critiques of the music residing just above "deep wells of homophobia, racism and longstanding anti-Eastern establishment senti-ments dating back to the dawn of the republic."[72] At a time when national economic tensions fueled white animosities, African American music be-came more pronounced on record company balance sheets. In 1977 Artie Mogull, president of United Artists Records, stated, "Black-oriented product represents in excess of 40% of our business."[73] The racism at the core of this adverse reaction seemed pronounced in the Midwest. While the smash hit 1977 film *Saturday Night Fever* downplayed the black and gay roots of disco, vociferous elements of this part of the country still connected the music to its original core audience.[74] One group in Detroit extended its derision toward the music to initially naming itself the "Disco Sucks Klan."[75] But the most infamous example of this backlash was Disco Demolition Night at Chicago's Comiskey Park on July 12, 1979.

Steve Dahl, who had been an on-air personality at the rock station WLUP, promoted the event, ostensibly as a protest because his previous radio out-let (WDAI) changed formats to disco. He claimed that blowing up records between the games of a Chicago White Sox double-header—which sparked the riot—did not have racist or fascist overtones.[76] In his words, it was "a declaration of independence from the tyranny of sophistication."[77] Such a statement seems either naive or disingenuous. If he had no racial animus, many of his followers at Comiskey Park pointedly did. The African Ameri-cans at the park noted the crowd's undisguised loathing for them in Joey Garfield's 2016 short documentary *Disco Demolition: Riot to Rebirth*.

One of these Comiskey ushers, a black teenager named Vince Lawrence, was also a budding instrumentalist and would go on to be one of the found-ers of what would be called house music. In Garfield's documentary, Law-rence detailed the confrontations he had with the Demolition Night crowd. His life up to that point had been different in some ways from the lives of a previous generation of young African American musicians and all too famil-iar in other regards. Lawrence attended Lake View High School on the North Side, and *Star Wars* fascinated him as much as anything else. This was a time when the Illinois state government had attempted to force Chicago Public Schools to comply with its desegregation decrees.[78] The plan failed, in part because of white antagonism.[79] Lawrence experienced such hostility directly when he walked a friend home in Bridgeport. A white thug beat him up, and his attacker turned out to be the son of a policeman. In that instance, not a lot had changed since Lowrell Simon was chased through that same neighborhood in the early 1960s.

Lawrence used the money he received for dropping the charges against his assailant (after weighty pressure) to buy a synthesizer—an instrument that enthralled him during his teen years as part of Captain Sky Cameron's stage crew. The keyboard allowed him to take a disco bass line and extend it. A couple of years later, he and his DJ friend Jesse Saunders were on the cutting edge of house, which took its name from the near West Side Warehouse Club, where Frankie Knuckles had become entrenched. Their primary contribution to this movement was an extended record in F-major called "On and On." For nine minutes, a repeated motif compels dancers, while a spooky disembodied voice occasionally drifts in to laugh demonically and then exhorts everyone to "dance until the beat is gone." While minimalism reverberated throughout the twentieth century, tracks like these brought it to Chicago dance floors.[80] According to Feldman's widow, Nancy Feldman, during the early 1980s Lawrence and Saunders charmed Paragon Studios owner Marty Feldman into recording them and charging them a lower rate. Such casual negotiations eventually became unnecessary, as house became an international phenomenon.

Just as house's rhythmic foundation connects to funk, its development happened within a media and social infrastructure that had been a part of Chicago's black communities for decades. The Hot Mix 5 DJ team on WBMX disseminated the new music just as WVON had done a generation earlier.[81] Like Herb Kent's 1960s teen dances, the Chosen Few DJ group would spin records at the far South Side's Catholic Mendel High. The attendees also mirrored an earlier era—according to writer Michelangelo Matos, gang members danced alongside other kids.[82] Kent's self-reinvention also sparked this musical direction: after the veteran radio personality moved to WXFM in 1978, he played American and European new wave and dance tracks for his program *Punk Out*. Keyboardist Larry Heard, who crafted an ambient form of deep house under the name Mr. Fingers, paid close attention to Kent's inclusive playlist.[83]

For Frankie Knuckles, house arose as a deliberate reaction against Dahl's racism and the musical void such actions may have engendered. He expressed this in a 1990 *Chicago Tribune* interview with writer Greg Kot. "I watched that caper that Steve Dahl pulled at Disco Demolition Night and it didn't mean a thing to me or my crowd," Knuckles told Kot. "But it scared the record companies, so they stopped signing disco artists and making disco records. So we created our own thing in Chicago to fill the gap."[84]

As Knuckles stated, the aftermath of disco corresponded to a major demise of Chicago R&B recording. But there were other reasons for this descent. The industry was, as always, mercurial. A slump hit album sales in 1979, even as Michael Jackson's *Off the Wall* sold more than nine million copies.[85] The nationwide decline in independent black music retail stores as chains increased also hurt local shops during the early 1980s.[86] But overall, black popular music remained big business at this time, with sales exceeding $500 million annually in 1981 and every major label creating separate departments devoted to it.[87] Trade magazines like *Cash Box* credited the crossover success of the Jacksons and Earth, Wind, and Fire, but to reach middle America, these artists served corporations that had consolidated their businesses on the Coasts. Likewise, these imposing selling operations saw no need to connect with lingering small and autonomous distributors in the Midwest. Ironically, the kinds of Chicago producers and entrepreneurs who created the circumstances for such hugely popular soul acts to ascend had only slight access to this new economy.

So during the 1980s, for the most part the earlier generation's major Chicago R&B musicians and producers packed it in. Curtom closed in 1980 as Mayfield made the Atlanta suburbs his permanent home. Getting away from Great Lakes winters to raise his family on a sprawling southern estate contributed heavily to his decision.[88] Carl Davis tried to keep Chi-Sound going, telling *Cash Box* in 1981 that independent entrepreneurs would come back and his city would once more emerge as a recording center.[89] He shut everything down three years later.[90] Jerry Butler had left the record industry and started running the profitable South Side beer distributorship Iceman Beverage Company.[91]

Yet younger house musicians and entrepreneurs like Lawrence still capitalized on previous decades' institutions—from record hops to personalized distribution. And another musical development was just over the horizon. WJPC program hosts—Tom Joyner, LaDonna Tittle, BB D'Banana, and Richard Pegue—called themselves The J-P-C Gang and self-released a 45 called "Christmas Delight 80." The record was their rhyming over the rhythm track to the Sugarhill Gang's "Rapper's Delight." Licensing may have been cleared, or maybe not. Also about that time, Demetrice Cantrell (Sugar Ray Dinke) and his friends from Cabrini-Green engaged in rap battles against kids from other neighborhoods at CopHerBox II.[92] Back then, the music industry largely did not think hip-hop would be anything more than a brief novelty.

Early in the 1980s, black Chicago musicians and media also took up another cause when Congressman Harold Washington ran to become the city's first African American mayor. He was elected on April 12, 1983, after a contentious battle against the seemingly inexorable Democratic political machine, Republicans, and other strident white opposition.[93] This campaign had deep roots in black radio through WVON journalist Lu Palmer, who had supported Washington since his first run for mayor in 1977. Washington also reached out to artists in that initial run, bringing on Oscar Brown Jr. to serve as special events director.[94] Musicians made a more pronounced contribution to the later, victorious, campaign. Former bassist Charles Colbert Jr. drew on his skills as a performer and his knowledge of advertising to take a lead role in crafting radio jingles for voter registration drives. Many of those spots were recorded at Paragon, which Colbert knew from the early 1970s.

Other musicians devoted their time and effort to the campaign. Mayfield returned from Atlanta to headline a Washington campaign event at the University of Illinois–Chicago Pavilion in February 1983.[95] He also supported Washington as one of the few nonpoliticians included in a *Chicago Sun-Times* article naming candidates' prominent endorsers during the mayoral primary.[96] Gene Barge, an activist since his time with Operation Breadbasket, brought his eighteen-piece orchestra to play at rallies for no charge. Phil Cohran recalled performing at thirty-five functions for Washington, and Syl Johnson also raised money for the campaign. Black public spaces continued to serve a political function; Woods said Washington held several events at the CopHerBox II. Radio DJ–concert promoter Pervis Spann introduced Washington to Butler, who had the mayoral candidate come onstage at the Arie Crown Theater when the singer shared a bill with Aretha Franklin. Although these musicians did not work collectively during the 1983 race, their actions affirmed that artistic advocacy had not vanished during the post–civil rights era. If nothing else, these efforts added to the exuberant atmosphere of the campaign, a quality lacking in Washington's opponents in the primary and general elections.[97] Meanwhile, an anonymous racist flyer that circulated during the election snarled that Washington would rename the Chicago Transit Authority the Soul Train.[98]

When white aldermen picked up on that racism to block Washington's initiatives during the 1980s, these musicians recognized the situation. It was one that would be repeated on a larger scale. Twenty-five years later, Syl Johnson said of Washington's administration, "Racism really hurt his ability to govern. Which was dumb on [white alderman Ed] Vrdolyak's part. Like some stupid idiot Republicans."[99] An equally infuriated Butler ran for office and in 1986 was elected to the Cook County Board of Commissioners.

That transition from musical performance to governance succeeded because serving is what artists like Butler always did. They convinced people to listen soulfully and to believe in the progress that made the political ascendancy of Harold Washington possible. Despite bitter segregation and harsh economic distress, they met indifference head-on, and they cultivated an infrastructure that produced enduring music that paralleled and often reinforced political activism. Musicians and music teachers organized to fight for unionization and to become entrepreneurial themselves. Washington's campaign touched diverse impulses that had thrived in Chicago for more than two decades—from the Afrocentric vision Phil Cohran espoused to the integrationist ideal as expressed through Rotary Connection to the cooperative workshop Butler assembled.

Away from the spotlight, other musicians kept working and augmented their legacies in other ways. Barge continued in his role as mentor and elder statesman. Others remained engaged more formally as teachers. This effort was imperative, since early 1980s government cutbacks of public school funding impeded the ambitions of students seeking the experiences that had benefited earlier performers (a trend that still continues).[100]

James Mack had arranged Tyrone Davis's hit "Turning Point" in 1975 as well as numerous other records, but then he resumed his focus on composing and education. During the mid-1980s, Mack was scoring a piece for the Chicago Chamber Orchestra that would draw on African American folk themes as well as Catholic and Jewish liturgical music. His ideal was to create music that eclipsed any hint of racism. He also continued teaching at Loop College (before it was renamed after Harold Washington) and sounded ready to inspire a future generation. "When I was at Crane, I loved it because I was the only music teacher and I taught them everything that they learned about music from the beginning," Mack said. "It was a wonderful circumstance. It was like the old apprenticeship method of learning something, where you just did it, did it and did it."[101]

EIGHT

Future Telling:
Reissues, Sampling, and Young
Artists Reconsider Soul History

Chaka Khan had a busy Chicago weekend in July 2013. She performed a free concert at the city's downtown Millennium Park, discussed issues with civic organizers, and spoke at a celebration when a stretch of Blackstone Avenue on the South Side was renamed in her honor. Khan's former Hyde Park neighbors came out in force for the street sign's unveiling, as did local officials and activists. For Khan, the ceremony "was more for a blanket reception than an intimate reflection." A few months later she mentioned to me returning to the city and encouraging students to pursue law and business courses, noting that young singers now confront different challenges than she encountered.

Much of the younger generation's music would have been unimaginable when Khan grew up in the city, but a great deal of it descends from what she and her contemporaries created there in the 1960s and 1970s. Sun Ra, Phil Cohran, Willie Henderson, and Daryl "Captain Sky" Cameron were forerunners of Afrofuturism; nowadays a number of Chicago artists make this worldview a key component of their work.[1] Musicians decades ago fought for empowerment within a world of union jobs and record companies; in the twenty-first century they make legal cases for demanding sampling royalties. Independent reissue producers have shown that the music's history contains more depth than chart listings showed. These compilers also recognize the dignity that the people who made this history have earned. Like the music, social and political issues have endured or evolved. But what remains constant, and inspiring, is that a number of Chicago artists continue to address those concerns. Their demand for respect has never wavered.

Throughout the past decade, Chicago has continued celebrating soul culture. The city commemorated its role in originating *Soul Train* with a Millennium Park concert on September 5, 2011, featuring Don Cornelius, the

Impressions, the Emotions, and the Chi-Lites. Tom Tom Washington and Willie Henderson led the accompanying orchestra that night, with the same kind of verve they displayed in studios forty years earlier. In June 2017 the city also renamed a stretch of Elm Street by Cabrini-Green after Terry Callier, five years after he died. That was a quieter event than other celebrations, but the low-key nature fit the way Callier sang and lived.

Throughout the city, performers like singer Gerald McClendon and Richie Davis's Chicago Catz draw on the popular soul repertoire in club, festival, and private performances. Meanwhile, younger rap, R&B, and spoken-word artists in Chicago are seeking connections with that earlier generation while also establishing their own voices. David Weathersby's 2017 documentary *Got the Love* offers an overview of a resurgent acoustic soul scene featuring interviews with vocalists Tiaybe and Adam Ness. Another singer, Zeshan "Zeshan B" Bagewadi, blends that source material with his own sharp political statements as well as his parents' South Asian traditions.[2] Not just music, but other artistic manifestations of Chicago's soul culture from the 1960s and 1970s have been saluted nearly fifty years later, including the paintings of Kerry James Marshall and the Wall of Respect that was once near the Affro-Arts Theater.[3]

Still, with the former home offices of such companies as Vee-Jay–Brunswick being neglected to various degrees, questions remain as to how deep this appreciation may be. Numerous great musicians who worked on Record Row, like vocalist Marvin Smith, bassist Bernard Reed, and guitarist Larry Blasingaine (Larry Abdul Hakeem), sound strong yet frequently remain underappreciated. As hip-hop, trip-hop, and indie rock artists have sampled long-forgotten Chicago soul records, who profits remains speculative. Some of the results of musical samples have benefited legacy artists, other artists await their royalty checks. And the industry continues to be unsettled, perhaps in ways that will prove transformative. Whereas in the 1950s black teenagers walked down Record Row in hopes of a record deal, new worlds opened to their descendants in the city sixty years later: In February 2017, twenty-three-year-old Chicagoan Chance the Rapper (Chancelor Bennett) took home three Grammy awards for *Coloring Book*, a gospel-inspired CD he released independently.[4]

On Chance's victory day, Numero Group had also been nominated for two Grammys in historical packaging categories, and it was not the first time for the Chicago-based reissue company. Five years earlier it received similar recognition for its boxed set *Syl Johnson: Complete Mythology*.[5] Johnson enjoyed a higher profile as a result of the release, including being the subject of Rob Hatch-Miller's 2015 documentary *Syl Johnson: Any Way the*

Wind Blows. Nor is Johnson the only one who has benefited from such collections: the Notations celebrated their longevity in 2015 with the collection *Still Here, 1967–1973,* and artists like Renaldo Domino saw their long-lost singles become available on such compilations as *Eccentric Soul: Twinight's Lunar Rotation* (2006). All of this led to more performance opportunities for these artists. While major record companies have always mined their own catalogs for vintage material to repackage, Numero Group and Minneapolis-based Secret Stash (which reissued some of the One-derful catalog) mark a bottom-up approach to soul collectors. British and Japanese fans have promoted this music for years through their determined pursuits of vinyl.[6] That passion increased and spread with the rise of online shopping and auction sites. Another reason for these new appraisals of vintage R&B records from the array of small labels that proliferated in Chicago has been evolving aesthetics. People who grew up with the do-it-yourself model of punk rock and post-punk, for instance, find value in 45s cut spontaneously in small studios.

Rob Sevier and Ken Shipley, who founded Numero Group in 2003, represent a distinctive spin on this collectors' drive, as well as a contrast to an earlier generation of blues advocates who helped forge the history of that genre. Historian Marybeth Hamilton described Numero Group's antecedents in her 2008 book *In Search of the Blues.* As Hamilton depicts 1950s disputes, it was folklorists and collectors—not musicians and their initial audiences—who invented such terms as "Delta blues."[7] Yet even if those people may have been self-righteous outsiders, they were the ones who made Robert Johnson and Leadbelly recordings widely accessible. Amanda Petrusich considers similar issues in her 2014 book about 78 rpm record collectors, *Do Not Sell at Any Price.* In writing about the recent reissue labels Tompkins Square and Dust-to-Digital, Petrusich wonders how much "the urge to romanticize lost cultures" captured on old vinyl infects its analysis and presentation.[8] She also describes how archivists' backgrounds determine what music becomes valuable. Ultimately though, as Hamilton and Petrusich state, pivotal audio documents might not have been preserved without those advocates' efforts. The same could be said for soul music, even if its 45s and LPs were from not that long ago.

Both Sevier and Shipley acknowledge these precedents. But for them narratives matter, as their compilations also tell musical stories of New York punk and pop as well as music from 1970s Burkina Faso (Upper Volta). Rather than search for some kind of purity test through vinyl (as blues collectors did), several of the Numero Group releases represent a historical continuum, more a neglected culture than a lost one. Sevier said that while collectors to this day can be insular and focus on niches—be it psychedelic garage, rock, or northern soul—he and Shipley came up with the name Eccentric Soul to create a sense of inclusion through not focusing on genre. Also, as part of a living tradition, the company has presented its artists in concerts and made sure they receive proper royalties, which their predecessors tended not to make a priority. Another key difference from previous generations is that artist-entrepreneurs often control the music that turns up on Numero Group compilations. The Syl Johnson collection, for one, would not have happened had he not allowed his recordings to be released. Shipley added that while their company tries to sell music conscientiously, a broader mission was not part of this incentive. Sevier concurred.

"Once we figured out how this business worked, we wanted to provide the people with royalties and provide a deeper look into their lives and stories," Sevier said. "I think there are 1,400 payees we deal with. We didn't have any funding for a mission. We had the ability to put together a record, write the notes, and make good decisions of what it looks like. I wouldn't call the ability to sell the record and pay the people royalties a mission— that's being responsible within our limited means to people who made music that we like."

Hip-hop and sampling have shifted the perceived value of such records, in artistic and monetary terms, since the DJ culture that sustains the system has become global. A gratifying example of this international society is DJ-producer and former Chicagoan Theo Parrish's exultation at finding Numero Group's *Universal Togetherness Band* reissue in a 2016 promo video for California's Amoeba Records store.[9] A few minutes on the whosampled .com site demonstrates that 1960s and 1970s performers from this city are valued as much as their better-known contemporaries. Some of these DJs have taken tips from Charles Stepney and turned avant-garde compositional theory into popular records. Those ideas hew closely to Stepney's own. The New York-based hip-hop group a Tribe Called Quest's 1990s albums are a noteworthy case: its 1997 "I'm the Black Gold of the Sun" not only samples Rotary Connection's song but adapts its title. The experimental-on-a-budget aesthetic that Stepney brought to electronic music preceded the thinking behind early hip-hop DJs' turntable manipulations. Captain Sky's "Super Sporm" shows up in Public Enemy and Kendrick Lamar records; he also got namechecked in the Sugarhill Gang hit "Rapper's Delight." But a sample that is perhaps as well recognized as any entire song mentioned in this book is the horn arrangement in the Chi-Lites' 1970 "Are You My Woman (Tell Me So)," which became the foundation for Beyoncé's 2003 smash "Crazy in Love." Eugene Record received a writing credit on the Grammy-winning track—an award he never achieved with his famous group. He died from cancer two years later.

If and how these older artists (or their estates) are getting paid for their contributions to recent performers' recordings remains debatable. In that regard the music industry remains incorrigible. Communications studies professor Kembrew McLeod and legal scholar Peter DiCola weighed these issues in *Creative License: The Law and Culture of Digital Sampling.* As they state, questions of publishing and record company ownership, along with the issue of who can obtain legal representation, remain complicated.[10] They hold up Curtis Mayfield as an example of an artist who secured his own publishing early on and whose family continues to benefit from sampling income.[11] Captain Sky has also been polite but aggressive in his demands for compensation. Still, over the course of writing this book, I've visited brilliant artists who sorely needed these deserved payouts, despite the diligence of such attorneys as the late Jay B. Ross, who represented numerous Chicago R&B and house musicians in their financial claims.[12]

A couple of musicians who shaped Chicago soul in its earliest days have profited especially well from sampling. Then and now, they've always stood up for themselves. Johnny Pate composed soundtracks in the early 1970s, including *Shaft in Africa* from 1973; more than thirty years later, Jay-Z used its horn loop for his "Show Me What You Got," and Diddy employed the same track for "Press Play." As a result, Pate and his publishers got paid twice.[13] The walls in Syl Johnson's house on Chicago's Near South Side display gold- and platinum-certified albums from the R&B, rap, and rock musicians who have used sounds from his recordings to craft their own. Like Mayfield, Johnson had an ownership stake in his music. And he remained as crafty as he was industrious, as is borne out through a litany of tales involving his time as a sheriff's deputy in south suburban Harvey, Illinois, or as the owner of the Solomon's Fishery fast food restaurants.[14] Johnson's chasing down the hundreds who sampled his recordings required listening to sounds overheard on the street, legal persistence, and sometimes the assistance of those artists who were sampling him. Robert Fitzgerald Diggs— better known as RZA from the Staten Island hip-hop collective the Wu-Tang Clan—was one such example. The rapper, born in Brooklyn about the time *Is It Because I'm Black* was released, became conscientious about compensating the sources for his tracks, like "Hollow Bones." Johnson told the story as only he can.

> I tried to call RZA, never could reach him. But he finally called me and said, "Hey man, what's up? OK, my brother, this motherfucking lawyer of mine,

he's got a hotline to me, he's going to call you up and get this motherfucking shit straight. We're going to blow Syl Johnson to the motherfucking sky!" I said, "Thank you, sir." When he said, "We're gonna pay the fuck out of you," I called him Sir. I counted up, they did seventeen tracks. A whole lot of other tracks. First check came, it was 110 [thousand], they knocked it off to 90, and then they gave me 130 for [Johnson's lawyer]. They put the other money on seven tracks. OK, whatever. You know what I'm saying? The check came bigger than that check—Airborne Express. It came from RCA/Victor. The next came from, I read it right there, "Wu-Tang Productions." I looked, and I said, "I don't believe this check is going to be any good." So I got an eighteen-month CD with it. It didn't bounce, so after eighteen months I built this house.[15]

Johnson's success also came from his wits and his diligence. So did his ability to delve into issues affecting the city and the nation, as the enduring "Is It Because I'm Black" continues to prove. More than forty years later, Bardo Martinez of the Los Angeles group Chicano Batman hailed it as a defiant statement of identity.[16] That declaration shows that affinities between California-based Mexican Americans and classic midwestern soul singers have not ended since the Latino rock band Thee Midniters covered McKinley Mitchell's "The Town I Live In" in 1967.

Meanwhile, younger Chicago artists are responding to contemporary conflicts, some of them connected to that earlier era. The city remains largely segregated along racial lines, with large parts of the South and West Sides devoid of such necessities as healthy food options. Mayor Rahm Emanuel's appointed school board adopted a budget in August 2013 that, among other harms, sharply cut educational music programs.[17] That same year, his administration abruptly closed forty-nine public schools outright.[18]

One performer who reflects on such topics in Chicago is poet-singer Jamila Woods, who released her debut *HEAVN* in summer 2016.[19] This was when Black Lives Matter demonstrations responded to police killings and to presidential candidate Donald Trump's making her city a target of his bombastic racism. Her lyrics praise black womanhood and offer affirmations that transcend ongoing conflicts. While the electronic loops and samples may seem a far cry from the 1960s and 1970s Record Row arrangements, Woods's words would have been applauded in the Affro-Arts Theater.[20] She also displays a consciousness of her city's musical legacy in her verses; Woods's affectionate poem "Ode to Herb Kent" was published ten months before the radio legend's death in October 2016 at age eighty-eight.[21] Another impressive young R&B singer, Ravyn Lenae, performed at the Pitchfork Music Festival in July 2018 when she was nineteen (meaning that at the time research on this book began in earnest she would have been twelve). Her positive ethos and fluid high notes came across vividly on the song "Spice," which Lenae introduced with the shout-out "Any Caribbean girls in the crowd? Black girls, brown girls—yeah, this is for us!" The diverse audience cheered.

South Side-based rapper Che "Rhymefest" Smith also combines his art-istry with civic engagement. This included running for alderman of Chicago's Twentieth Ward in 2011 with a progressive platform including improving buildings' environmental impact and building healthy grocery options.[22] He also codirects the youth outreach initiative Art of Culture, Inc. While Rhymefest may be best known for his collaborations with former Chicago-ans Kanye West (on "Jesus Walks") and Common (on "Glory"), his own re-cordings, such as *Blue Collar* in 2006 (Allido/J-Records), provide more vivid narratives about life in the city he makes his home. At the time Rhymefest spoke with me from his house in the Chatham neighborhood, he expanded his palette to include an acoustic performance at the Hyde Park venue the Promontory. The following year, he performed at the 2017 Chicago Blues Festival in Millennium Park, where harmonica player–singer Billy Branch jammed with his group. Connecting the musical history and social history of the city remained on Rhymefest's mind. He focuses on developing smaller entrepreneurs who engage with a neighborhood, not unlike the indepen-dent record companies, distributors, and one-stops that once flourished south of the Loop, or, for that matter, echoing the time when Clarence Ludd allowed start-up shoe salesmen to set up their wares at the High Chaparral in the mid-1970s. As Rhymefest tells it, the ties between music, economics, and a shared culture formed a holistic sensibility.

> You start with community, everybody knows everyone, everybody can depend on everyone. It's like an economic cooperative, or cooperative economics. Community has that. I know where I'm going to order my next shipment from. You can build economics from community. From community comes economics. Once we are communally strong, then we can build our wealth. Once the wealth building is there, then we build our politics. What are our values? How do we cement our values and policies? From this community, from these economics, from these values, you have the subcultures of music and education—all these little things that accentuate and make it all strong and blend together.

Stepping back and discussing the role of musicians in all of this, Rhymefest added that his city's history provides examples who inspired his outlook. He mentioned Maurice White's spirituality as one and Mayfield's social consciousness as another. "They were living in the future," Rhymefest said of those artists. "You have to live tomorrow, you can't think today. If you really go into it, think about it, Curtis Mayfield was talking about the War on Drugs before there was a War on Drugs. And the real beauty is not the music, but the reflection of what it shows. I'm ready to get back to future telling."

ACKNOWLEDGMENTS

I am grateful to everyone who helped make this book a reality. All endeavors grow from communities as much as from individuals, and that is true with the terrific people on this team.

Everyone at the University of Chicago Press has my deep gratitude and admiration. I have been fortunate to write this book under the guidance of the brilliant editor Elizabeth Branch Dyson. She knew what I wanted to say, and her insights made the results better than I could have imagined. I've also relied on the sharp and enthusiastic Dylan Joseph Montanari, Alice Bennett, and Mollie McFee. The press's anonymous manuscript reviewers' suggestions improved the book, and they have my great thanks for their comments.

The National Endowment for the Humanities Public Scholar fellowship provided critical support for my research and writing. May this agency and the National Endowment for the Arts always continue to preserve and enrich American culture.

The more than a hundred people I interviewed generously shared their memories, and I can't thank them enough for their insights. I am honored that several of them have become my friends. Eleven have died since they offered me their stories, and I hope this book complements their families' memories. Many others are active performers. See them now.

A legion of friends and relatives offered needed advice, suggestions, introductions, connections, resources, and the occasional admonishment. Thanks for all of it go out to Francisco Arcaute, Jake Austen, Peter Berkowitz, Jonas Bernholm, Mitchell Bluitt, Rob Bowman, Rob Buerglener, Donald Burnside, John Ciba, Rodney Clark, Matthew Cohen, Mariama Cosey, Bill Dahl, Julio Davis, Matthew DeLeon, Andy Downing, Nancy Feldman, Garland Floyd, Joey Garfield, Travers Gauntt, Donald and Margaret Gay, Bob Gendron, Kevin Goins, Mark Guarino, Travis Jackson, Virginia Jahnke,

Earlene Jones, Robert Kendrick, E. Tammy Kim, Jason Koransky, Greg Kot, Jessica Linker, Mike Maggiore, Robert Marovich, Steve Marquette, Portia Maultsby, Curtis Mayfield III, John Murph, David Nathan, Brenda Nelson-Strauss, Jim and Susan Neumann, Raúl Niño, Marlyn Paul, Jeremy Perney, Zach Phillips, James Porter, Kenneth "Kip" Rainey, Guthrie Ramsey, Bill Randle, Howard Reich, Noah Schaffer, Mel, Sherie, and Helen Scheer, Evan Schofer, Paul Shanahan, Adam Shatz, Scott Sherman, RJ Smith, Richard Steele, Eddie and Verlene Thomas, Pat Thomas, Jack and Linda Vartoogian, Ivan Watkins, Lynn Orman Weiss, Stephan Wender, Chris Weston, Matt Weston, Jakobi Williams, Lois Wilson, Rick Wojcik, and Wolfie.

Michael Orlove listened as I initially brainstormed this idea, and his support has been crucial at every step. When Mike Reed gave his encouragement, I knew I had to keep on pushing. Arno Rotbart's judicious manuscript editing imparted the right kind of organizational challenges.

The best thing about social media is the Chicago Soul to Soul page on Facebook. Its leader, Gregory Moore, and the M-Squad team keep the musical discussions lively, informative, and often hilarious. Edward "Skipper" Keyes offered numerous contacts with musicians who deeply respect his longtime advocacy. I also admire Robert Pruter's groundbreaking work in this field and thank him for allowing me to use photos from his personal archive. Even though Thomas "Tom Tom" Washington declined to speak about his past, he allowed me to sit in on his South Side Big Band's rehearsals and showed kindness during a challenging time.

Several library employees assisted me as I conducted research. These included the staff of the Chicago Public Library, especially everyone involved with the Vivian G. Harsh research collection at the Carter G. Woodson regional branch, as well as the dedicated teams at the Conrad Sulzer regional branch and Harold Washington library center downtown. I also received help from the team at the Chicago History Museum and the Stony Island Arts Bank as I looked through its Johnson Publishing Archive and Frankie Knuckles Collection. As I traveled out of town, everyone at the Schomburg Center for Research in Black Culture, New York Public Library, and the Archives of African American Music and Culture, Indiana University, in Bloomington, Indiana, was equally conscientious.

The National Gallery of Art and the Smithsonian Institution's National Museum of African American History and Culture in Washington, DC, offered me platforms to talk about this book as it was being completed in 2017. A work-in-progress chapter also constituted my presentation at the Association for Recorded Sound Collections Conference, Indiana University, Bloomington, Indiana, in 2016.

Some top musicians and scholars helped immensely with discerning the technical sides to music making and expressing those details on the printed page, particularly Chris Greene, Charles Rumback, and Suzanne Wint.

My father, Sheldon Cohen, and my mother, Kayla Cohen, encouraged me to create the kind of book I wanted to write and gave me the fascination with history and the written word to make it happen. It's impossible for me to be more grateful to them.

All my forever love goes to my wonderful wife, Lavonne. She saved my life in more ways than one.

Interviews Conducted by the Author

Ron Alexenburg, July 13, 2014

Dan Alfano, March 31, 2016

Ruby Andrews, October 29, 2012, April 21, 2018

"Joshie" Jo Armstead, January 6, 2016

Gene Barge, September 10, 2013

Chuck Barksdale, October 7, 2016

Sidney Barnes, March 24, 2014

Ahmed Benbayla, November 13, 2015

Cicero Blake, April 11, 2016

Larry Blasingaine (Larry Abdul Hakeem), December 14, 2016

Byron Bowie, March 7, 2013

Elmer Brown, February 13, 2015

Donald Burnside, July 22, 2014

Thomas Burrell, May 18, 201

Jerry Butler, July 4, 2016

Terry Callier, January 1997

Daryl "Captain Sky" Cameron, April 7, 2015

Gene Chandler, March 11, 2016

Marshall Chess, March 21, 2014

Gavin Christopher, February 26, 2016

Otis Clay, December 2012

Linda Clifford, May 29, 2014

Kelan Phil Cohran, April 18, 2013, March 31, 2016

Charles Colbert Jr., April 21, 2014

Paul Coleman, April 18, 2016

Mitty Collier, June 29, 2016

General Crook, December 12, 2014

Cliff Curry, January 9, 2014

Helen Curry, June 29, 2016

Jack Daniels, March 23, 2015

Andrew Davis, August 17, 2017

George Davis, April 14, 2015

Richie Davis, March 2, 2016

Larry Dixon, May 11, 2018

Renaldo Domino, November 3, 2016

Patti Drew, April 28, 2017

Millard Edwards, August 23, 2016

Shelley Fisher, August 28, 2015

Emmett Garner, August 4, 2015

Rev. Donald Gay, June 5, 2014

Vernon Gibbs, November 29, 2016

Will Gilbert, October 7, 2014

Garland Green, June 8, 2016

Cecil Hale, March 30, 2016

Judy Hauff, June 19, 2015

Marv Heiman, November 25, 2013

Finis Henderson III, January 20, 2017

Willie Henderson, July 16, 2015

Art Hoyle, June 15, 2017

Elbert Hunter, March 25, 2015

Bobby Hutton, April 15, 2016

Don Jackson, April 6, 2016

Maurice Jackson, December 19, 2014

Chris James, January 12, 2017

Jay Johnson, January 22, 2014

Syl Johnson, January 2010, February 20, 2012

Melvyn "Deacon" Jones, January 9, 2016

Chaka Khan, September 28, 2013

Denise LaSalle, November 2013

Vince Lawrence, January 31, 2017

Eric Leaner, October 8, 2014

Benneth "Benny" Lee, May 26, 2016

Tim Long, October 4, 2014

Beverly Shaffer Longmire, October 8, 2014

Clarence Ludd, August 11, 2014

Elaine Mack, August 6, 2014

Hollee Thee Maxwell (Holly Maxwell), August 11, 2014

Gerald McClendon, March 9, 2014

Nadine McKinnor, March 17, 2017

Raynard Miner, January 24, 2017

Roscoe Mitchell, March 5, 2016

Anna Morris, June 27, 2016

Larry Nestor, May 26, 2016

Johnny Pate, August 29, 2013, February 29, 2016

Velma Perkins (Vee Allen), April 11, 2017

Eddie Perrell, August 6, 2015

Rollo Radford, July 29, 2015

Gus Redmond, September 10, 2014

Bernard Reed, February 25, 2013, October 24, 2015

Derf Reklaw (Fred Walker), March 7, 2016

Don Rose, July 15, 2014

Jackie Ross, June 8, 2015

Jay B. Ross, April 4, 2016

Rob Sevier, July 29, 2016

Marlena Shaw, August 26, 2013

Ken Shipley, July 29, 2016

Fred Simon, March 25, 2015

Lowrell Simon, June 25, 2015

Che "Rhymefest" Smith, March 30, 2016

Marvin Smith, March 30, 2015

Richard Steele, August 29, 2016

Morris "Butch" Stewart, June 10, 2015

Jackie Taylor, September 12, 2013

Larry Hill Taylor, April 28, 2016

Bobby Thomas, March 25, 2015

Eddie Thomas, July 29, 2014, July 14, 2015

Lowell Thompson, June 13, 2016

Marshall Thompson, August 5, 2015

Reginald Torian, July 24, 2014

Wanda Hutchinson Vaughn, July 14 and 15, 2015

Larry Wade, April 19 and 20, 2015

Shirley Wahls, June 24, 2016

Danae Williams, September 19, 2015

Willie Woods, July 20, 2016

Benjamin Wright, December 9, 2013

NOTES

INTRODUCTION

1. Historian Jeffrey Helgeson describes this attitude of black self-help among local politically focused organizations: "Even in the worst of times black Chicagoans generally responded not with resignation but with a commitment to the hard work of improving their quality of life and increasing their control over their everyday lives." *Crucibles of Black Empowerment: Chicago's Neighborhood Politics from the New Deal to Harold Washington* (Chicago: University of Chicago Press, 2014), 242.

CHAPTER ONE

1. Jerry Butler, *Only the Strong Survive: Memoirs of a Soul Survivor* (Bloomington: University of Indiana Press, 2004), 39. The singer's memoir suggests the date as sometime in March 1958, but it could have been earlier. Curtis Mayfield also related variations of this story to Michael McAlpin, Sue Cassidy Clark, and other journalists.
2. Robert Pruter, *Chicago Soul* (Urbana: University of Illinois Press, 1992), 3–5.
3. Curtis Mayfield interview, Michael McAlpin Collection.
4. Aaron Cohen, "History in a Boxed Set: New Release Celebrates African-American Owned Record Label Based Here," *Chicago Tribune*, December 23, 2007, retrieved from chicagotribune.com.
5. Mayfield's son, Todd Mayfield, doubts the spontaneity of this series of encounters, stating that entrepreneur Vi Muszynski had scheduled an April audition at Vee-Jay for the Impressions. Todd Mayfield with Travis Atria, *Traveling Soul: The Life of Curtis Mayfield* (Chicago: Chicago Review Press, 2016), 45. Todd Mayfield states that it was unlikely the group visited Chess, because Thomas had previously tried to interest that company in his group and was rejected. However, the insistent nature of teenagers suggests they might not have accepted just one rebuff. Adding to this complexity of events is that the Impressions recorded an earlier version of "For Your Precious Love" for Muszynski's tiny Bandera label, according to Bill Dahl's liner notes for *Birth of Soul*, special Chicago edition (Kent, 2009).
6. Historian Adam Green mentions Chicago's melding of musical idioms and rhythms in his *Selling the Race: Culture, Community, and Black Chicago, 1940–1955* (Chicago: University of Chicago Press, 2009). He emphasizes that new sounds were synthesized from older ones—like R&B coming from gospel—and combined with production structures to help create "what is perhaps black folk's most universally acclaimed modernism" (13).

7. Green also states that "lines of symbiosis" connected artists, producers, club owners, and audiences such that Bronzeville (as a neighborhood or as a signifier of black Chicago) controlled its own identity in the era just before the late 1950s. Green, *Selling the Race*, 80.

8. Butler, *Only the Strong Survive*, 24–28.

9. Jeffrey Helgeson, *Crucibles of Black Empowerment: Chicago's Neighborhood Politics from the New Deal to Harold Washington* (Chicago: University of Chicago Press, 2014), 195.

10. Isabel Wilkerson, *The Warmth of Other Suns* (New York: Vintage, 2011), 190.

11. Ibid., 262.

12. Ibid.

13. "CPS Stats and Facts," Chicago Public Schools website: cps.edu. Charter schools and private academies are not included in these statistics.

14. Dionne Danns, *Something Better for Our Children: Black Organizing in Chicago Public Schools, 1963–1971* (New York: Routledge, 2003), 26–27.

15. Leon Forrest, *Relocations of the Spirit* (Wakefield, RI: Asphodel Press, 1994), 49.

16. Howard Reich, "Walter Dyett: A Captain Courageous," *Chicago Tribune*, September 6, 1998, retrieved from chicagotribune.com.

17. Barbara R. Lundquist and Winston T. Sims, "African-American Music Education: Reflections on an Experience," *Black Music Research Journal* 16 (Fall 1996): 316–17.

18. Nancy MacLean, *Freedom Is Not Enough: The Opening of the American Workplace* (New York: Russell Sage Foundation, 2006), 28.

19. Roosevelt University website, roosevelt.edu.

20. John Evans, "Colleges Here to Enroll 90,000," *Chicago Daily Tribune*, September 19, 1954, 1.

21. Ibid.

22. "James Mack to Conduct UC Contemporary Choir," *Chicago Daily Defender*, September 26, 1968, 19.

23. Stepney's attending Roosevelt was mentioned in the liner notes to the Johnny Pate album *Jazz Goes Ivy League* (King, 1958), on which he plays vibraphone. At Wilson Junior College he conducted the dance band, as mentioned in the newspaper article "College Plans 3D 'Parade of Stars' Night," *Chicago Tribune*, November 15, 1953, SW_A16.

24. Curtis Mayfield to Sue Cassidy Clark, September 19, 1968. Sue Cassidy Clark Papers, Center for Black Music Research Library and Archives, Columbia College Chicago.

25. Butler, *Only the Strong Survive*, 11; Robert Pruter, *Chicago Soul* (Urbana: University of Illinois Press, 1992), 137.

26. Aaron Cohen, *Aretha Franklin's "Amazing Grace"* (New York: Bloomsbury, 2011), 20–27.

27. Wallace D. Best describes these complexities throughout an earlier era in *Passionately Human, No Less Divine: Religion and Culture in Black Chicago, 1915–1952* (Princeton: Princeton University Press, 2005).

28. From The Flamingos' official website, theflamingos.com, and the Rock and Roll Hall of Fame website, rockhall.com.

29. The Nation of Islam considers mathematics the highest meaning of Islam: noi.org.

30. Unsigned liner notes, Barbara Acklin, *Love Makes a Woman* (Brunswick, 1968).

31. Bill Dahl, liner notes, *The One-derful! Collection* (Secret Stash, 2014).

32. In 1967 Thee Midniters, a Mexican American rock group in East Los Angeles, covered Mitchell's song, and its popularity within that community attests to the universality of the migratory experience.

33. Andrew J. Diamond, *Chicago on the Make: Power and Inequality in a Modern City* (Oakland: University of California Press, 2017), 123.

34. Natalie Y. Moore, *The South Side: A Portrait of Chicago and American Segregation* (New York: St. Martin's Press, 2016), 49.

35. Ibid., 50.

36. Wendy Plotkin, "'Hemmed In': The Struggle against Racial Restrictive Covenants and Deed Restrictions in Post-WW II Chicago," *Journal of the Illinois State Historical Society*, Spring 2001, 57–61.

37. Diamond, *Chicago on the Make*, 127.

38. Roscoe Mitchell with the Art Ensemble of Chicago, Don Myrick with Earth, Wind, and Fire.

39. Neither Drew nor Chandler recalls any actual Latino membership in their gangs. They just liked the names.

40. Brian Ward, *Just My Soul Responding: Rhythm and Blues, Black Consciousness, and Race Relations* (Berkeley: University of California Press, 1998), 57–59.

41. Big Herm's served the same function when I hung out there as an eleven-year-old in 1980, but I did not attempt to sing.

42. Mike Lenehan, "Vocal History: Conversations with the Dells: 28 Years of Rhythm and Blues, from Doowop to Disco," *Chicago Reader*, November 14, 1980, 22.

43. Amy Absher, *The Black Musician and the White City: Race and Music in Chicago, 1900–1967* (Ann Arbor: University of Michigan Press, 2014), 72.

44. At the time I wrote this, psychology professor Angela Duckworth's *Grit: The Power of Passion and Perseverance* (New York: Scribner, 2016) was a best seller.

45. Musicologist Guthrie P. Ramsey Jr. refers to cultural critics Hazel Carby and Evelyn Brooks Higginbotham when he observes that the many voices from a city like Chicago reflected diverse subcultures rather than merely a multipronged response to established racial hegemony. *Race Music: Black Cultures from Bebop to Hip-Hop* (Berkeley: University of California Press, 2004), 23–24.

46. Ben Austen, *High-Risers: Cabrini-Green and the Fate of American Public Housing* (New York: HarperCollins, 2018), 38.

47. Leonard S. Rubinowitz and James E. Rosenbaum, *Crossing the Class and Color Lines: From Public Housing to White Suburbia* (Chicago: University of Chicago Press, 2000), 23.

48. D. Bradford Hunt, *Blueprint for Disaster: The Unraveling of Chicago Public Housing* (Chicago: University of Chicago Press, 2009), 92–93.

49. J. S. Fuerst, *When Public Housing Was Paradise: Building Community in Chicago* (Urbana: University of Illinois Press, 2005), 3.

50. Austen, *High-Risers*, 14.

51. *70 Acres in Chicago: Cabrini Green* (Ronitfilms, 2014). The documentary shows a photo of the Impressions, yet the names of musicians who were Cabrini residents are not mentioned.

52. Butler, *Only the Strong Survive*, 68.

53. Lynn Van Matre, "Mayfield: Films, Disks Get His Soul Support," *Chicago Tribune*, November 27, 1977, E3.

54. Fuerst, *When Public Housing Was Paradise*, 3.

55. Ibid., 6.

56. Austen, *High-Risers*, 28.

57. Allan H. Spear, *Black Chicago: The Making of a Negro Ghetto, 1890–1920* (Chicago: University of Chicago Press, 1967), 105.

58. Michael Winston, "Racial Consciousness and the Evolution of Mass Communications," *Daedalus*, 111 (Fall 1982): 177.

59. Susan J. Douglas, *Listening In: Radio and the American Imagination* (New York: Times Books, 1999), 224.

60. Clovis E. Semmes, *The Regal Theater and Black Culture* (New York: Palgrave Macmillan, 2006), 129.

61. Norman Spaulding, "History of Black Oriented Radio in Chicago, 1927–1963" (PhD diss., Communications Department, University of Illinois Urbana-Champaign, 1981), 71–73.

62. Mark Newman, *Entrepreneurs of Profit and Pride: From Black-Appeal to Radio Soul* (New York: Praeger, 1988), 142.

63. Vintage recordings of Al Benson's broadcasts appear on YouTube and other websites, although their provenance is questionable.

64. Spaulding, "History of Black Oriented Radio in Chicago," 124.

65. "Promises Good Music over WBEE," *Chicago Defender*, April 1, 1958, A8.

66. "Urban League Staffer WBEE Radio Guest," *Chicago Defender*, December 22, 1958, A21; "Radio Survey Shows Southsiders Choose Best Foods, Clothes," *Chicago Defender*, May 7, 1958, 17.

67. Mitty Collier's first appearance on the R&B charts was with "I'm Your Part Time Love" in 1963. Tony Rounce, liner notes, *Shades of Mitty Collier: The Chess Singles* (Kent, 2008).

68. Green, *Selling the Race*, 86.

69. Lucky Cordell interview, Michael McAlpin Collection.

70. Susan J. Douglas makes the salient point that song plugging and bribery became a law enforcement concern in the 1950s only because "it was undermining the hegemony of white, middle-class and upper-middle-class culture and economic interests and favoring black culture, working-class culture and youth culture." Douglas, *Listening In*, 251.

71. Terry Barnes, "Everyone Knows the Hits, but How about the Men behind Them?" *Billboard*, June 12, 1993, R16.

72. "Al Benson Sends Plane to Dixie," *Chicago Daily Defender*, February 23, 1956, 3. His use of "ironic" probably was meant to critique the United States government's lack of progress in fighting segregation while it sought to highlight human rights abuses in the Soviet bloc.

73. Spaulding, "History of Black Oriented Radio in Chicago," 80–81. More information about the Chez Paree's history is on its official website, chezpareechicago.com; Benson's advocacy is not mentioned on the site.

74. Bill Dahl, artist biography, allmusic.com. Dahl notes that Merriweather tried to record and perform after 1946, but the effects of the stroke were too severe and he died in 1953.

75. That's how it seemed when I visited the building. Of course, my imagination likely influenced my perception.

76. Leon Forrest, *Divine Days* (Chicago: Another Chicago Press, 1992), 1009.

77. Michael Ribas, "The Sounds of Vee-Jay," liner notes, *Vee-Jay: The Definitive Collection* (Shout Factory, 2007), 20.

78. Phil Upchurch's playing added strong resonance to Dee Clark's 1961 pop hit "Raindrops."

79. Robert Pruter, *Doowop: The Chicago Scene* (Urbana: University of Illinois Press, 1996), 1.

80. John Broven, *Record Makers and Breakers: Voices of the Independent Rock 'n' Roll Pioneers* (Urbana: University of Illinois Press, 2009), 15.
81. Ibid., 23.
82. Mike Callahan, "The Vee-Jay Story: Part One, Scenes from a Family Owned Company," *Goldmine*, May 1981, 6.
83. James B. Lane, "'Good Nite Sweetheart': Vivian Carter and Vee Jay Records," *Traces*, Winter 2011, 48.
84. Ewart Abner interview with Portia Maultsby, October 21, 1984, Indiana University.
85. Robert Pruter and Robert L. Campbell, "The Chance Label: Nexus of Doowop and Jazz," *Stop-Time!*, Center for Black Music Research, Columbia College Chicago, Fall 1999, 6.
86. Mike Callahan, "The Vee-Jay Story," *Goldmine*, May 1981, 7. The pawnbroker's name was Maurice Tepper, and those first records were four tunes by the Spaniels, who were also from Gary.
87. Music historian David Sanjek challenged the conventional notion of white record companies' carving up the independent market among themselves during the 1950s in "One Size Does Not Fit All: The Precarious Position of the African American Entrepreneur in Post–World War II American Popular Music," *American Music* 15 (Winter 1997): 538–39.
88. Herb Kent and David Smallwood, *The Cool Gent: The Nine Lives of Radio Legend Herb Kent* (Chicago: Lawrence Hill Books, 2009), 179.
89. Bruce Swedien, *Make Mine Music* (Milwaukee, WI: Hal Leonard Books, 2009), 34–38.
90. Greg Milner, *Perfecting Sound Forever: An Aural History of Recorded Music* (New York: Faber and Faber, 2009), 146.
91. "Disks and Tapes Boom Stereo Trade," *Chicago Daily Tribune*, October 12, 1958, SW_A8.
92. Ewart Abner interview with Portia Maultsby, October 21, 1984, Indiana University.
93. Broven, *Record Makers and Breakers*, 13.
94. Douglas, *Listening In*, 250.
95. Broadcast Music, Incorporated, website, bmi.com.
96. Hilda See, "New Writers Invade Rhythm, Blues Field as Pix Okay New Tune Style," *Chicago Defender*, March 12, 1955, 7.
97. Ibid.

CHAPTER TWO

1. "'Duke of Earl' Hits Million Record Sales," *Chicago Daily Defender*, April 2, 1962, 16.
2. Fred Goodman, "The Windy City's Leading Independent," *Cash Box*, May 30, 1981, SBM-22.
3. Pruter, *Chicago Soul*, 58.
4. Ibid., 59–60.
5. Ewart Abner interview with Portia Maultsby, October 21, 1984, Indiana University.
6. Douglas, *Listening In*, 242–46.
7. Motown released Marv Johnson's "Come to Me" on January 21, 1959. *The Complete Motown Singles*, vol. 1, *1959–1961* (Motown/Hip-O Select, 2004).
8. Butler, *Only the Strong Survive*, 49–50.
9. When Butler was reminded that such reggae musicians as Bob Marley would go on to cite Mayfield as their primary inspiration, he quietly responded, "You take some, you give some."
10. Helgeson, *Crucibles of Black Empowerment*, 164–65.

11. Neal Samors, *Chicago in the Sixties: Remembering a Time of Change* (Chicago: Chicago's Books, 2006), 276.
12. "Vee-Jay Boss Joins Urban League Board," *Chicago Defender*, July 9, 1962, 17.
13. That same year, Atlantic released the compilation album *Jamaica Ska* (thanks to Heather Augustyn for making that point). Epic Records released *The Real Jamaica Ska* in 1964; Carl Davis and Curtis Mayfield are listed as its producers.
14. Dungill Family Papers, Vivian G. Harsh Research Collection, Carter G. Woodson Branch, Chicago Public Library.
15. Peter Jones, "Betty Everett: At Last Betty Hits Our Charts," *Record Mirror*, January 15, 1965, retrieved from rocksbackpages.com. Her version of "Getting Mighty Crowded," written by Van McCoy, proved durable in England; Elvis Costello reinterpreted it in 1980 on his *Get Happy!!!* album (Columbia).
16. Bob Spitz, *The Beatles* (New York: Little, Brown, 2005), 389.
17. Ray Brack, "Vee Jay Returns to Chi. Roost: Aims Sights at 'Great Heights,'" *Billboard*, October 23, 1965, 3.
18. "Government Slaps Liens on Vee Jay Materials in L.A.," *Billboard*, October 23, 1965, 3.
19. *Record Row: Cradle of Rhythm and Blues* documentary (WTTW, 1997).
20. Allan Kozinn, "Ewart Abner, Jr., 74, President of Motown Label," *New York Times*, January 12, 1998, retrieved from nytimes.com.
21. Peter Guralnick, *Dream Boogie: The Triumph of Sam Cooke* (New York: Little, Brown, 2005), 330.
22. Agnes R. Smith, "Curtis Mayfield Puts on a Business Suit," *Sepia*, September 1977, 30–33.
23. Liner notes, *People Get Ready! The Curtis Mayfield Story* (Rhino Records, 1996).
24. "Columbia Men to New Posts," *Billboard*, October 16, 1961, 3.
25. Carl H. Davis Sr., *The Man behind the Music* (Matteson, IL: Life to Legacy, 2009), 34.
26. "'Marketable' Formula Proves OK in Okeh's Bid for Buildup," *Billboard*, February 13, 1965, 40.
27. A number of sources analyze Mayfield's guitar playing. Michael Ross's article "Forgotten Heroes: Curtis Mayfield," *Premier Guitar*, October 6, 2014, retrieved from premierguitar.com, includes a helpful brief instructional on the best way to try reproducing his approach.
28. Sue Cassidy Clark Papers, Center for Black Music Research Library and Archives, Columbia College Chicago.
29. Liner notes, *People Get Ready! The Curtis Mayfield Story* (Rhino Records, 1996).
30. The Library of Congress's including "People Get Ready" in its National Recording Registry on March 23, 2016, is one of many examples of its recognition in terms of the civil rights movement: loc.gov/today/pr/2016/16–056.html.
31. Gail Schechter, "The North Shore Summer Project," in *The Chicago Freedom Movement: Martin Luther King Jr. and Civil Rights Activism in the North*, ed. Mary Lou Finley et al. (Lexington: University Press of Kentucky, 2016), 166.
32. *The Murder of Fred Hampton* (1971, Howard Alk, director). Jakobi Williams's history of the Illinois Black Panther Party, *From the Bullet to the Ballot* (Chapel Hill: University of North Carolina Press, 2013), describes the spurious nature of the charges against Hampton for stealing ice cream.
33. Andrew Young's comments are included on the documentary *Movin' On Up: The Music and Message of Curtis Mayfield and the Impressions* (Reelin' in the Years, 2008).
34. Ward, *Just My Soul Responding*, 13–14.
35. Clark Walker, "History of Local 208 and the Struggle for Racial Equality in the

American Federation of Musicians," *Black Music Research Journal* 8 (Autumn 1988): 208.

36. Fred Farrar, "Chicago No. 1 Spot for Do-Re-Mi Boys," *Chicago Tribune*, October 15, 1962, C6.

37. "Hire Negroes to Help Merge Music Unions," *Chicago Tribune*, June 21, 1963, A2.

38. Absher, *Black Musician and the White City*, 121–23.

39. Ibid.

40. Plan of Merger of Chicago Federation of Musicians, Local 10 of AFM with Musicians' Protective Union, Local 208 of AFM, April 1, 1964, Charles Walton Papers, Chicago Public Library, Carter G. Woodson branch.

41. "Two Ministers Fight to Control Radio Station," *Chicago Defender*, July 17, 1948, 8.

42. "New Station WVON Aimed at Negro Market Debuts Monday," *Chicago Defender*, March 30, 1963, 10.

43. Nick Biro, "R&B Roundup," *Billboard*, June 1, 1963, 24.

44. Bob Hunter, "WVON New King of Chicago Radio Says Hooper," *Chicago Defender*, September 21, 1963, 10.

45. Biro, "Chicago Radio: Kings Remain Assumptive; Heirs Presumptive," *Billboard*, March 28, 1964, 12.

46. Jennifer Searcy describes such inventive engineering in "The Voice of the Negro: African American Radio, WVON, and the Struggle for Civil Rights in Chicago" (PhD diss., Loyola University Chicago, August 2013), 76–77.

47. Nadine Cohodas, *Spinning Blues into Gold: The Chess Brothers and the Legendary Chess Records* (New York: St. Martin's Press, 2000), 217–18.

48. Ibid.

49. Pervis Spann, with Linda C. Walker, *The 40 Year Spann* (Chicago: National Academy of Blues, 2003), 17

50. This source will remain anonymous.

51. This is a different source, who will also remain anonymous.

52. "Race Relations to Be Analyzed Weekly on WVON," *Chicago Defender*, April 24, 1963, 5.

53. "WVON Donates $2,000 to Ala. Victims," *Chicago Defender*, May 7, 1963, 16.

54. Brian Ward, *Radio and the Struggle for Civil Rights in the South* (Gainesville: University Press of Florida, 2004), 127.

55. James Allen, "Reader Places Thumbs Down: WYNR, WVON," *Chicago Defender*, February 22, 1964, 9.

56. Historian George Lipsitz mentions this process nationwide in *Time Passages: Collective Memory and American Popular Culture* (Minneapolis: University of Minnesota Press, 1991), 116–17.

57. While Johnson's account of his life story includes no small amount of mythmaking, the biographical account that constitutes Ken Shipley's liner notes to the aptly titled boxed set *Syl Johnson: Complete Mythology* (Numero Group, 2010) is reliably cross-checked with other data.

58. Pruter, *Chicago Soul*, 152.

59. Bob Mehr, "The Godfather of King Drive," *Chicago Reader*, April 21, 2005, retrieved from chicagoreader.com.

60. The compilation *Eccentric Soul: The Bandit Label* (Numero Group, 2004) showed that while the company was not upstanding, many of its singles from groups like the Majestic Arrows are a lot of fun. These are also early examples of the work of excellent musical arranger Benjamin Wright.

61. "The Need to Produce," *Ebony*, June 1961, 70.

62. Ibid.

63. "Park Manor Unit to Meet Tonight," *Chicago Defender*, June 6, 1960, A8.

64. "Scene in Boycott Hq.: Hope, Anxiety, Elation," *Chicago Defender*, February 27, 1964, 15.

65. Ethan Michaeli, *The "Defender": How the Legendary Black Chicago Newspaper Changed America* (New York: Houghton Mifflin Harcourt, 2016), 377–89.

66. Bob Hunter, "WVON New King of Chicago Radio Says Hooper," *Chicago Defender*, September 21, 1963, 10.

67. Dionne Danns writes about mid-1960s Marshall student protests in "Chicago High School Students' Movement for Quality Public Education, 1966–1971," *Journal of African American History* 88 (Spring 2003): 138–50.

68. "Young Troupers Make Hit Debut," *Ebony*, May 1963, 156–61.

69. Ibid., 157.

70. Ramsey, *Race Music*, 77.

71. Arthur Kempton, *Boogaloo: The Quintessence of American Popular Music* (Ann Arbor: University of Michigan Press, 2005), 364. The book's title comes from a 1965 Chicago record by the duo Tom and Jerrio.

72. Michaeli, *"Defender,"* 377–89.

73. Unsigned album liner notes, Alvin Cash and the Registers, *Twine Time* (Mar-V-Lus, 1965).

74. Untitled photo caption, *Chicago Defender*, January 2, 1965, 16.

75. Along with Kempton, Malcolm Baumgart and Mick Patrick make this claim in their liner notes to Jackie Ross's *Jerk and Twine: The Complete Chess Recordings* (Kent, 2012).

76. Kent and Smallwood, *Cool Gent*, 122.

77. Marc Clemens, "Teens: Point of View, an Editorial," *Chicago Defender*, October 13, 1962, 16.

78. "Tony Visconti on Recording *The Gouster* and *Young Americans*," liner notes, David Bowie, *Who Can I Be Now? [1974–1976]* (Parlophone Records, 2016).

CHAPTER THREE

1. Davis, *Man behind The Music*, 82.

2. Earl Calloway, "Carl Davis, Producer of Talent on the Go and Rising," *Chicago Defender*, October 16, 1969, 19.

3. Recording Industry Association of America Certifications, riaa.com.

4. Ibid.

5. "Carl Davis Is Brunswick V.P.," *Cash Box*, February 28, 1970, 10.

6. In newspaper articles during the early and middle 1960s, Crane Junior College's address was listed as 2250 West Van Buren Street. Later in the decade the campus address was cited as about one block north at 2245 West Jackson Boulevard. Now named Malcolm X College, its address is 1900 West Jackson.

7. Lillian Calhoun, "Chicago Schools Rewrite Bible: 'Suffer, Children; Come to Me,'" *Chicago Defender*, October 21, 1964, 4.

8. Ibid.

9. James Mack interview with Bill Dahl, mid-1980s.

10. "James Mack and City College Teachers Awarded Ford Grant," *Chicago Defender*, August 19, 1969, 11.

11. James Mack interview with Bill Dahl, mid-1980s.

12. Caspar Melville, liner notes, the Pharaohs, *In the Basement* (Luv 'n' Haight, 1997).

13. Maurice White with Herb Powell, *My Life with Earth, Wind and Fire* (New York: Amistad, 2016), 37–38.

14. Arthur Siddon, "Crane Tunes Curriculum to Fit City's Job Market," *Chicago Tribune*, February 11, 1965, W2.

15. Ibid.

16. "Winning a War," *Ebony*, May 1963, 112.

17. Charles L. Hughes, *Country Soul: Making Music and Making Race in the American South* (Chapel Hill: University of North Carolina Press, 2015), 60.

18. Indeed, when writer Nelson George addressed them in *The Death of Rhythm and Blues* (New York: Pantheon, 1988), he suggested that such debates hadn't gone away decades later.

19. Clovis E. Semmes, "The Dialectics of Cultural Survival and the Community Artist: Phil Cohran and the Affro-Arts Theater," *Journal of Black Studies* 24 (June 1994): 449.

20. Mary Lou Finley, Bernard Lafayette Jr., James R. Ralph Jr., and Pam Smith, eds., *The Chicago Freedom Movement* (Lexington: University Press of Kentucky, 2016), 26.

21. Ronald E. Shaw, "A Final Push for National Legislation: The Chicago Freedom Movement," *Journal of the Illinois State Historical Society* 94 (Autumn 2001): 318.

22. Michaeli, *"Defender,"* 404.

23. "30,000 Hear Dr. King at Soldier Field Rally," *Chicago Defender*, July 11, 1966, 3.

24. Bernadine C. Washington, "King's Dream Shared by Thousands," *Chicago Defender*, July 16, 1966, 18.

25. Michaeli, *"Defender,"* 417.

26. Ward speculates on this in *Just My Soul Responding*, 331.

27. Nelson George, *The Hippest Trip in America: "Soul Train" and the Evolution of Culture and Style* (New York: William Morrow, 2014), 7.

28. Ibid., 9.

29. Christopher P. Lehman, *A Critical History of "Soul Train" on Television* (Jefferson, NC: McFarland, 2008), 18–19.

30. Jennifer Medina, "When the Music Stopped for Don Cornelius," *New York Times*, March 9, 2012, retrieved from nytimes.com.

31. Susan Gregory, *Hey, White Girl!* (New York: W. W. Norton, 1970).

32. Although not an immediate hit, the Ivories' 1967 single "Please Stay" (Wand) would become sought by British "Northern Soul" record collectors twenty years later.

33. For instance, the line "move up a little higher" in "Keep On Pushing" may have derived from William H. Brewster's 1940s gospel hit, "Move On Up a Little Higher." Robert Marovich describes the earlier song's trajectory in his 2015 book *A City Called Heaven: Chicago and the Birth of Gospel Music* (Urbana: University of Illinois Press, 2015).

34. Sadly, Griffin's potential was never fully realized: he died in a car crash along with bassist Leonard Brown and guitarist Joe Thomas while touring with the Impressions that spring. Dave Potter, "Sad Impressions Go into Seclusion: Rock Stars Here Mourn Musicians," *Chicago Defender*, May 11, 1968, 1.

35. Craig Werner, *Higher Ground: Stevie Wonder, Aretha Franklin, Curtis Mayfield and the Rise and Fall of American Soul* (New York: Crown, 2004), 140.

36. Earl Ofari, "Curtis Mayfield: A Man for All People," *Soul Illustrated*, Summer 1972, 20.

37. In 2017 Gregory Moore posted on the Chicago Soul to Soul Facebook page a WLS weekly playlist from June 16, 1967. Of the forty acts listed, only five were R&B (including Dionne Warwick, who some would contend was a pop singer). The number two song that week was Music Explosion's "Little Bit of Soul," a fitting title.

38. "Impressions' Tune, 'We're a Winner' Stirs Racial Fuss," *Jet*, February 15, 1968, 58–59.
39. Ibid.
40. Liner notes, *People Get Ready! The Curtis Mayfield Story* (Rhino, 1996).
41. Arnold Shaw, *The World of Soul* (New York: Cowles, 1970), 88. Shaw was not the only white critic at the time who attacked black R&B personages deemed too upwardly mobile. In Detroit, White Panther radical John Sinclair frequently derided Motown founder Berry Gordy, whom he considered exploitative; Stuart Cosgrove, *Detroit 67: The Year That Changed Soul* (Edinburgh: Polygon, 2016), 14.
42. Michael Haralambos, *Soul Music: The Birth of a Sound in Black America* (New York: Da Capo Press, 1974), 125.
43. Michael Alexander, "The Impressions," *Rolling Stone*, December 27, 1969, 29.
44. Lara Langer Cohen and Jordan Alexander Stein, eds., *Early African American Print Culture* (Philadelphia: University of Pennsylvania Press, 2012), describes the history of African Americans in this industry.
45. Albert Murray, *The Omni-Americans: Black Experience and American Culture* (New York: Da Capo Press, 1990), 61.
46. "Curtis Mayfield Has Own Label," *Soul*, April 22, 1968, 1.
47. Earl Ofari, "Curtis Mayfield: A Man for All People," *Soul Illustrated*, Summer 1972, 20.
48. Mayfield, Sue Cassidy Clark interview, September 19, 1968, Sue Cassidy Clark Papers.
49. Liner notes, The Five Stairsteps and Cubie, *Our Family Portrait* (Buddah Records, 1967).
50. Keni Burke interview with Bob Abrahamian, June 14, 2009, retrieved from sittinginthepark.com.
51. Also, Caribbean sounds had been at least an understated presence within American popular music throughout the twentieth century.
52. "New Faces to Watch: Keni Burke," *Cash Box*, June 27, 1981, 8.
53. Emily J. Lordi, *Donny Hathaway Live* (New York: Bloomsbury Academic, 2016), 25.
54. Mayfield, Sue Cassidy Clark interview, September 19, 1968, Sue Cassidy Clark Papers.
55. Werner, "Curtis Mayfield," *Goldmine*, July 4, 1997, retrieved from rocksbackpages.com.
56. Sel Yackley, "The Sound: Music and Radio for Young Listeners," *Chicago Tribune*, February 13, 1968, B7.
57. Jon Savage, *1966: The Year the Decade Exploded* (London: Faber and Faber, 2015), 242.
58. Ibid., 246.
59. Malcolm Baumgart and Mick Patrick, liner notes, Jackie Ross, *Jerk and Twine: The Complete Chess Recordings* (Kent, 2012). As their notes also state, *Billboard* had suspended its R&B charts at this time.
60. "R&B Sells 40% in UK," *Soul*, November 24, 1966, 10.
61. "SBA Raises Direct Loans Ceiling to $100,000," *Chicago Defender*, September 10, 1966, 31.
62. "Small Business Loans up to $25,000 Now Available," *Chicago Defender*, December 31, 1966, 21.
63. Mary Smith, "Big Boost for Small Business," *Ebony*, September 1968, 76–87.
64. "Five Here Get $25,000 in Loans from SBA," *Chicago Defender*, May 8, 1965, 4.
65. "Superachiever Barbara Proctor," sellingpower.com.
66. Johnson has given different answers about his ownership role in Twinight to me and various other journalists, so as the liner notes to Syl Johnson, *Complete Mythology* (Numero Group, 2010), state, the musician's ownership percentage in the company remains unknown.

67. Rob Sevier, Ken Shipley, and Tom Lunt, liner notes, *Eccentric Soul: Twinight's Lunar Rotation* (Numero Group, 2006).

68. The sales number comes from Ryan Boyle's liner notes to the Notations, *Still Here, 1967–1973* (Numero Group, 2015); Chart position from "Best Selling Soul Singles," *Billboard*, December 19, 1970, 36.

69. Pruter, *Chicago Soul*, 178.

70. Jim Bessman, "Armstead Remains 'Red Hot,'" *Billboard*, October 1, 2005, 67.

71. Andrews's "Casanova" reached number nine on the *Billboard* R&B singles chart (September 23, 1967, 34).

72. "Best Selling Soul Singles," *Billboard*, September 6, 1969, 46; Pruter, liner notes, Garland Green, *The Very Best of Garland Green* (Kent Records, 2008).

73. Unfortunately, as Armstead later told Christian John Wikane, she wound up losing the masters during the 1990s in a bad business deal with the record label Collectibles. But not being one to take a punch, by 2017 she had regained them. Christian John Wikane, "The Brill Building, Broadway, and Beyond: R&B and Soul Singer-Songwriter Joshie Armstead," *Pop Matters*, September 11, 2017, retrieved from popmatters.com.

74. "Chess Developing $1.5 Million Recording Center at New Chi HQ," *Cash Box*, March 18, 1967, 7.

75. Ibid.

76. Sam Sutherland, "Maurice White: From Sessionman to Producer," *Record World*, January 7, 1978, 36.

77. Cohodas, *Spinning Blues into Gold*, 200–203.

78. In *My Life with Earth, Wind and Fire*, White posits that he took center stage in protesting directly to Leonard Chess (46). Cohodas writes that both White and Satterfield refused to punch a clock (225–26). Either way, this was an example of younger musicians' feeling a growing empowerment.

79. Cohodas, *Spinning Blues into Gold*, 225–26.

80. That song was adapted from Barge's 1961 instrumental with the Church Street Five, "A Night with Daddy 'G.'" Daddy G became Barge's own nickname when Bonds namechecked him in his hit.

81. According to Barge's interview with Allegra Moore, this was a rally that Chicago civil rights organizations put together in support of their schools campaign. Gene Barge with Allegra Malone, "Music and the Movement II," in *Chicago Freedom Movement*, 350.

82. Pete Cosey interview with Joan Richards, WNUR-FM, May 7, 1983.

83. Michael McAlpin Collection, Archives of African American Music and Culture, Indiana University, Bloomington.

84. Nearly forty years later, Barack Obama used Wilson's version of "Higher and Higher" during his 2008 presidential campaign and victory rallies.

85. Bass's opinions on this issue were included in her conversation with Michael McAlpin.

86. This cars-for-royalties practice is depicted in the 2008 dramatic film about Chess, *Cadillac Records*. But this movie's accounts are dubious, since several people who worked at the company pointed out the film's inaccuracies and fabrications.

87. Cohodas, *Spinning Blues into Gold*, 239.

88. Broven, *Record Makers and Breakers*, xi.

89. Davis, *Man behind the Music*, 77–82.

90. The link between Brunswick and organized crime may have been alluded to in an episode of the television drama *The Sopranos* when New Jersey gang boss Tony Soprano

overhears the Chi-Lites' "Oh Girl" playing in a locker room and identifies the song and its record company during a conversation. YouTube.com.

91. Davis, *Man behind the Music*, 93. "Dakar" is a mashup of Davis's first and last name and was not intended as a tribute to the Senegalese city.

92. Information from the late Sonny Sanders's LinkedIn page at linkedin.com.

93. I will describe the Acklin-Record ascendancy in more detail in chapter 6.

94. Robert Pruter, "Barbara Acklin," *Goldmine*, July 1983, 169.

95. William K. Defossett Jr., "From a Young Point of View," *New York Amsterdam News*, March 8, 1969, 29.

96. Pruter, "Barbara Acklin," 170.

97. Recording Industry Association of America, riaa.com. Eldee Young's or Red Holt's actual participation on this recording will always be subject to dispute. Young died in 2007.

98. Jake Austen, "The Jackson Find," *Chicago Reader*, September 10, 2009, retrieved from chicagoreader.com.

CHAPTER FOUR

1. George Lewis, *A Power Stronger Than Itself: The AACM and American Experimental Music* (Chicago: University of Chicago Press, 2008), 51.

2. June Sawyers, "The Main Streets of Old Town," *Chicago Tribune*, July 5, 1991, F20.

3. Nyala Joan Smith Cooper, "Rebel Worker about Change: Person to Nation," in *Rise of the Phoenix: Voice from Chicago's Black Struggle, 1960–1975* (Chicago: Third World Press Foundation, 2017), 165–66.

4. Paul Gapp, "Wells Street," *Chicago Tribune*, July 28, 1974, 37.

5. Michael Simmons, "Michael Bloomfield: Who Is That Guitar Player?," liner notes to Michael Bloomfield, *From His Head to His Heart to His Hands* (Sony Music, 2014), 14. Bloomfield's own blues-rock guitar playing became legendary, and he also covered Curtis Mayfield's "Man's Temptation" on the Bloomfield, Al Kooper, Steve Stills album, *Super Session* (Columbia, 1968).

6. Ibid.

7. Austen, *High-Risers*, 54–55.

8. "The Low Down," *Chicago Defender*, September 25, 1965, 27.

9. "It's Love, Love, Love!," *Ebony*, July 1967, 100.

10. Donald R. Hopkins, "In the 'Now' Generation," *Ebony*, August 1967, 111–15; "The Hippies of Hashberry," *Ebony*, August 1967, 116–20.

11. Pruter, *Doowop*, 177–78.

12. Marv David, liner notes, Willie Wright, *I'm on My Way* (Argo, 1963).

13. Will Hodgkinson, "Terry Callier," *Guardian*, October 15, 2004. retrieved from theguardian.com.

14. Different sources offered diverging reasons for the delay.

15. Jimmy Collier with Allegra Malone, "Music and the Movement I," in *Chicago Freedom Movement*, 328.

16. Margalit Fox, "Billy Davis, Who Developed Iconic TV Ads, Dies at 72," *New York Times*, September 10, 2004, retrieved from nytimes.com.

17. Absher, *Black Musician and the White City*, 80–81.

18. Edwin Black, "For the Record: Charles Stepney," *DownBeat*, November 26, 1970, 12.

19. Ibid.

20. Murray, *Omni-Americans*, 141.

21. Lewis, *Power Stronger Than Itself*, 58–59.
22. Aaron Cohen, "The Faces of Chicago Soul: Compilations, Reissues Attest to the City's Vibrant 70s Scene," *Chicago Tribune*, June 10, 2007, retrieved from chicagotribune.com.
23. In 1974, when Marshall Chess was serving as president of Rolling Stones Records, he brought Roland Binzer on board to complete the concert documentary *Ladies and Gentlemen: The Rolling Stones*. Vicki Hodgetts, "Ladies and Gentlemen: The Rolling Stones," *Rolling Stone*, May 9, 1974, retrieved from rollingstone.com.
24. Mary Merryfield, "Are Hippie Motives Love or Fear?," *Chicago Tribune*, July 23, 1967, sec. 5, 4.
25. Bob Lucas, "Minnie Riperton," *Ebony*, December 1976, 34; "Former Rotary Connection Star Joins Comedian Kirby," *Chicago Defender*, December 8, 1970, 11.
26. Penny Valentine, "Minnie Riperton: Perfect Angel in Flight," *Sounds*, April 12, 1975, retrieved from rocksbackpages.com.
27. Lynn Norment, "Minnie Riperton: 'Perfect Angel' Leaves Legacy of Love," *Ebony*, October 1979, 95.
28. Chris Charlesworth, "Minnie Riperton," *Melody Maker*, April 12, 1975, retrieved from rocksbackpages.com.
29. Michaeli, "*Defender*," 420–21.
30. Robb Baker, "Records with a Rock: The Vanilla Fudge Shatters a Credo," *Chicago Tribune*, March 10, 1968, N11.
31. Will Leonard, "Soulful Strings Fill Room with People, Music," *Chicago Tribune*, June 23, 1968, N13.
32. Baker, "Take It from the Top, Group!," *Chicago Tribune*, October 27, 1968, E1.
33. Baker, "Bright Future for Local Group," *Chicago Tribune*, October 10, 1968, B22.
34. Ron Schlachter, "Ward's Boycotts Cadet's 'Peace,'" *Billboard*, December 14, 1968, 3.
35. Cohodas, *Spinning Blues into Gold*, 295–96.
36. Kevin Le Gendre, *Soul Unsung: Reflections on the Band in Black Popular Music* (Sheffield, UK: Equinox, 2012), 200.
37. "Rock Star Baby Huey Found Dead," *Chicago Tribune*, October 29, 1970, B18. Jones disputes this article's statement about the choir, saying he does not recall Huey's singing in that school vocal ensemble.
38. Baker, "Teens Dance Almost Everywhere," *Chicago Tribune*, April 16, 1967, M1.
39. Pruter, *Chicago Soul*, 304.
40. "Gordon High Plans 'Super Soul Dance,'" *Chicago Tribune*, March 16, 1969, NW8.
41. Baker, "Calm Vibrations at Rock Festival," *Chicago Tribune*, April 27, 1970, B16.
42. "Indiana Rites for Baby Huey Rock Musician," *Chicago Tribune*, October 30, 1970, C14.
43. "Best Selling *Billboard* Soul LPs," *Billboard*, May 8, 1971, 41.
44. Lenny Kaye, "Baby Huey: The Baby Huey Story: The Living Legend," *Rolling Stone*, April 15, 1971, retrieved from rocksbackpages.com.
45. This information is from Paragon session logs that the late Marty Feldman's wife Nancy Feldman kindly shared with me.
46. Samors, *Chicago in the Sixties*, 223.
47. Ollan Christopher Bell [Chris James], *Music Saved My Life: From Darkness into the Light* (n.p.: Ollan Christopher Bell, 2017), 93.
48. Album review, *Billboard*, September 11, 1971, 21.
49. Earl Calloway, "Stars Add Color to Billiken Parade: Stardom," *Chicago Defender*, August 13, 1975, 18; Calloway, "A Boss Time at 'Soul Explosion '75,'" *Chicago Defender*, April 21, 1975, 20.

50. Lynn Van Matre, "Music: The Beach Boys: Still Surfin' in the '70s," *Chicago Tribune*, August 18, 1972, B8; the *Chicago Seed* office address was listed on the newspaper's masthead.

51. Those sessions would come out in 2016 on a CD, *Hidden Stash*, on Anthem of the North Records.

52. Back cover advertisement, *Chicago Seed*, vol. 5, no. 6 (June 1970).

53. Stephan Benzkofer, "1970 rock concert at Grant Park was a true riot fest," *Chicago Tribune*, July 25, 2015, retrieved from chicagotribune.com.

54. Timothy White, "Elton John: The *Billboard* Interview," *Billboard*, October 4, 1997, EJ-8.

55. whosampled.com.

56. Lynn Van Matre, "A Show That Is Saturated with Soul," *Chicago Tribune*, January 8, 1973, C13.

CHAPTER FIVE

1. Gwendolyn Brooks's poem is titled "Two Dedications, II: The Wall August 27, 1967." chicagofilmarchives.org.

2. "Mecca for Blackness," *Ebony*, May 1970, 96.

3. Paul Gilroy, *The Black Atlantic: Modernity and Double Consciousness* (Cambridge, MA: Harvard University Press, 2002), 76.

4. Howard Reich, "Phil Cohran, Influential Chicago Composer-Bandleader, Dies at 90," *Chicago Tribune*, June 29, 2017, retrieved from chicagotribune.com.

5. White, *My Life with Earth, Wind and Fire*, 66.

6. Maurice White once said dismissively of Sun Ra, "I saw him in Chicago. He had a light on top of his head. I thought he was crazy." Richard Williams, "Earth, Wind & Fire: Flying Sorcerers," *Melody Maker*, February 25, 1978, retrieved from rocksbackpages.com. But Chaka Khan fondly recalled seeing the Art Ensemble of Chicago as a teenager and referred to the group as "my boys."

7. Bill V. Mullen, *Popular Fronts: Chicago and African-American Cultural Politics, 1935–46* (Urbana: University of Illinois Press, 2015), 75.

8. Ibid., 83.

9. John F. Szwed, *Space Is the Place: The Life and Times of Sun Ra* (New York: Da Capo, 1997), 50, 66.

10. These singles and the stories behind them are included in the two-disc set, Sun Ra, *The Singles* (Evidence, 1996).

11. Baker E. Morten, "5,000 Hear Muhammad," *Chicago Defender*, March 5, 1960, 2.

12. "Etta Moten Brings Africa to Chicago," *Ebony*, May 1961, 100.

13. "Ahmad Jamal's Alhambra Supper Club Is New Concept in Nightspots," *Ebony*, October 1961, 53–58.

14. Ibid.

15. Clovis E. Semmes, "The Dialectics of Cultural Survival and the Community Artist: Phil Cohran and the Affro-Arts Theater," *Journal of Black Studies* 24 (June 1994): 450.

16. Ibid., 451.

17. Lewis, *Power Stronger Than Itself*, 96–98.

18. The Miles Davis album *Dark Magus* (Columbia, 1977), which was recorded at New York's Carnegie Hall on March 30, 1974, shows Pete Cosey's contributions to the trumpeter's band.

19. Phil Cohran, "The Spiritual Musician," unpublished manuscript, December 1965, Leonard Wash Papers, Vivian Harsh Collection, Carter G. Woodson Branch, Chicago Public Library.

20. "Cohran 'Keeps It Cool,'" *Chicago Defender*, August 24, 1967, 18.

21. Semmes, "Dialectics of Cultural Survival and the Community Artist," 456.

22. Mary Pattillo, *Black on the Block: The Politics of Race and Class in the City* (Chicago: University of Chicago Press, 2007), 70.

23. Ibid., 72–74.

24. Larry Neal, "Any Day Now: Black Art and Black Liberation," *Ebony*, August 1969, 54.

25. Margo Natalie Crawford, "Black Light on the Wall of Respect: The Chicago Black Arts Movement," in *New Thoughts on the Black Arts Movement* (New Brunswick, NJ: Rutgers University Press, 2006), 23. Patrick T. Reardon, "Chicago's 'Wall of respect' Inspired Outdoor Tributes across U.S.," *Chicago Tribune*, July 30, 2017, sec. 1, 21.

26. Crawford, "Black Light on the Wall of Respect," 24–25.

27. "Ali Visits New Afro-Arts Theater," *Chicago Defender*, January 2, 1968, 10.

28. Danns, *Something Better for Our Children*, 81. According to Danns, between 27,000 and 35,000 students citywide participated in the boycott.

29. Neal, "Any Day Now," 58.

30. The Soul Messengers' R&B recordings and story were collected for the CD *Soul Messages from Dimona* (Numero Group, 2008); Fran Markowitz describes the faith's adherents in "Israel as Africa, Africa as Israel: 'Divine Geography' in the Personal Identity of the Black Hebrew Israelites," *Anthropological Quarterly* 69 (October 1996): 193–205.

31. Naturally a single was attached to the dance, the Five Du-Tones' "The Woodbine Twine" (One-derful, 1965).

32. Historian George Lipsitz mentions a similar acculturation process in his 1991 book *Time Passages*. He describes how California-based Chicano bands like los Lobos featured the folkloric accordion and guitarron within a rock 'n' roll context. They were using such instruments to define their identity as both open-ended and rooted in specific traditions. *Time Passages: Collective Memory and American Popular Culture* (Minneapolis: University of Minnesota Press, 1991), 152. The Pharaohs, among others, applied the same way of thinking to their use of African percussion.

33. Paul Steinbeck, *Message to Our Folks: The Art Ensemble of Chicago* (Chicago: University of Chicago Press, 2017), 176.

34. Michael Bourne, album review, *DownBeat*, August 17, 1972, 26.

35. Ibid.

36. Williams, *From the Bullet to the Ballot*, 62–63.

37. Jakobi Williams's book provides ample details about these events surrounding Hampton's killing, especially government agencies' surveillance of the Black Panthers.

38. "New Afro-Arts Theatre to Open on Southside Dec. 1," *Chicago Defender*, November 28, 1967, 5.

39. Jimmy Collier with Allegra Malone, "Music and the Movement I," in *Chicago Freedom Movement*, 330.

40. Donald Mosby, "Westside Gang Plans Business Ventures: Vice Lords Set Investment Program," *Chicago Defender*, April 4, 1968, 1.

41. James Porter, "Oscar Brown Jr.," *Flying Saucers Rock 'n' Roll* (Durham, NC: Duke University Press), 25.

42. Howard Reich, "Chicago Jazz Artists Address Violence Head-On," *Chicago Tribune*, November 11, 2016, retrieved from chicagotribune.com.

43. Mayfield, *Traveling Soul*, 217.

44. David Johnson, "Black P Stone Nation: America's Toughest Black Gang," *Sepia*, April 1971, 18.

45. The liner notes to the 2010 reissue of Lou Bond's self-titled 1974 album, *Lou Bond (Light in the Attic)*, do not mention Bond's gang activities but state that he had a troubled upbringing in Chicago and that much of his life story remained mysterious. In a 2010 interview posted on the *Light in the Attic* website, Bond credited Barnes for introducing him to Jimmy Webb's songs (blog.lightintheattic.net/r-i-p-lou-bond/). Bond died in 2013.

46. Barbara Reynolds, "You'd Never Believe He Was a Cop," *Ebony*, July 1969, 106.

47. Rev. Jesse Jackson had brought Ben Branch to Memphis to perform at a meeting that night in the midst of that city's sanitation workers' strike.

48. Marshall Frady, *Martin Luther King, Jr.: A Life* (New York: Penguin Books, 2006), 204.

49. Michaeli, "*Defender*," 444–45.

50. Robert M. Marovich, *A City Called Heaven: Chicago and the Birth of Gospel Music* (Urbana: University of Illinois Press), 312.

51. *Cliff Kelley Show*, WVON 1690 AM, July 8, 2015.

52. Kent and Smallwood, *Cool Gent*, 146.

53. "Affro-Arts Theater Stalled in Bid for License," *Chicago Defender*, August 11, 1968, SC_A4.

54. "King's Death Sparks a Package by Chess," *Billboard*, May 18, 1968, 3.

55. I am grateful to Jonas Bernholm for emailing me a recently revised and translated version of his diary, which is the text I'm referring to here.

56. Williams, *From the Bullet to the Ballot*, 58–59.

57. Ibid.

58. *The Essence of Fred Hampton: An Attempt to Capture the Spirit of a Young Man Who Influenced So Many and to Pass It on to Those Who Didn't Have the Opportunity to Meet Him* (Chicago: Salsedo Press, 1989), 52. Not every copy of this booklet includes Tyrone Davis's account. I'm grateful to Jakobi Williams for sending me this page. Davis's reserved attitude toward politics is recounted in the article "Tyrone Davis: Upstairs Partner," *Soul*, April 7, 1969, 12.

59. Numero Group reissued *Boscoe* on CD in 2007, and detailed information about the group is in the liner note booklet by Judson Picco, Rob Sevier, and Ken Shipley.

60. Mitchell Duneier, *Ghetto: The Invention of a Place, the History of an Idea* (New York: Farrar, Straus and Giroux, 2016), 82–84.

61. Marovich, *City Called Heaven*, 313–14.

62. Doug McAdam, *Political Process and the Development of Black Insurgency, 1930–1970* (Chicago: University of Chicago Press, 1982), 203.

63. Hans J. Massaquoi, "Elijah Muhammad: Prophet and Architect of the Separate Nation of Islam," *Ebony*, April 1970, 78–79.

64. D. Bradford Hunt details the Robert Taylor Homes' severe structural flaws and inadequacies in housing families with large ratios of children to adults during the 1960s and 1970s in *Blueprint for Disaster*, 155–57.

65. Austen, *High-Risers*, 53.

66. Sudhir Alladi Venkatesh, *American Project* (Cambridge, MA: Harvard University Press, 2000), 17.

67. franksmasonryinc.com.

68. Austen's beautifully written *High-Risers* is the most recent, and most heartbreaking, account of life in Cabrini-Green.

69. Marvin Gaye's *What's Going On* was released on May 21, 1971, and Sly Stone's *There's a Riot Goin' On* was completed in September of that year.

70. Harold M. Barger, "Political Content of Black Newspapers, Chicago and Nation, 1969–1970" (PhD diss., Political Science Department, Northwestern University, 1971), 153.

71. Helgeson, *Crucibles of Black Empowerment*, 199.

72. Simeon B. Osby, "Ask Hanrahan to Resign," *Chicago Defender*, May 20, 1970, 1.

73. Earl Calloway, "Wright Arranges for the Dells," *Chicago Defender*, March 11, 1974, 10.

74. "Earth, Wind and Fire Elements of an Unusual Group," *Soul*, October 11, 1971, 13.

75. Lewis, *Power Stronger Than Itself*, 461.

76. "Conservatives Sing for Theatre Benefit," *Chicago Defender*, February 28, 1970, 16. The group later recorded for Memphis-based Hi Records under the somewhat appropriate name Teacher's Edition.

77. Ron Chepesiuk, *Black Gangsters of Chicago* (Fort Lee, NJ: Barricade Books, 2007), 175.

78. Ibid., 198–99.

79. Lewis discusses this debate in terms of Amiri Baraka, sociologist E. Franklin Frazier, and the AACM in *Power Stronger Than Itself*, 206–14.

80. Ben Ratliff provides an insightful description of how Mayfield's tenor/falsetto voice and guitar tone affect listeners throughout this performance in *Every Song Ever: Twenty Ways to Listen in an Age of Musical Plenty* (New York: Farrar, Straus and Giroux, 2016), 65–66.

CHAPTER SIX

1. Bob Fisher, "The Chi-Lites," *New Musical Express*, February 22, 1975, retrieved from rocksbackpages.com.

2. Richard Pegue, "Richard Pegue's Chicago," *Soul*, November 6, 1972, 8.

3. Robert C. Smith, "The Changing Shape of Urban Black Politics: 1960–1970," *Annals of the American Academy of Political and Social Science* 439 (September 1978): 17.

4. Ibid.

5. Emily J. Lordi offers enlightened analyses of Hathaway's albums throughout her *Donny Hathaway Live* (New York: Bloomsbury Academic, 2016).

6. These musicians included guitarist Phil Upchurch, drummer Morris Jennings, saxophonist Don Myrick, and tuba player Aaron Dodd.

7. Patricia Krizmis, "Negro's Business, Culture Show Keeps Crowd of 100,000 Buzzing," *Chicago Tribune*, October 4, 1969, N14.

8. Ibid.

9. Diamond, *Chicago on the Make*, 59.

10. "Three Shows Offered at Black Expo," *Chicago Tribune*, November 14, 1970, W5.

11. Chester Higgins, "Black Expo Boasts Pride, Progress," *Jet*, November 26, 1970, 12.

12. Marshall Frady, *Jesse: The Life and Pilgrimage of Jesse Jackson* (New York: Random House, 1996), 264–66.

13. "Black Expo," *Ebony*, December 1969, 112.

14. Gene Barge with Allegro Malone, "Music and the Movement II," in *Chicago Freedom Movement*, 347.

15. Ibid.

16. "Black Expo Comes of Age," *Ebony*, December 1971, 68.

17. "Quincy and Cannonball Lead Confab on Black American Music at Dunbar," *Chicago Defender*, November 10, 1970, 11.

18. Paramount released *Save the Children* in 1973, and Motown issued its soundtrack that year. Despite receiving positive reviews from such critics as Gene Siskel in the *Chicago*

Tribune and A. H. Weiler in the *New York Times*, the film has since fallen out of circulation. Ownership rights issues involving the music and performances are likely the reason.

19. "Gary Coalition Holds Black Business Fair," *Chicago Defender*, September 14, 1970, 14.

20. "Complete Schedule of Black Political Parley," *Chicago Defender*, March 9, 1972, 2.

21. "Blacks Map National Political Strategies at Convention in Gary," *Jet*, March 16, 1972, 6.

22. Ward, *Just My Soul Responding*, 388–89.

23. Bernard E. Garnett, "Soul Radio *Must* Serve Community Needs," *Billboard*, August 22, 1970, 14.

24. Those artists with soul chart placement on page 13 in the August 22, 1970, issue of *Billboard* included Tyrone Davis, the Dells, the Impressions, and Jerry Butler.

25. Curtis Mayfield, "A Whole New Thing," *Billboard*, August 22, 1970, 16. But Mayfield may also have been prescient: his friend Major Lance's daughter, Keisha Lance Bottoms, was elected mayor of Atlanta on December 5, 2017. On her website she notes that her father "left Chicago in the 1960s and moved back to the deeply segregated south because of the potential for excellence he saw in this city" (keishalancebottoms.com).

26. When asked about that article's headline sixteen years later, Butler quipped, "Did I spell it correctly?"

27. Butler expressed no ill will toward Gamble and Huff, since their issue was not getting paid sufficiently from Mercury; G. Fitz Bartley, "Jerry Butler . . . the Survivor," *Soul*, August 14, 1972, 4. He wound up recording for their Philadelphia International company in the 1970s.

28. Pruter, *Chicago Soul*, 297.

29. Earl Calloway, "Recordings and Stuff," *Chicago Defender*, August 17, 1974, A13.

30. Norman Jopling, "The Iceman Talking: The Life and Times of Jerry Butler," *Creem*, June 1973, retrieved from rocksbackpages.com.

31. "Chicago to Build a Creative Soul Center," *Billboard*, August 22, 1970, 20.

32. Lacy J. Banks, "Jerry Butler: The Anti-perspirant Iceman," *Black Stars*, August 1972, 26.

33. ASCAP website, ascap.com/press/2014/1203-top-holiday-songs-100-years; pitchfork.com.

34. Hank Fox, "Chess to Be Sold to GRT," *Billboard*, November 2, 1968, 1.

35. "Broadened Musical Scope of Chess Underscored in New Product Sounds," *Cash Box*, January 24, 1970, 9.

36. Earl Paige, "Chess Steps Up Chicago Set Up—'Refine' Shipping Operations," *Billboard*, August 1, 1970, 4.

37. "Dells to Aid Black Composers," *Soul*, June 2, 1969, 1.

38. *Billboard* website, billboard.com/artist/399697/dells/chart.

39. Wade is listed as "Al Wade" on the album's credits because "L. Wade" was misheard in a telephone conversation in the Chess office.

40. Reklaw said all these sessions were completed within one week.

41. Tony Rounce, liner notes, the Independents, *Just As Long: The Complete Wand Recordings, 1972–74* (Kent, 2016). This Chuck Jackson is not the singer by that same name who recorded such hits as "Any Day Now" for Wand.

42. Steve Guarnori, *Scepter Wand Forever!* (Stephen Guarnori, 2016), 420.

43. "Fountain of Life Fund Drive Ends with Music, Song," *Chicago Defender*, April 18, 1964, 15.

44. Pruter, *Chicago Soul*, 339.

45. Pruter, "The Independents: The Chuck Jackson and Marvin Yancy Jr. Brainchild," *Goldmine*, January 15, 1988, 16.

46. As seen on YouTube.

47. Simon Reynolds describes and analyzes this nostalgia trend within rock music in his *Retromania: Pop Culture's Addiction to Its Own Past* (New York: Farrar, Straus and Giroux, 2011).

48. Jean Williams, "Production Team Won't Switch Over," *Billboard*, December 4, 1976, 26.

49. Ibid., 299.

50. riaa.com.

51. These recordings included Simtec and Wylie's relentlessly funky 1971 album *Gettin' over the Hump*, which also used Evans's arrangements.

52. Carl Davis, *Man behind the Music*, 100–101.

53. Ibid. Also, journalist Fred Goodman contended that once Dakar had substantial hits with Tyrone Davis, Brunswick demanded a taste of that success, and the deal was made for that reason. Goodman, "The Windy City's Leading Independent," *Cash Box*, May 30, 1981, SBM-22.

54. Loop College at 30 East Lake Street was renamed in 1987 to honor Chicago mayor Harold Washington.

55. Indeed, Daniels's story about this affair is too tangled for the scope of this book.

56. Ed Ochs, "Soul Sauce," *Billboard*, November 6, 1971, 32.

57. The Lost Generation's Fred Simon confirmed that Quinton Joseph played in this unusual position while at Brunswick.

58. When Alonzo Tucker (Mister T), covered "Love Uprising" on Dakar a few years later, his spoken introduction calling for putting down guns clarified the message. It's one that remains relevant.

59. I am indebted to Suzanne Wint for her transcription and perspective on this track. And it says a lot for Bernard Reed that Wint—a classical flutist and music professor—considered taking up the bass after hearing him.

60. Searcy, "Voice of the Negro," 287.

61. These included the Chicago-based WGRT as well as suburban WBEE (in Harvey, Illinois), WMPP (Chicago Heights, Illinois), and WOPA (Oak Park, Illinois). "Soul Radio Stations," *Billboard*, August 16, 1969, S-30.

62. Faith C. Christmas, "Pact Makes WVON jockeys 'Highest Paid,'" *Chicago Defender*, February 16, 1971, 2.

63. Ibid.

64. Dan Kening, "Yvonne Daniels, 'First Lady of Radio,'" *Chicago Tribune*, June 23, 1991, retrieved from chicagotribune.com.

65. Pruter, liner notes, *South Side Soul Survey* (Soulscape Records, 2007).

66. "Youth Action Aired on WGRT," *Chicago Defender*, July 6, 1968, 15.

67. "Charlie Cherokee," *Chicago Defender*, July 17, 1972, 5.

68. Jesse Louis Jackson, "'Country Preacher' on the Case," *Chicago Defender*, June 12, 1971, 11.

69. Ibid.

70. "John Johnson buys WGRT," *Chicago Defender*, October 18, 1972, 2. I will address WJPC in the next chapter.

71. Ellis Cashmore, *The Black Culture Industry* (London: Routledge, 1997), 51.

72. Earl Paige, "Black Artists Find a Home on Jukeboxes in White Neighborhoods," *Billboard*, January 29, 1972, 42.

73. Ibid.

74. Ibid.

75. For example, during the late 1950s, Department of Justice special prosecutor Richard B. Ogilvie announced his federal investigation of gangsters and extortion within the Chicago jukebox industry. Sandy Smith, "Jury Probe of Juke Mob to Open Here," *Chicago Tribune*, February 24, 1959, 1. Reading newspaper reports from the ensuing decades indicates that, if anything, such prosecutions just drove the associations further underground.

76. Kerry Segrave, *Jukeboxes: An American Social History* (Jefferson, NC: McFarland, 2002), 304–5.

77. Ibid.

78. US Department of Housing and Urban Development website (hud.gov); Gary Puckrein, "Moving Up," *Wilson Quarterly* 8 (Spring 1984): 75.

79. "Will the Suburbs Beckon?," *Ebony*, July 1971, 112.

80. Moore, *South Side*, 162. In 2016 the city had 762 homicides, an alarming number, yet still considerably fewer than in the early 1970s. Katherine Rosenberg-Douglas and Tony Briscoe, "2016 Ends with 762 Homicides; 2017 Opens with Fatal Uptown Gunfight," *Chicago Tribune*, January 2, 2017, retrieved from chicagotribune.com.

81. Semmes, *Regal Theater and Black Culture*, 4.

82. Ibid., 8–9.

83. African American studies professor Mark Anthony Neal states that, nationwide in the 1970s, "the dance hall represented one of the primary institutions which attracted the black middle class to the very urban spaces that they abandoned." Neal, *What the Music Said: Black Popular Music and Black Public Culture* (New York: Routledge, 1999), 120.

84. Angela Parker, "The Soul Scene—South and West," *Chicago Tribune*, August 13, 1971, sec. 2, 9.

85. Ibid.

86. "Charlie Cherokee Says," *Chicago Defender*, August 31, 1970, 5.

87. Parker, "Soul Scene—South and West." Also, Carl Davis alludes to his underworld connections as helping him establish and control his club. Davis, *Man behind the Music*, 102–3.

88. Maureen O'Donnell, "Barbara Trent Balin, 1929–2014, Ran West Side Club Peppermint Lounge," *Chicago Sun-Times*, December 22, 2014, 42.

89. "Stars Perform for Guys and Gals Club," *Chicago Defender*, February 28, 1973, 10.

90. "'New Image' in WCIU-TV's Future," *Chicago Defender*, May 2, 1967, 9.

91. Ibid.

92. WTTW website, interactive.wttw.com/a/chicago-stories-jim-tilmon.

93. Christopher P. Lehman, *A Critical History of "Soul Train" on Television* (Jefferson, NC: McFarland, 2008), 13.

94. Ibid., 14–15.

95. Ibid., 18.

96. [No title], *Chicago Defender*, August 5, 1969, 14. Unfortunately, the article did not reveal what Cornelius's comments were.

97. Jake Austen, "'Soul Train' Local," *Chicago Reader*, October 2, 2008, retrieved from chicagoreader.com.

98. George, *Hippest Trip in America*, 9.

99. Don Cornelius, interview with Andy Downing, August 2011.

100. As Austen and Lehman state, Cornelius's associate Clinton Ghent hosted a Chicago version of *Soul Train* that ran concurrently with the national broadcast until June 11, 1976.

101. "'Soul Train' Is Great: Goes National," *Chicago Defender*, November 1, 1971, 10.

102. Kathryn Sederberg, "Syndicated 'Soul Train' Heads down TV Track to Young, Black Market," *Advertising Age*, February 7, 1972, 34.

103. George, *Hippest Trip in America*, 16.

104. Joseph P. Cahill, "Debt Swipes Star Who Beat the Odds," *Crain's Chicago Business*, September 16, 1995, retrieved from chicagobusiness.com; Advertising Hall of Fame website (advertisinghall.org); "Vince Cullers Advertising," *Advertising Age*, September 15, 2003 (advertisingage.com).

105. Susannah Walker, "Black Dollar Power: Assessing African American Consumerism since 1945," *African American History since World War II* (Chicago: University of Chicago Press, 2009), 388.

106. White, *My Life with Earth, Wind and Fire*, 71.

107. Marilyn Kern-Foxworth, *Aunt Jemima, Uncle Ben, and Rastus: Blacks in Advertising, Yesterday, Today, and Tomorrow* (Westport, CT: Praeger, 1994), 116.

108. Ibid., 132.

109. Jason Chambers, *Madison Avenue and the Color Line: African Americans in the Advertising Industry* (Philadelphia: University of Pennsylvania Press, 2008), 206–7.

110. Ibid.

111. Allan Jaklich, "Black Ad Market Is Gray Area," *Chicago Tribune*, June 25, 1970, D10 (yet another unfortunate headline from this period).

112. Lynn Taylor, "Black Ad Agencies Look to the Future," *Chicago Tribune*, February 23, 1972, C12.

113. "Vince Cullers Advertising," *Advertising Age*, adage.com website.

114. Edwin Henry, "Hair: The Quickest Way to Make a Million in the Business World," *Sepia*, April 1971, 63–68.

115. Patrick Salvo, "'Soul Train': Television's Most Successful Black Show," *Sepia*, August 1976, 38.

116. "Vince Cullers Advertising," *Advertising Age*, adage.com website.

117. Chambers, *Madison Avenue and the Color Line*, 245–46.

118. "Top Ten International Billings" and "Agency Profiles," *Advertising Age*, February 22, 1972, 40, 45.

119. "Burrell Communications Group," *Advertising Age*, adage.com.

120. Kern-Foxworth, *Aunt Jemima, Uncle Ben, and Rastus*, 140.

121. Two accounts of advertisers co-opting the general counterculture in the 1960s are Thomas Frank's *The Conquest of Cool* (Chicago: University of Chicago Press, 1997) and the fictional HBO television series *Mad Men*, which ran from 2007 to 2015.

122. As of 2017, that commercial's appearance on YouTube yielded a wide array of comments—some derisive, others admiring.

123. Leninka Cruz, "'Dinnertimin' and 'No Tipping': How Advertisers Targeted Black Consumers in the 1970s," *Atlantic*, June 7, 2015; Chris Bodenner, "When Do Multicultural Ads Become Offensive? Your Thoughts," *Atlantic*, June 22, 2015, both retrieved from theatlantic.com.

124. This clip was included in Raoul Peck's 2016 documentary about Baldwin, *I Am Not Your Negro*.

CHAPTER SEVEN

1. "Curtis Mayfield's 33rd Birthday Party," *Black Stars*, September 1975, 72–74. Mayfield was born on June 3, so the event was likely held on or around that date.

2. The Recording Industry Association of America certified gold status (500,000) sales of

Super Fly on September 7, 1972. Mayfield's 1970 album *Curtis* received this designation on June 6, 1973, and his 1973 album *Back to the World* also achieved it on that date. riaa.com.

3. James P. Murray, "Dollars Flow Fast for Black Superstars . . . and Many Retire, or Die with Only Pennies," *New York Amsterdam News*, March 29, 1975, D12.

4. Alex Poinsett, "Annual Progress Report: 1975: Another Year of Erosion," *Ebony*, January 1976, 120.

5. US Census Bureau figures, included in Abdul Alkalimat, Romi Crawford, and Rebecca Zorach, *The Wall of Respect: Public Art and Black Liberation in 1960s Chicago* (Evanston, IL: Northwestern University Press, 2017).

6. "The Ten Best Cities for Blacks," *Ebony*, February 1978, 97. Three of these ten cities were in the Midwest, the other two being Indianapolis and Minneapolis.

7. Ibid.

8. William Julius Wilson, *When Work Disappears: The World of the New Urban Poor* (New York: Vintage Books, 1997), 29–30.

9. Ibid., 34–35.

10. Vernon E. Jordan Jr., "Black Youth: The Endangered Generation," *Ebony*, August 1978, 86.

11. Alvin Poussaint, "What Makes Them Tick? A Psychological Profile of the New Generation," *Ebony*, August 1978, 80.

12. Bill Berry, "Beyond the Here and Now: New Generation Blacks Search for Religion," *Ebony*, August 1978, 93–98.

13. Lerone Bennett Jr., "Lost Found Generation: New Group with New Values Changes Racial Dialogue," *Ebony*, August 1978, 37.

14. Ibid.

15. Album review (no byline), *Black Radio Exclusive*, November 20, 1978, 12.

16. Cashmore, *Black Culture Industry*, 177.

17. Kembrew McLeod and Peter DiCola, *Creative License: The Law and Culture of Digital Sampling* (Durham, NC: Duke University Press, 2011), 55.

18. This segment can be seen on YouTube.

19. Earl Calloway, "Stars Perform for Bell's Defense Fund," *Chicago Defender*, December 24, 1975, 24.

20. Greg Kot, *I'll Take You There: Mavis Staples, the Staple Singers and the March up Freedom's Highway* (New York: Scribner, 2014), 212–13.

21. The name derived from the copper-colored building as well as the lascivious term that means what you think it does.

22. "Young Chicagoans Build Million Dollar Shoe Empire," *Ebony*, December 1978, 78.

23. George Lazarus, "Johnson Publishing Co. 'Is on the Air,'" *Chicago Tribune*, July 11, 1973, E8.

24. Display ad, *Chicago Defender*, October 31, 1973, 12.

25. Earl Calloway, "Working Together or Working Apart, It Works," *Chicago Defender*, March 22, 1975, A3.

26. "Charlie Cherokee Says," *Chicago Defender*, June 16, 1975, 22.

27. Lucky Cordell interview, *The History Makers*, January 16, 2002, retrieved from thehistorymakers.com.

28. Susan J. Douglas describes the sonic developments of FM, which involves modulating the frequency instead of the amplitude of a radio wave, in *Listening In*, 259–61.

29. "More FM Radio Sets," *Chicago Tribune*, May 10, 1960, A6; "Radio Stations Post Big Gains," *Chicago Tribune*, December 23, 1979, N6.

30. Jerry Boulding, "Routes: The Saga of Black Radio," *Black Radio Exclusive*, November 9, 1979, 42. Boulding also expanded on these ideas in "Who's Right and What's Left and Who's Out of Step," *Black Radio Exclusive*, January 25, 1980, 6.

31. At least the stations that were cited in the *Chicago Tribune* radio station listings emphasized these formats.

32. Boulding, "Routes: The Saga of Black Radio," 42.

33. "Charlie Cherokee Says," *Chicago Defender*, December 26, 1973, 8.

34. "WBMX Radio Sold for $27 Million," *Chicago Tribune*, September 9, 1987, B3; "Egmont Sonderling, 91; Founded Company," *New York Times*, August 4, 1997, retrieved from newyorktimes.com.

35. "Arbitron Analysis," *Black Radio Exclusive*, July 11, 1977, 6.

36. Ibid.

37. "Arbitron Study Shows Blacks Favor AM Radio Dial over FM," *Cash Box*, March 26, 1977, 41.

38. Ibid.

39. Gary Deeb, "WBMX: No Jive for the 'Giant Killer,'" *Chicago Tribune*, December 10, 1975, E15. James expressed similar sentiments in Joy Darrow's article, "A Master of the Sound Game," *Chicago Defender*, December 22, 1975, 19.

40. Ibid.

41. "Top Firms Back Sickle Bike-a-Thon," *Chicago Defender*, August 30, 1975, 2.

42. Sharron Kornegay, "Stress Broadcast Ethics: Jackson," *Chicago Sun-Times*, November 13, 1976, 50; "Charlie Cherokee Says," *Chicago Defender*, January. 12, 1974, 5.

43. Fred Goodman, "The Windy City's Leading Independent," *Cash Box*, May 30, 1981, SBM-24.

44. George, *Death of Rhythm and Blues*, 136.

45. Alexenburg is referring to an often-told account that CBS Records threatened to pull all its videos from MTV in 1983 unless the network aired Michael Jackson's "Billie Jean." Author Steve Knopper addresses this issue in his Jackson biography, *MJ: The Genius of Michael Jackson* (New York: Scribner, 2015), 116–17. As Knopper states, different sides of this story present conflicting claims, but what remains irrefutable is that Jackson accelerated integration at MTV and that Alexenburg deserves credit for helping put him in a position to do so.

46. Wright arranged the strings on "Don't Stop 'til You Get Enough," "Rock with You," and "Get on the Floor." Producer Quincy Jones was born in Chicago but left the city as a child.

47. White describes the contributions that Washington and Wright made to his music at this time in *My Life with Earth, Wind and Fire*, 248, 254, 258–59.

48. Ibid., 180.

49. "Black Music Marketing Delivers for CBS; Dept. of Specialists Functions as a Team," *Cash Box*, January 28, 1978, 23.

50. Marovich, *City Called Heaven*, 286–87.

51. White, *My Life with Earth, Wind and Fire*, 196.

52. Fredric Dannen discusses the trial as part of a wider federal sweep into the record industry in *Hit Men: Power Brokers and Fast Money inside the Music Business* (New York: Vintage Books, 1991), 103–7. Davis discusses it in *The Man behind the Music*, ii–iv and 129–43. The trial was held in New Jersey because of federal jurisdiction. Although

Davis was the only defendant acquitted outright at the first trial, his Brunswick code-fendants' convictions were overturned.

53. Sidney Miller Jr., "Chi-Town's Carl Davis, Pres. of Chi-Sound Records," *Black Radio Exclusive*, May 11, 1979, 12.

54. Davis, *Man behind the Music*, 146. In the book he also misidentifies the address as 20 East Huron.

55. Miller, "Chi-Town's Carl Davis," 12.

56. In the film *Sparkle*, cast members Lonette McKee and Irene Cara sang its songs, but Aretha Franklin is the sole lead voice on the album.

57. These soundtracks include the Staple Singers' *Let's Do It Again* (Curtom, 1976), Mavis Staples's *A Piece of the Action* (Curtom, 1977), and Gladys Knight and the Pips' *Claudine* (Buddah, 1974).

58. At least one blogger, Gregory V. Boulware, brought up *Three the Hard Way* in the wake of the Flint, Michigan, water crisis that began in 2014. He's likely not the only one. Retrieved from boulwareenterprises.wordpress.com.

59. Earl Calloway, "'No Place to Run' Scenes Filmed at Roberts Motel," *Chicago Defender*, January 14, 1974, 13; Calloway, "Producer Films Movie at Roberts Motel," *Chicago Defender*, February 9, 1974, 32. No other evidence can be found of the film's existence; the costumes, or lack thereof, as photographed in the *Defender* article, seem outrageous even by blaxploitation standards.

60. From an interview with Andrew Davis on the website thehollywoodinterview .blogspot.com/2012/04/andrew-davis-hollywood-interview.html.

61. "Rites For 'Stony Island' Star Edward Robinson of Chicago," *Chicago Tribune*, April 10, 1979, 13.

62. Charles Shaar Murray, *Crosstown Traffic: Jimi Hendrix and the Rock 'n' Roll Revolution* (New York: St. Martin's Press, 1989), 86.

63. *Stony Island* DVD release (Cinema Libre Studio, 2012). *Stony Island* may have exerted another influence: six years after its release, *Purple Rain* told Prince's loosely autobiographical story of his years assembling a band in Minneapolis. Both pictures presented young interracial music ensembles in the Midwest, and the story arcs end with climactic concert performances. Susanna Hoffs (daughter of Tamar Hoffs) acted in *Stony Island*; in the mid-1980s Prince offered her band, the Bangles, his song "Manic Monday." When the Prince connection was mentioned to Andrew Davis, he seemed dubious but did not dismiss the idea.

64. Mayfield explained in detail to Pruter in *Chicago Soul* that he did not feel comfortable recording disco but others persuaded him to make the record, 310.

65. Gil Askey composed, produced, and arranged the song.

66. Tim Lawrence, *Love Saves the Day: A History of American Dance Music Culture, 1970–1979* (Durham, NC: Duke University Press, 2003), 156–58, 297–99.

67. Most of this book's information about Dogs of War is from interviews with Eddie Thomas and from the Spring and Fall 1979 editions of its newsletter that he graciously shared.

68. Pruter mentions in *Chicago Soul* that the spank was "Chicago's last great contribution to black popular dance," 208. That was the case when his book was published, but in 2003, R. Kelly globalized the audience for a slow Chicago dance, stepping, through his song and video, "Step in the Name of Love."

69. Peter Brown, who grew up in the Chicago suburbs, recorded his 1977 album *A Fantasy Love Affair* (T. K. Productions) in Miami. The LP's credits acknowledge Lucky Cordell but not Eddie Thomas.

70. Jacob Arnold, liner notes, Larry Dixon, *Star Time: Larry Dixon and LAD Productions Inc., Chicago 1971–87* (Past Due Records, 2016).

71. Jefferson Cowie, *Stayin' Alive: The 1970s and the Last Days of the Working Class* (New York: New Press, 2010), 321.

72. Ibid., 322.

73. Cookie Amerson, "Presidents Discuss Trends to Black Oriented Product," *Cash Box*, February 26, 1977, 10.

74. Tim Lawrence describes how *Saturday Night Fever* "established an imaginative framework for the stabilization of disco culture" in *Love Saves the Day*, 307.

75. Cowie, *Stayin' Alive*, 322.

76. Steve Dahl with Dave Hoekstra and Paul Natkin, *Disco Demolition: The Night Disco Died* (Chicago: Curbside Splendor, 2016), 16.

77. Ibid.

78. Dionne Danns, "Chicago School Desegregation and the Role of the State of Illinois, 1971–1979," *American Educational History Journal* 37, no. 1 (2010): 10.

79. Ibid.

80. Will Hermes connects disco, early hip-hop, and punk rock to classical minimalism in 1970s New York in *Love Goes to Buildings on Fire* (New York: Faber and Faber, 2011).

81. Michaelangelo Matos, *The Underground Is Massive: How Electronic Dance Music Conquered America* (New York: Dey Street, 2015), 11.

82. Ibid., 12.

83. Jacob Arnold, "Solitary Refinement," *Wire*, May 2018, 38; "Inside Track," *Billboard*, July 8, 1978, 82.

84. Greg Kot, "House: What It Is, How It Began, and Why It's an Orphan Here at Home," *Chicago Tribune*, August 19, 1990, J4.

85. George, *Death of Rhythm and Blues*, 167–68.

86. Nelson George, "Times Even Tougher for Black Retailers," *Billboard*, November 13, 1982, 58.

87. Michael Martinez, "Will This Be the Year?," *Cash Box*, May 30, 1981, SBM-7.

88. Craig Werner, "Curtis Mayfield," *Goldmine*, July 4, 1997, retrieved from rocksbackpages.com.

89. Fred Goodman, "The Windy City's Leading Independent," *Cash Box*, May 30, 1981, SBM-24.

90. Davis, *Man behind the Music*, 156.

91. Butler, *Only the Strong Survive*, 214.

92. Leor Galil, "Pioneering Chicago Rapper Sugar Ray Dinke speaks on the legacy of 'Cabrini Green Rap,'" *Chicago Reader*, February 1, 2018, retrieved from chicagoreader.com.

93. Gary Rivlin, *Fire on the Prairie: Chicago's Harold Washington and the Politics of Race* (New York: Henry Holt, 1992).

94. Ben Joravsky, "The Lost Harold Washington Files," *Chicago Reader*, November 30, 2017, 10.

95. Michaeli, *"Defender,"* 484.

96. "Endorsements," *Chicago Sun-Times*, February 20, 1983.

97. At least that's how it seemed when I attended a Washington campaign rally at the Hotel Belmont a few months before my fourteenth birthday. But my strongest recollection of the event was meeting Muhammad Ali.

98. Diamond, *Chicago on the Make*, 248.

99. This interview was conducted while congressional Republicans fought to block several of President Barack Obama's policies.

100. Mitchell Locin, "Third of State's Schools Face Fiscal Problems," *Chicago Tribune*, September 3, 1981, N_A2.

101. James Mack interview with Bill Dahl, mid-1980s.

CHAPTER EIGHT

1. A couple of articles in *Chicago* magazine highlighted these Afrofuturist artists, who include jazz saxophonist David Boykin, rapper Lupe Fiasco, electronic musician Jamal Moss, and poet Eve Ewing. Matthew Hendrickson, "Why Sun Ra Is Dominating Chicago's Culture Scene," *Chicago*, April 30, 2014, and Adam Morgan, "The Next Generation of Chicago Afrofuturism," *Chicago*, August 17, 2017, retrieved from chicagomag.com.

2. Bagewadi included footage of Chicago's Black Lives Matter protests and demonstrations against President Donald Trump's policies in the 2017 video of his cover of George Perkins's 1970 R&B song "Cryin' in the Streets."

3. Kerry James Marshall's paintings were celebrated through major exhibitions at Chicago's Museum of Contemporary Art and New York's Met Breuer in 2016. Alkalimat, Crawford, and Zorach, *Wall of Respect*, was published in 2017.

4. Frank Guan, "Chance the Rapper's Grammy Wins Were a Breakthrough, but He Was No Underdog," *Vulture*, February 12, 2017, retrieved from vulture.com. As Guan states, while Chance the Rapper's wins were accomplishments, he also benefited from strategic alliances; *Coloring Book* was streamed through Apple Music. Chance's father, Ken Bennett, had served as an aide to Harold Washington in the 1980s and continued his political involvement in the years that followed. Andy Grimm, "Chance the Rapper to Rauner: 'Take Our Kids Off the Table,'" *Chicago Sun-Times*, March 3, 2017, retrieved from chicago.suntimes.com.

5. While Rob Hatch-Miller's documentary *Syl Johnson: Any Way the Wind Blows* shows the singer upset about his Grammy loss, he seemed nonchalant in a conversation a couple days after the ceremony. Johnson simply shrugged and said, "How can you beat Paul McCartney? He's an icon."

6. British journalist Stuart Cosgrove describes this British fascination in his book *Young Soul Rebels: A Personal History of Northern Soul* (Edinburgh, UK: Polygon, 2016).

7. Marybeth Hamilton, *In Search of the Blues* (New York: Basic Books, 2008), 231–33.

8. Amanda Petrusich, *Do Not Sell at Any Price: The Wild, Obsessive Hunt for the World's Rarest 78 RPM Records* (New York: Scribner, 2014), 176.

9. "New 'What's in My Bag?' Episode with Theo Parrish, Zernell and Marcellus Pittman," *Amoebite*, April 25, 2016, amoeba.com.

10. McLeod and DiCola, *Creative License*, 80–82.

11. Ibid., 86.

12. As "the Rappin' Lawyer," Jay B. Ross recorded his own hip-hop track called "Sue the Bastards." The accompanying video includes Jackie Ross and Gene Chandler.

13. "Same Sample, Different Ditty," *Billboard*, November 25, 2006, 9. During a casual conversation in June 2017, Pate said he and his wife Carolyn are living comfortably, in part from their share of that amount.

14. One of Johnson's former producers compared him to the African American folklore trickster figure Br'er Rabbit.

15. While these numbers seem significantly higher than the typical amount for licensing

fees that McLeod and DiCola describe, RZA also expressed his eagerness to richly compensate Johnson in Hatch-Miller's documentary. So it likely all adds up.

16. Lanre Bakare, "Syl Johnson's 'Is It Because I'm Black?' and a 'World of No Pity'— Protest Playlist No. 2," *Guardian*, March 13, 2017, retrieved from theguardian.com.

17. Diamond, *Chicago on the Make*, 327.

18. Eve L. Ewing, "'We Shall Not Be Moved': A Hunger Strike, Education, and Housing in Chicago," *New Yorker*, September 21, 2015, retrieved from newyorker.com.

19. Leor Galil, "Soul Singer Jamila Woods Makes Music about Black Womanhood That Speaks to Everyone," *Chicago Reader*, July 13, 2016, retrieved from chicagoreader.com.

20. Jamila Woods performed at the July 2017 Pitchfork Music Festival in Chicago's Union Park (as did a Tribe Called Quest), the year before Ravyn Lenae's set at the event. Jazz drummer Mike Reed, who runs the festival, is also a member of the AACM, which Phil Cohran cofounded. So there are just a few degrees of separation among Woods, Lenae, and the Affro-Arts Theater.

21. Jamila Woods, "Ode to Herb Kent," *Poetry*, December 2015, retrieved from poetryfoundation.org.

22. Dennis Rodkin, "Che 'Rhymefest' Smith's Green Hopes for the 20th Ward," *Chicago Magazine*, February 9, 2011, retrieved from chicagomag.com; Moore, *South Side*, 139.

SELECTED DISCOGRAPHY

ALBUMS

Acklin, Barbara. *The Brunswick Singles As and Bs*. Edsel, 1999.

———. *I Call It Trouble*. Brunswick, 1973.

———. *I Did It*. Brunswick, 1970.

———. *Love Makes a Woman*. Brunswick, 1968.

———. Seven Days of Night. Brunswick, 1969.

———. *Someone Else's Arms*. Brunswick, 1970.

Amuzement Park. *Amuzement Park*. Mirus, 1982.

Andrews, Ruby. *Black Ruby*. Zodiac, 1972.

———. *Just Loving You: The Zodiac Sessions, 1967–1973*. Grapevine, 2004.

Art Ensemble of Chicago. *Les Stances à Sophie*. Pathé, 1970.

Artistics. *The Articulate Artistics*. Brunswick, 1968.

———. I'm Gonna Miss You. Brunswick, 1967.

———. *I Want to Make My Life Over*. Brunswick, 1970.

———. *What Happened*. Brunswick, 1970.

B, Zeshan. *Vetted*. Minty Fresh, 2017.

Baby Huey. *The Baby Huey Story: The Living Legend*. Curtom, 1971.

Bass, Fontella. *Rescued: The Best of Fontella Bass*. MCA Records, 1992.

Bond, Lou. *Lou Bond*. Light in the Attic, 2010.

Boscoe. *Boscoe*. Numero Group, 2007.

Brighter Side of Darkness. *Love Jones*. 20th Century Records, 1973.

Brown, Peter. *A Fantasy Love Affair*. Drive, 1977,

Butler, Billy. *The Right Tracks: The Complete Okeh Recordings, 1963–1966*. Kent, 2007.

Butler, Billy, and Infinity. *Hung Up on You*. Pride, 1973.

Butler, Jerry. *Aware of Love*. Vee-Jay, 1961.

———. *Jerry Butler Sings Assorted Sounds with the Aid of Assorted Friends and Relatives*. Mercury, 1971.

———. *The Sagittarius Movement*. Mercury, 1971.

———. *The Spice of Life*. Mercury, 1972.

Callier, Terry. *I Just Can't Help Myself*. Cadet, 1973.

———. *New Folk Sound of Terry Callier*. Prestige, 1965.

———. *Occasional Rain*. Cadet, 1972.

———. *What Color Is Love*. Cadet, 1972.

Captain Sky. *The Adventures of Captain Sky*. AVI, 1978.
———. *Pop Goes the Captain*. AVI, 1979.
Chandler, Gene. *The Duke of Earl*. Vee-Jay, 1962.
———. *Get Down*. 20th Century Fox, 1978.
———. *There Was a Time*. Brunswick, 1968.
———. *The Two Sides of Gene Chandler*, Brunswick, 1969.
Chandler, Gene, Situation. *The Gene Chandler Situation*. Mercury, 1970.
Chandler, Gene, and Jerry Butler. *Gene and Jerry One and One*. Mercury, 1970.
Chi-Lites. *(For God's Sake) Give More Power to the People*. Brunswick, 1971.
———. *Give It Away*. Brunswick, 1969.
———. *I Like Your Lovin'*. Brunswick, 1970.
———. *A Letter to Myself*. Brunswick, 1973.
———. *A Lonely Man*. Brunswick, 1972.
———. *Toby*. Brunswick, 1974.
Christopher, Gavin. *Gavin Christopher*. Curtom, 1979.
Clifford, Linda. *If My Friends Could See Me Now*. Curtom, 1978.
Cohran, Phil, and the Artistic Heritage Ensemble. *Armageddon*. Zulu/Tizona, 2010.
———. *On the Beach*. Zulu, 1968.
———. *The Spanish Suite*. Zulu, 1968.
Collier, Mitty. *Shades of Mitty Collier: The Chess Singles, 1961–1968*. Kent, 2008.
Crook, General. *General Crook*. Wand, 1974.
Davis, Tyrone. *Best of Tyrone Davis*. Rhino, 2002.
———. *Can I Change My Mind*. Dakar, 1969.
———. *Home Wrecker*. Dakar, 1974.
———. *I Had It All the Time*. Dakar, 1972.
———. *It's All in the Game*. Dakar, 1973.
———. *Turn Back the Hands of Time*. Brunswick, 1970.
———. *Turning Point!* Dakar, 1975.
Dells. *The Dells Sing Dionne Warwick's Greatest Hits*. Cadet, 1972.
———. *Freedom Means*. Cadet, 1971.
———. *Give Your Baby a Standing Ovation*. Cadet, 1973.
———. *Like It Is/Like It Was*. Cadet, 1969.
———. *Love Is Blue*. Cadet, 1969.
———. *Musical Menu*. Cadet, 1968.
———. *There Is*. Cadet, 1968.
Dixon, Larry, and LAD Products, Inc. *Star Time, Chicago 1971–87*. Still Music, 2015.
Drew, Patti. *Tell Him*. Capitol, 1967.
———. *Wild Is Love*. Capitol, 1969.
———. *Workin' on a Groovy Thing*. Capitol, 1968.
Dungills. *Africa Calling*. Vee-Jay, 1963.
Dyson, Ronnie. *Love in All Flavors*. CBS, 1977.
Earth, Wind, and Fire. *Head to the Sky*. CBS, 1973.
Emotions. *Flowers*. Columbia, 1976.
———. *Rejoice*. CBS, 1977.
Esquires. *Get on Up and Get Away*. Bunky, 1967.
Everett, Betty. *There'll Come a Time*. Universal City, 1969.
Five Stairsteps and Cubie. *Our Family Portrait*. Buddah, 1967.
Franklin, Aretha. *Sparkle*. Atlantic, 1976.
Green, Garland. *The Very Best of Garland Green*. Kent, 2008.

Hathaway, Donny. *Everything Is Everything*. Atco, 1970.

Heaven and Earth. *Heaven and Earth*. Mercury, 1978.

Henderson, Willie, and the Soul Explosions. *Funky Chicken*. Brunswick, 1970.

Hutson, Leroy. *Love, Oh Love*. Curtom, 1973.

Hutton, Bobby. *Piece of the Action*. ABC, 1973.

Impressions. *Check Out Your Mind*. Curtom, 1970.

———. *People Get Ready*. ABC-Paramount, 1966.

———. *Ridin' High*. ABC-Paramount, 1966.

———. *This Is My Country*. Curtom, 1968.

———. *Three the Hard Way*. Curtom, 1974.

———. *The Young Mod's Forgotten Story*. Curtom, 1969.

Independents. *Just as Long: The Complete Wand Recordings, 1972–1974*. Kent, 2016.

Interpreters. *"The Knack."* Cadet, 1965.

Jackson, Michael. *Off the Wall*. Epic, 1979.

Jackson, Walter. *Feeling Good*. Chi-Sound, 1976.

———. *It's All Over: The Okeh Recordings, Volume 1*. Kent, 2006.

———. *Speak Her Name: The Okeh Recordings, Volume 3*. Kent, 2007.

———. *Welcome Home: The Okeh Recordings, Volume 2*. Kent, 2006.

James, Ginji. *Love Is a Merry-Go-Round*. Brunswick, 1971.

Johnson, Syl. *Complete Mythology*. Numero Group, 2010.

Lance, Major. *Everybody Loves a Good Time! The Best of Major Lance*. Legacy, 1995.

Lenae, Ravyn. *Crush*. Atlantic, 2018.

Lost Generation. *The Sly, Slick and the Wicked*. Brunswick, 1970.

———. *Young, Tough and Terrible*. Brunswick, 1972.

Lovelites. *The Lovelite Years*. Lovelite Records, 1999.

Mayfield, Curtis. *Curtis*. Curtom, 1970.

———. *Curtis in Chicago*. Curtom, 1973.

———. *Curtis/Live*. Curtom, 1971.

———. *Roots*. Curtom, 1971.

———. *Short Eyes*. Curtom, 1977.

———. *Super Fly*. Curtom, 1972.

———. *(There Is No Place Like) America Today*. Curtom, 1975.

Mighty Marvelows. *The Mighty Marvelows*. ABC Records, 1968.

Mystique. *Mystique*. Curtom, 1977.

Natural Four, *Heaven Right Here on Earth*. Curtom, 1975.

———. *Natural Four*. Curtom, 1974.

———. *Nightchaser*. Curtom, 1976.

New Rotary Connection. *"Hey, Love."* Cadet Concept, 1971.

Notations. *Notations*. Gemigo, 1975.

———. *Still Here, 1967–1973*. Numero Group, 2015.

Pate, Johnny. *Jazz Goes Ivy League*. King, 1958.

———. Outrageous. MGM Records, 1970.

Pate, Johnny, and Orchestra. *Set a Pattern*. ABC Records, 1968.

Pharaohs. *Awakening*. Luv 'n' Haight, 1996.

———. *In the Basement*. Luv 'n' Haight, 1997.

Pieces of Peace. *Pieces of Peace*. Cali-Tex, 2007.

Rasputin's Stash. *The Devil Made Me Do It*. Gemigo, 1974.

———. *Hidden Stash*. Athens of the North, 2016.

———. *Rasputin's Stash*. Cotillion, 1971.

Rhymefest. *Blue Collar*. Allido/J-Records, 2006.

Riperton, Minnie. *Come to My Garden*. GRT, 1970.

——. *Perfect Angel: Deluxe Edition*. Universal Music, 2017.

Ross, Jackie. *Jerk and Twine: The Complete Chess Recordings*. Kent, 2012.

Rotary Connection. *Aladdin*. Cadet Concept, 1968.

——. *Dinner Music*. Cadet Concept, 1970.

——. *Peace*. Cadet Concept, 1968.

——. *The Rotary Connection*. Cadet Concept, 1967.

——. *Songs*. Cadet Concept, 1969.

Rufus. *Rufus*. ABC, 1973.

Shades of Brown. *S.O.B.* Dusty Groove, 2008.

Sheppards. *The Sheppards*. Solid Smoke, 1980.

Simon, Lowrell. *Lowrell*. AVI, 1979.

Simtec and Wylie. *Gettin' Over the Hump*. Mister Chand, 1971.

South Shore Commission. *South Shore Commission*. Wand, 1975.

Staple Singers. *Let's Do It Again*. Curtom, 1975.

Stewart, Billy. *The Greatest Sides*. Sugar Hill Records, 1984.

——. *Unbelievable*. Chess, 1965.

Sun Ra. *The Singles*. Evidence, 1996.

Universal Togetherness Band. *Universal Togetherness Band*. Numero Group, 2014.

Various Artists. *Birth of Soul: Special Chicago Edition*. Kent, 2009.

——. *Chicago Cool Breezin'*. Demon/Westside, 1999.

——. *Curtis Mayfield's Chicago Soul*. Legacy, 1995.

——. *Eccentric Soul: The Bandit Label*. Numero Group, 2004.

——. *Eccentric Soul: The Cash Label*. Numero Group, 2018.

——. *Eccentric Soul: The Nickel and Penny Labels*. Numero Group, 2011.

——. *Eccentric Soul: Sitting in the Park*. Numero Group, 2015.

——. *Eccentric Soul: Twinight's Lunar Rotation*. Numero Group, 2006.

——. *The One-derful Collection: M-Pac! Records*. Secret Stash, 2015.

——. *The One-derful Collection: Mar-V-Lus Records*. Secret Stash, 2015.

——. *The One-derful Collection: One-derful Records*. Secret Stash, 2014.

——. *Stony Island*. Glades, 1978.

——. *Ultra High Frequencies: The Chicago Party*. Numero Group, 2014.

——. *Vee-Jay: The Definitive Collection*. Shout Factory, 2007.

Weapons of Peace. *Weapons of Peace*. Playboy Records, 1977.

Wilson, Jackie. *Whispers*. Brunswick, 1966.

Woods, Jamila. *HEAVN*. SoundCloud, 2016.

Wright, Willie. *I'm on My Way*. Argo, 1963.

Young-Holt Unlimited. *Soulful Strut*. Brunswick, 1968.

SINGLES

Armstead, Jo. "A Stone Good Lover." Giant, 1968.

——. "There's Not Too Many More (Left Like Him)." Giant, 1969.

Artistics. "This Heart of Mine." Okeh, 1965.

Baby Huey and the Baby Sitters. "Monkey Man." St. Lawrence, 1965.

Brothers and Sisters. "I Am Somebody." Toddlin' Town, 1969.

——. "Nobody Is Gonna Turn Us 'Round." Toddlin' Town, 1970.

Chandler, Gene. "Soul Hootenanny." Constellation, 1965.

Chandler, Gene, and Barbara Acklin. "From the Teacher to the Preacher." Brunswick, 1968.

————. "Show Me the Way to Go." Brunswick, 1968.

C.O.D.s. "Michael (The Lover)." Kellmac, 1965.

Coffee. "Your Lovin' Ain't as Good as Mine." Love Lite Records, 1977.

Conservatives. "That's All." Ebonic Sound, 1969.

Crook, General. "Do It for Me." Down to Earth, 1970.

————. "Gimme Some (Parts I and II)." Down to Earth, 1970.

Curry, Helen. "A Prayer for My Soldier." Daran, 1969.

Dumas, Martin L. "Attitude, Belief and Determination." Taurean Connection, ca. late-1970s.

Fisher, Shelley. "Elegy (to a Plain Black Boy)." Aries, 1966.

Five Du-Tones. "The Gouster." One-derful, 1963.

Flamingos. "Golden Teardrops." Chance, 1953.

Franklin, Bobby's, Insanity. Bring It on Down to Me (Parts I and II). Thomas, 1969.

Garner, Emmett, Jr. "So Much Better." Maxwell, ca. 1970.

Garrett, Jo Ann. "One Woman." Duo, 1968.

Green, Garland. "You Can't Get Away That Easy." Cotillion, 1972.

Hathaway, Donny. "This Christmas." ATCO, 1970.

Hi-Lites. "I'm So Jealous." Daran, 1964.

Hutton, Bobby. "Come See What's Left of Me." Phillips, 1969.

J-P-C Gang. "Christmas Delight 80." WJPC, 1979.

Jackson, Maurice. "Step by Step." Plum, 1972.

Lewis, Barbara. "Hello Stranger." Atlantic, 1963.

Love's Children. "Soul Is Love." Curtom, 1971.

Maxwell, Holly. "No One Else." Curtom, 1969.

————. "Suffer." Curtom, 1969.

Miller, Bobby. "Take It in Stride." Constellation, ca. 1964.

Notations. "Judy Blue Eyes." Mercury, 1977.

Radiants. "Hold On." Chess, 1968.

————. "Voice Your Choice." Chess, 1964.

Ross, Jackie. "Hard Times." SAR, 1962.

Russell, Saxie. "Psychedelic Soul, Part 1 and Part 2." Thomas, 1968.

Salty Peppers. "La, La, La, Part 1 and Part 2." TEC, 1969.

Saunders, Jesse. "On and On." Jess-Say, 1984.

Smith, Marvin. "Time Stopped. Brunswick, 1966.

Soul Majestics. "I Done Told You Baby." Chicago Music Bag Recording, 1968.

South Side Movement. "I' Been Watchin' You." Wand, 1972.

Starlets. "My Baby's Real." Cadet, 1967.

Vondells. "Lenora." Marvello, 1964.

Vontastics. "Peace of Mind." St. Lawrence, 1965.

Wahls, Shirley. "We've Got to Keep On Movin' On." Smash, 1969.

SELECTED BIBLIOGRAPHY

BOOKS AND OTHER PRINTED SOURCES

Absher, Amy. *The Black Musician and the White City: Race and Music in Chicago, 1900–1967*. Ann Arbor: University of Michigan Press, 2014.

Alkalimat, Abdul, Romi Crawford, and Rebecca Zorach, eds. *The Wall of Respect: Public Art and Black Liberation in 1960s Chicago*. Evanston, IL: Northwestern University Press, 2017.

Anderson, Alan B., and George W. Pickering. *Confronting the Color Line: The Broken Promise of the Civil Rights Movement in Chicago*. Athens: University of Georgia Press, 1986.

Austen, Ben. *High-Risers: Cabrini-Green and the Fate of American Public Housing*. New York: HarperCollins, 2018.

Austen, Jake, ed. *Flying Saucers Rock 'n' Roll: Conversations with Unjustly Obscure Rock 'n' Roll Eccentrics*. Durham, NC: Duke University Press, 2011.

Banfield, William C. *Cultural Codes: Makings of a Black Music Philosophy*. Lanham, MD: Scarecrow Press, 2010.

Barger, Harold M. "Political Content of Black Newspapers, Chicago and Nation, 1969–1970." PhD diss., Political Science Department, Northwestern University, June 1971.

Bell, Ollan Christopher [Chris James]. *Music Saved My Life: From Darkness into the Light*. N.p.: Ollan Christopher Bell, 2017.

Beltramini, Enrico. "SCLC Operation Breadbasket: From Economic Civil Rights to Black Economic Power." In "Expanding the Narrative: Exploring New Aspects of the Civil Rights Movement Fifty Years Later," special issue, *Fire!!!* 2, no. 2 (2013): 5–47.

Best, Wallace D. *Passionately Human, No Less Divine: Religion and Culture in Black Chicago, 1915–1952*. Princeton, NJ: Princeton University Press, 2005.

Biondi, Martha. *The Black Revolution on Campus*. Berkeley: University of California Press, 2012.

Blain, Keisha N. "'Confraternity among All Dark Races': Mittie Maude Lena Gordon and the Practice of Black (Inter)nationalism in Chicago, 1932–1942." *Palimpsest: A Journal on Women, Gender, and the Black International* 5, no. 2 (2016): 151–81.

Boyd, Robert L. "Black Business Transformation, Black Well-Being, and Public Policy." *Population Research and Policy Review* 9 (May 1990): 117–32.

———. "A Contextual Analysis of Black Self-Employment in Large Metropolitan Areas, 1970–1980." *Social Forces* 70 (December 1991): 409–29.

Branch, Taylor. *At Canaan's Edge: America in the King Years, 1965–68.* New York: Simon and Schuster, 2006.

Broven, John. *Record Makers and Breakers: Voices of the Independent Rock 'n' Roll Pioneers.* Urbana: University of Illinois Press, 2009.

Brown, Tamara Lizette. "So You Think You Can Dance." In *Soul Thieves: The Appropriation and Misrepresentation of African American Popular Culture.* New York: Palgrave Macmillan, 2014.

Burnim, Mellonee V., and Portia K. Maultsby, eds. *African American Music: An Introduction.* New York: Routledge, 2006.

Butler, Jerry. *Only the Strong Survive: Memoirs of a Soul Survivor.* Bloomington: Indiana University Press, 2000.

Caponi, Gena Dagel, ed. *Signifyin(g), Sanctifyin', and Slam Dunking: A Reader in African American Expressive Culture.* Amherst: University of Massachusetts Press, 1999.

Cashmore, Ellis. *The Black Culture Industry.* New York: Routledge, 1997.

Chambers, Jason. *Madison Avenue and the Color Line: African Americans in the Advertising Industry.* Philadelphia: University of Pennsylvania Press, 2008.

Chandler, Johnny. Liner notes to *Black Gold: The Very Best of Rotary Connection.* Universal/Island, 2006.

Chapple, Steve, and Reebee Garofalo. *Rock 'n' Roll Is Here to Pay: The History and Politics of the Music Industry.* Chicago: Nelson-Hall, 1977.

Cogan, Jim, and William Clark. *Temples of Sound: Inside the Great Recording Studios.* San Francisco: Chronicle Books, 2003.

Cohen, Aaron. *Aretha Franklin's "Amazing Grace."* New York: Bloomsbury, 2011.

Cohodas, Nadine. *Spinning Blues into Gold: The Chess Brothers and the Legendary Chess Records.* New York: St. Martin's Press, 2000.

Cosgrove, Stuart. *Detroit 67: The Year That Changed Soul.* Edinburgh, UK: Polygon, 2016.

———. *Young Soul Rebels: A Personal History of Northern Soul.* Edinburgh, UK: Polygon, 2016.

Cowie, Jefferson. *Stayin' Alive: The 1970s and the Last Days of the Working Class.* New York: New Press, 2010.

Dahl, Steve, with Dave Hoekstra and Paul Natkin. *Disco Demolition: The Night Disco Died.* Chicago: Curbside Splendor, 2016.

Dannen, Fredric. *Hit Men: Power Brokers and Fast Money inside the Music Business.* New York: Vintage Books, 1991.

Danns, Dionne. "Chicago High School Students' Movement for Quality Public Education, 1966–1971." *Journal of African American History* 88 (Spring 2003): 138–50.

———. "Chicago School Desegregation and the Role of the State of Illinois, 1971–1979." *American Educational History Journal* 37, no. 1 (2010): 55–73.

———. *Something Better for Our Children: Black Organizing in Chicago Public Schools, 1963–1971.* New York: Routledge, 2003.

Dates, Jannette L., and William Barlow, eds. *Split Image: African Americans in the Mass Media.* Washington, DC: Howard University Press, 1993.

Davis, Carl H., Sr. *The Man behind the Music: The Legendary Carl Davis.* Matteson, IL: Life to Legacy, 2009.

Diamond, Andrew J. *Chicago on the Make: Power and Inequality in a Modern City.* Oakland: University of California Press, 2017.

Douglas, Susan J. *Listening In: Radio and the American Imagination.* New York: Times Books, 1999.

Duneier, Mitchell. *Ghetto: The Invention of a Place, the History of an Idea.* New York: Farrar, Straus and Giroux, 2016.

Dyja, Thomas. *The Third Coast: When Chicago Built the American Dream*. New York: Penguin Press, 2013.

Early, Gerald. ed. *Speech and Power*. Vol. 1, *The African-American Essay and Its Cultural Content from Polemics to Pulpit*. Hopewell, NJ: Ecco Press, 1992.

———, ed. *Speech and Power*. Vol. 2, *The African-American Essay and Its Cultural Content from Polemics to Pulpit*. Hopewell, NJ: Ecco Press, 1993.

Fink, Robert. "Goal-Directed Soul? Analyzing Rhythmic Teleology in African American Popular Music." *Journal of the American Musicological Society* 64 (Spring 2011): 179–238.

Finley, Mary Lou, Bernard Lafayette Jr., James R. Ralph Jr., and Pam Smith, eds. *The Chicago Freedom Movement: Martin Luther King Jr. and Civil Rights Activism in the North*. Lexington: University Press of Kentucky, 2016.

Fitzgerald, Jon. "Black Pop Songwriting 1963–1966: An Analysis of U.S. Top Forty Hits by Cooke, Mayfield, Stevenson, Robinson, and Holland-Dozier-Holland." *Black Music Research Journal* 27 (Fall 2007): 97–140.

Floyd, Samuel A., Jr. *The Power of Black Music: Interpreting Its History from Africa to the United States*. New York: Oxford University Press, 1995.

Forrest, Leon. *Divine Days*. Chicago: Another Chicago Press, 1992.

———. *Relocations of the Spirit*. Wakefield, RI: Asphodel Press, 1994.

Frady, Marshall. *Jesse: The Life and Pilgrimage of Jesse Jackson*. New York: Random House, 1996.

———. *Martin Luther King, Jr.: A Life* New York: Penguin Books, 2006.

Freeland, Gregory K. "'We're a Winner': Popular Music and the Black Power Movement." *Social Movement Studies* 8 (August 2009): 261–88.

Fuerst, J. S. *When Public Housing Was Paradise: Building Community in Chicago*. Urbana: University of Illinois Press, 2005.

Garofalo, Reebee. "From Music Publishing to MP3: Music and Industry in the Twentieth Century." *American Music* 17 (Autumn 1999): 318–54.

George, Nelson. *The Death of Rhythm and Blues*. New York: Pantheon, 1988.

———. *The Hippest Trip in America: "Soul Train" and the Evolution of Culture and Style*. New York: William Morrow, 2014.

Gillett, Charlie. *The Sound of the City: The Rise of Rock and Roll*. New York: Da Capo Press, 1996.

Gilroy, Paul. *The Black Atlantic: Modernity and Double Consciousness*. Cambridge, MA: Harvard University Press, 2002.

Green, Adam. *Selling the Race: Culture, Community, and Black Chicago, 1940–1955*. Chicago: University of Chicago Press, 2009.

Gregory, Susan. *Hey, White Girl!* New York: W. W. Norton, 1970.

Grossman, James R. *Land of Hope: Chicago, Black Southerners and the Great Migration*. Chicago: University of Chicago Press, 1989.

Guarnori, Steve. *Scepter Wand Forever!* N.p.: Stephen Guarnori, 2016.

Guillory, Monique, and Richard C. Green, eds. *Soul: Black Power, Politics, and Pleasure*. New York: New York University Press, 1998.

Guralnick, Peter. *Sweet Soul Music: Rhythm and Blues and the Southern Dream of Freedom*. New York: Harper and Row, 1986.

Hale, Casey. "Different Placements of Spirit: African Americans Historicizing in Sound." PhD diss., Music Department, City University of New York, October 2014.

Halker, Clark. "A History of Local 208 and the Struggle for Racial Equality in the American Federation of Musicians." *Black Music Research Journal* 8 (Autumn 1988): 207–22.

Hamilton, Marybeth. *In Search of the Blues*. New York: Basic Books, 2008.

Haralambos, Michael. *Soul Music: The Birth of a Sound in Black America*. New York: Da Capo Press, 1974.

Helgeson, Jeffrey. *Crucibles of Black Empowerment: Chicago's Neighborhood Politics from the New Deal to Harold Washington*. Chicago: University of Chicago Press, 2014.

Hepworth, David. *Never a Dull Moment: 1971–the Year That Rock Exploded*. New York: St. Martin's Press, 2016.

Hughes, Charles L. *Country Soul: Making Music and Making Race in the American South*. Chapel Hill: University of North Carolina Press, 2015.

Hunt, D. Bradford. *Blueprint for Disaster: The Unraveling of Chicago Public Housing*. Chicago: University of Chicago Press, 2009.

Hutchinson, Earl Ofari. "The Continuing Myth of Black Capitalism." In "The Urban Crisis 1993," special issue, *Black Scholar* 23 (Winter/Spring 1993): 16–21.

Iton, Richard. *In Search of the Black Fantastic: Politics and Popular Culture in the Post–Civil Rights Era*. New York: Oxford University Press, 2008.

Jefferson, Margo. *Negroland: A Memoir*. New York: Pantheon, 2015.

Jewell, Frank. *Annotated Bibliography of Chicago History*. Chicago: Chicago Historical Society, 1979.

Jones, LeRoi [Amiri Baraka]. *Black Music*. New York: Quill, 1967.

Joseph, Peniel E. *Waiting 'til the Midnight Hour: A Narrative History of Black Power in America*. New York: Henry Holt, 2006.

Kempton, Arthur. *Boogaloo: The Quintessence of American Popular Music*. Ann Arbor: University of Michigan Press, 2005.

Kent, Herb, and David Smallwood. *The Cool Gent: The Nine Lives of Radio Legend Herb Kent*. Chicago: Lawrence Hill Books, 2009.

Kern-Foxworth, Marilyn. *Aunt Jemima, Uncle Ben, and Rastus: Blacks in Advertising, Yesterday, Today, and Tomorrow*. Westport, CT: Praeger, 1994.

Khan, Chaka. *Chaka! Through the Fire*. New York: Rodale, 2003.

Knopper, Steve. *MJ: The Genius of Michael Jackson*. New York: Scribner, 2015.

Kohl, Paul Robert. "Who Stole the Soul? Rock and Roll, Race, and Rebellion." PhD diss., Communications Department, University of Utah, June 1994.

Kot, Greg. *I'll Take You There: Mavis Staples, the Staple Singers and the March up Freedom's Highway*. New York: Scribner, 2014.

Kurlansky, Mark. *Ready for a Brand New Beat: How "Dancing in the Street" Became the Anthem for a Changing America*. New York: Riverhead Books, 2013.

Kusmer, Kenneth L., and Joe W. Trotter, eds. *African American Urban History since World War II*. Chicago: University of Chicago Press, 2009.

Lauterbach, Preston. *The Chitlin' Circuit and the Road to Rock 'n' Roll*. New York: W. W. Norton, 2011.

Lawrence, Tim. *Love Saves the Day: A History of American Dance Music Culture, 1970–1979*. Durham, NC: Duke University Press, 2003.

Le Gendre, Kevin. *Soul Unsung: Reflections on the Band in Black Popular Music*. Sheffield, UK: Equinox, 2012.

Lehman, Christopher P. *A Critical History of "Soul Train" on Television*. Jefferson, NC: McFarland, 2008.

Levine, Lawrence W. *Black Culture and Black Consciousness: Afro-American Folk Thought from Slavery to Freedom*. New York: Oxford University Press, 2007.

Lewis, George E. *A Power Stronger Than Itself: The AACM and American Experimental Music*. Chicago: University of Chicago Press, 2008.

Lipsitz, George. *Time Passages: Collective Memory and American Popular Culture*. Minneapolis: University of Minnesota Press, 1991.

Lordi, Emily J. *Donny Hathaway Live*. New York: Bloomsbury Academic, 2016.

MacLean, Nancy. *Freedom Is Not Enough: The Opening of the American Workplace*. New York: Russell Sage Foundation, 2006.

Markowitz, Fran. "Israel as Africa, Africa as Israel: 'Divine Geography' in the Personal Narratives and Community Identity of the Black Hebrew Israelites." *Anthropological Quarterly* 69 (October 1996): 193–205.

Marovich, Robert M. *A City Called Heaven: Chicago and the Birth of Gospel Music*. Urbana: University of Illinois Press, 2015.

Mason, Phillip L. "Soul in the Culture of African Americans." *Music Educators Journal* 79 (November 1992): 49–52.

Matos, Michaelangelo. *The Underground Is Massive: How Electronic Dance Music Conquered America*. New York: Dey Street, 2015.

Mayfield, Todd, with Travis Atria. *Traveling Soul: The Life of Curtis Mayfield*. Chicago: Chicago Review Press, 2016.

McAdam, Doug. *Political Process and the Development of Black Insurgency, 1930–1970*. Chicago: University of Chicago Press, 1982.

McLeod, Kembrew, and Peter DiCola. *Creative License: The Law and Culture of Digital Sampling*. Durham, NC: Duke University Press, 2011.

Michaeli, Ethan. *The "Defender": How the Legendary Black Chicago Newspaper Changed America*. New York: Houghton Mifflin Harcourt, 2016.

Milner, Greg. *Perfecting Sound Forever: An Aural History of Recorded Music*. New York: Faber and Faber, 2009.

Monson, Ingrid. *Freedom Sounds: Civil Rights Call Out to Jazz and Africa*. New York: Oxford University Press, 2007.

Moore, Natalie Y. *The South Side: A Portrait of Chicago and American Segregation*. New York: St. Martin's Press, 2016.

Moore, Natalie Y., and Lance Williams. *The Almighty Black P Stone Nation: The Rise, Fall and Resurgence of an American Gang*. Chicago: Lawrence Hill Books, 2011.

Mullen, Bill V. *Popular Fronts: Chicago and African-American Cultural Politics, 1935–46*. Urbana: University of Illinois Press, 2015.

Murray, Albert. *The Omni-Americans: Black Experience and American Culture*. New York: Da Capo Press, 1990.

Myers, Marc. *Why Jazz Happened*. Berkeley: University of California Press, 2013.

Neal, Mark Anthony. *What the Music Said: Black Popular Music and Black Public Culture*. New York: Routledge, 1999.

Newman, Mark. *Entrepreneurs of Profit and Pride: From Black-Appeal to Radio Soul*. New York: Praeger, 1988.

Ngwainmbi, Emmanuel K. "The Black Media Entrepreneur and Economic Implications for the 21st Century." *Journal of Black Studies* 36 (September 2005): 3–33.

Pacyga, Dominic A. *Chicago: A Biography*. Chicago: University of Chicago Press, 2009.

Parris, Guichard, and Lester Brooks. *Blacks in the City: A History of the National Urban League*. New York: Little, Brown, 1971.

Pattillo, Mary. *Black on the Block: The Politics of Race and Class in the City*. Chicago: University of Chicago Press, 2007.

Perkins, Useni Eugene, ed. *Rise of the Phoenix: Voices from Chicago's Black Struggle, 1960–1975*. Chicago: Third World Press Foundation, 2017.

Petrusich, Amanda. *Do Not Sell at Any Price: The Wild, Obsessive Hunt for the World's Rarest 78 RPM Records*. New York: Scribner, 2014.

Plastic Crimewave [Steve Krakow]. *My Kind of Sound: The Secret History of Chicago Music Compendium*. Chicago: Curbside Splendor, 2015.

Pruter, Robert. *Chicago Soul*. Urbana: University of Illinois Press, 1992.

———. *Doowop: The Chicago Scene*. Urbana: University of Illinois Press, 1996.

Puckrein, Gary. "Moving Up." *Wilson Quarterly* 8 (Spring 1984): 74-87.

Quinn, Eithne. "'Tryin' to Get Over': 'Super Fly,' Black Politics, and Post-Civil Rights Film Enterprise." *Cinema Journal* 49 (Winter 2010): 86-105.

Ramsey, Guthrie P., Jr. "The Pot Liquor Principle: Developing a Black Music Criticism in American Music Studies." American Music 22 (Summer 2004): 284-95.

———. *Race Music: Black Cultures from Bebop to Hip-Hop*. Berkeley: University of California Press, 2004.

Ratliff, Ben. *Every Song Ever: Twenty Ways to Listen in an Age of Musical Plenty*. New York: Farrar, Straus and Giroux, 2016.

Record, Brian A., Sr. *My Father in Lites: A Father's Story from a Son's Perspective*. Chicago: Record Family Music Group, 2015.

Rickford, Russell. *We Are an African People: Independent Education, Black Power, and the Radical Imagination*. New York: Oxford University Press, 2016.

Rivlin, Gary. *Fire on the Prairie: Chicago's Harold Washington and the Politics of Race*. New York: Henry Holt, 1992.

Rubinowitz, Leonard S., and James E. Rosenbaum. *Crossing the Class and Color Lines: From Public Housing to White Suburbia*. Chicago: University of Chicago Press, 2000.

Rudinow, Joel. *Soul Music: Tracking the Spiritual Roots of Pop from Plato to Motown*. Ann Arbor: University of Michigan Press, 2010.

Samors, Neal. *Chicago in the Sixties: Remembering a Time of Change*. Chicago: Chicago's Books, 2006.

Sanjek, David. "One Size Does Not Fit All: The Precarious Position of the African American Entrepreneur in Post-World War II American Popular Music." *American Music* 15 (Winter 1997): 535-62.

Saunders, Jesse, with James Cummins. *House Music . . . the Real Story*. Baltimore: Publish America, 2007.

Savage, Jon. *1966: The Year the Decade Exploded*. London: Faber and Faber, 2015.

Searcy, Jennifer. "Voice of the Negro: African American Radio, WVON, and the Struggle for Civil Rights in Chicago." PhD diss., History Department, Loyola University Chicago, August 2013.

Semmes, Clovis E. "The Dialectics of Cultural Survival and the Community Artist: Phil Cohran and the Affro-Arts Theater." *Journal of Black Studies* 24 (June 1994): 447-61.

———. *The Regal Theater and Black Culture*. New York: Palgrave Macmillan, 2006.

Shaw, Arnold. *The World of Soul*. New York: Cowles, 1970.

Shelton, Jason E., and Michael O. Emerson. "Extending the Debate over Nationalism versus Integration: How Cultural Commitments and Assimilation Trajectories Influence Beliefs about Black Power." *Journal of African American Studies* 14 (September 2010): 312-36.

Smith, Preston H., II. *Racial Democracy and the Black Metropolis: Housing Policy in Postwar Chicago*. Minneapolis: University of Minnesota Press, 2012.

Smith, R. J. *The Great Black Way: L.A. in the 1940s and the Lost African American Renaissance*. New York: Public Affairs, 2006.

Smith, Robert C. "The Changing Shape of Urban Black Politics: 1960-1970." In "Urban

Black Politics," special issue, *Annals of the American Academy of Political and Social Science* 439 (September 1978).

Smith, Suzanne E. *Dancing in the Street: Motown and the Cultural Politics of Detroit.* Cambridge, MA: Harvard University Press, 1999.

Southern, Eileen. *The Music of Black Americans: A History.* 2nd ed. New York: W. W. Norton, 1983.

Spann, Pervis, with Linda C. Walker. *The 40 Year Spann.* Chicago: National Academy of Blues, 2003.

Spaulding, Norman. "History of Black Oriented Radio in Chicago 1929–1963." PhD diss., Communications Department, University of Illinois at Urbana-Champaign, 1981.

Spear, Allan H. *Black Chicago: The Making of a Negro Ghetto, 1890–1920.* Chicago: University of Chicago Press, 1967.

Steinbeck, Paul. *Message to Our Folks: The Art Ensemble of Chicago.* Chicago: University of Chicago Press, 2017.

Stephens, Robert W. "Soul: A Historical Reconstruction of Continuity and Change in Black Popular Music." *Black Perspective in Music* 12 (Spring 1984): 21–43.

Stewart, James B. "Message in the Music: Political Commentary in Black Popular Music from Rhythm and Blues to Early Hip Hop." *Journal of African American History* 90 (Summer 2005): 196–225.

Strickland, Arvarh E. *History of the Chicago Urban League.* Columbia: University of Missouri Press, 2001.

Swedien, Bruce. *Make Mine Music.* Milwaukee, WI: Hal Leonard Books, 2009.

Sykes, Charles E. "A Conceptual Model for Analyzing Rhythmic Structure in African American Popular Music." PhD diss., School of Music, Indiana University, May 1992.

Thompson, Lowell. *African Americans in Chicago.* Charleston, SC: Arcadia, 2012.

Todd-Breland, Elizabeth Shana. "'To Reshape and Redefine Our World': African American Political Organizing for Education in Chicago, 1968–1988." PhD diss., History Department, University of Chicago, August 2010.

Van Deburg, William L. *New Day in Babylon: The Black Power Movement and American Culture, 1965–1975.* Chicago: University of Chicago Press, 1992.

Van Horne, Winston A. "The Concept of Black Power: Its Continued Relevance." *Journal of Black Studies* 37 (January 2007): 365–89.

Vincent, Rickey. *Party Music: The Inside Story of the Black Panthers' Band and How Black Power Transformed Soul Music.* Chicago: Lawrence Hill Books, 2013.

Vivian, C. T. *Black Power and the American Myth.* Philadelphia: Fortress Press, 1970.

Wald, Gayle. *It's Been Beautiful: Soul! and Black Power Television.* Durham, NC: Duke University Press, 2015.

Ward, Brian. *Just My Soul Responding: Rhythm and Blues, Black Consciousness, and Race Relations.* Berkeley: University of California Press, 1998.

———, ed. *Media, Culture, and the Modern African American Freedom Struggle.* Gainesville: University Press of Florida, 2003.

———. *Radio and the Struggle for Civil Rights in the South.* Gainesville: University Press of Florida, 2004.

Werner, Craig. *Higher Ground: Stevie Wonder, Aretha Franklin, Curtis Mayfield and the Rise and Fall of American Soul.* New York: Crown, 2004.

———. "'Meeting over Yonder': Using Music to Teach the Movement in the North." *OAH Magazine of History* 26, no. 1 (2012): 41–45.

White, Maurice, with Herb Powell. *My Life with Earth, Wind and Fire.* New York: Amistad, 2016.

Wilkerson, Isabel. *The Warmth of Other Suns*. New York: Vintage, 2011.
Williams, Jakobi. *From the Bullet to the Ballot: The Illinois Chapter of the Black Panther Party and Racial Coalition Politics in Chicago*. Chapel Hill: University of North Carolina Press, 2013.
Wilson, Olly. "Black Music as an Art Form." *Black Music Research Journal* 3 (1983): 1–22.
Wilson, William Julius. *When Work Disappears: The World of the New Urban Poor*. New York: Vintage Books, 1997.

COLLECTIONS

Sue Cassidy Clark Papers, Center for Black Music Research Library and Archives, Columbia College Chicago.
Dungill Family Papers, Vivian G. Harsh Research Collection, Carter G. Woodson Branch, Chicago Public Library.
Michael McAlpin Collection, 1993-97, Archives of African American Music and Culture, Indiana University, Bloomington.
Leonard Wash Papers, Vivian Harsh Collection, Carter G. Woodson Branch, Chicago Public Library.

DVDS, FILMS, AND ONLINE DOCUMENTARIES

Disco Demolition: Riot to Rebirth. Red Bull Music Academy, 2016.
Got the Love. City Vanguard, 2017.
I Am Not Your Negro. Magnolia Pictures, 2016.
Movin' On Up: The Music and Message of Curtis Mayfield and the Impressions. Reelin' in the Years, 2008.
Record Row: Cradle of Rhythm and Blues. WTTW, 1997.
Stony Island. Cinema Libre Studio DVD edition, 2012.
Syl Johnson: Any Way the Wind Blows. Robert Hatch-Miller, 2015.

PERIODICALS

Advertising Age
Billboard
Black Music Research Journal
Black Radio Exclusive
Black Stars
Blues and Soul
Cash Box
Chicago Defender
Chicago Magazine
Chicago Reader
Chicago Seed
Chicago Sun-Times
Chicago Tribune
Crawdaddy
Creem
DownBeat
Ebony
Goldmine
Jet
Melody Maker

Mojo
New Music Express
New York Amsterdam News
Rolling Stone
Sepia
Soul
Soul Illustrated
Souls
Wax Poetics

EXHIBITIONS

Kerry James Marshall: Mastry. Museum of Contemporary Art, Chicago, April 23 – September 25, 2016.

Move Your Body: The Evolution of House Music. Chicago Cultural Center, Chicago, May 21 – August 16, 2015.

Never a Lovely So Real: Photography and Film in Chicago, 1950–1980. Art Institute of Chicago, May 12 – October 28, 2018.

Windy City Breakdown. Arts Incubator, Chicago, May 8 – 29, 2015.

INDEX